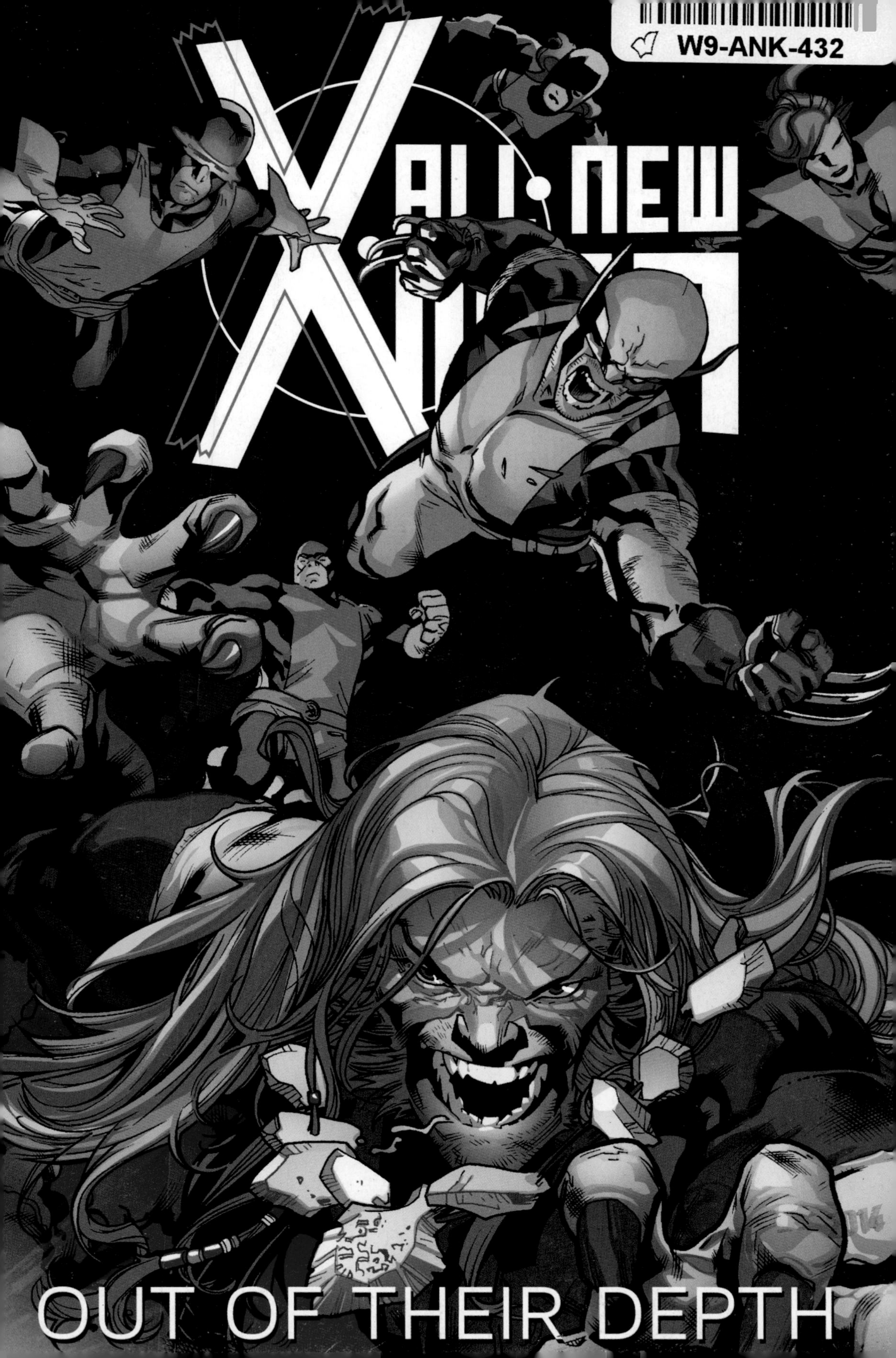
ALL-NEW
OUT OF THEIR DEPTH

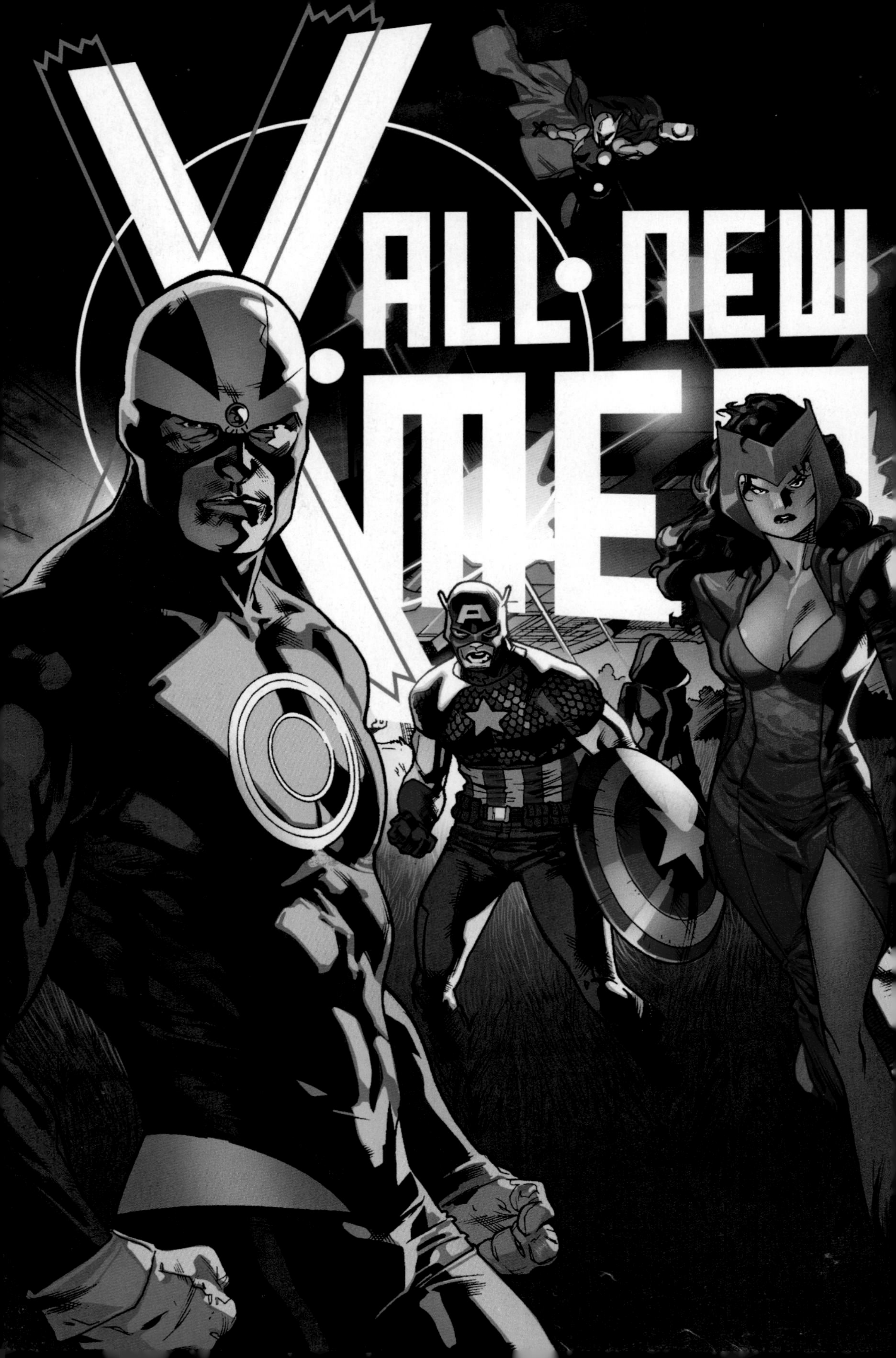
ALL-NEW
X-MEN

BEAST
HANK McCOY

MARVEL GIRL
JEAN GREY

CYCLOPS
SCOTT SUMMERS

ANGEL
WARREN WORTHINGTON III

ICEMAN
BOBBY DRAKE

OUT OF THEIR DEPTH

BRIAN MICHAEL
BENDIS
WRITER

STUART
IMMONEN
PENCILER, #11-14

WADE VON
GRAWBADGER
INKER, #11-14

DAVID
LAFUENTE
ARTIST, #15

MARTE
GRACIA
COLORIST, #11 & #14

RAIN
BEREDO
COLORIST, #12-13

JAMES
CAMPBELL
COLORIST, #15

COVER ART: **STUART IMMONEN, WADE VON GRAWBADGER & MARTE GRACIA** WITH RAIN BEREDO (COLORS, #15)

VC'S CORY
PETIT
LETTERER

JORDAN D.
WHITE
ASSISTANT EDITOR

NICK
LOWE
EDITOR

COLLECTION EDITOR: **JENNIFER GRUNWALD**
ASSISTANT EDITOR: **SARAH BRUNSTAD**
ASSOCIATE MANAGING EDITOR: **ALEX STARBUCK**
EDITOR, SPECIAL PROJECTS: **MARK D. BEAZLEY**
SENIOR EDITOR, SPECIAL PROJECTS: **JEFF YOUNGQUIST**
SVP PRINT, SALES & MARKETING: **DAVID GABRIEL**
BOOK DESIGNER: **RODOLFO MURAGUCHI**

EDITOR IN CHIEF: **AXEL ALONSO**
CHIEF CREATIVE OFFICER: **JOE QUESADA**
PUBLISHER: **DAN BUCKLEY**
EXECUTIVE PRODUCER: **ALAN FINE**

ALL-NEW X-MEN VOL. 3: OUT OF THEIR DEPTH. Contains material originally published in magazine form as ALL-NEW X-MEN #11-15. First printing 2014. ISBN# 978-0-7851-6639-9. Published by MARVEL WORLDWIDE, INC., a subsidiary of MARVEL ENTERTAINMENT, LLC. OFFICE OF PUBLICATION: 135 West 50th Street, New York, NY 10020. Copyright © 2013 and 2014 Marvel Characters, Inc. All rights reserved. All characters featured in this issue and the distinctive names and likenesses thereof, and all related indicia are trademarks of Marvel Characters, Inc. No similarity between any of the names, characters, persons, and/or institutions in this magazine with those of any living or dead person or institution is intended, and any such similarity which may exist is purely coincidental. **Printed in the U.S.A.** ALAN FINE, EVP - Office of the President, Marvel Worldwide, Inc. and EVP & CMO Marvel Characters B.V.; DAN BUCKLEY, Publisher & President - Print, Animation & Digital Divisions; JOE QUESADA, Chief Creative Officer; TOM BREVOORT, SVP of Publishing; DAVID BOGART, SVP of Operations & Procurement, Publishing; C.B. CEBULSKI, SVP of Creator & Content Development; DAVID GABRIEL, SVP Print, Sales & Marketing; JIM O'KEEFE, VP of Operations & Logistics; DAN CARR, Executive Director of Publishing Technology; SUSAN CRESPI, Editorial Operations Manager; ALEX MORALES, Publishing Operations Manager; STAN LEE, Chairman Emeritus. For information regarding advertising in Marvel Comics or on Marvel.com, please contact Niza Disla, Director of Marvel Partnerships, at ndisla@marvel.com. For Marvel subscription inquiries, please call 800-217-

Born with genetic mutations that gave them abilities beyond those of normal humans, mutants are the next stage in evolution. As such, they are feared and hated by humanity. A group of mutants known as the X-Men fight for peaceful coexistence between mutants and humankind. But not all mutants see peaceful coexistence as a reality.

The original X-Men — Cyclops, Angel, Iceman, Beast and Marvel Girl — have travelled from past to present and, after learning of the tragedies awaiting them, voted to stay. They want to help realize Xavier's dream before their destinies get in the way, but it might be too late for Jean Grey, who's been prematurely burdened by her psychic powers and adult memories.

Meanwhile, the shape-shifting mutant known as Mystique recruited Sabretooth and Mastermind to take the humans for everything they can. Posing as X-Men during robberies, they're driving the wedge between mutants and humans even deeper.

Modern-day Cyclops is more interested in mutant prosperity than mutant-human relations. His mission to bring new mutants to his Xavier school took him all over the world, and finally to the Jean Grey School.

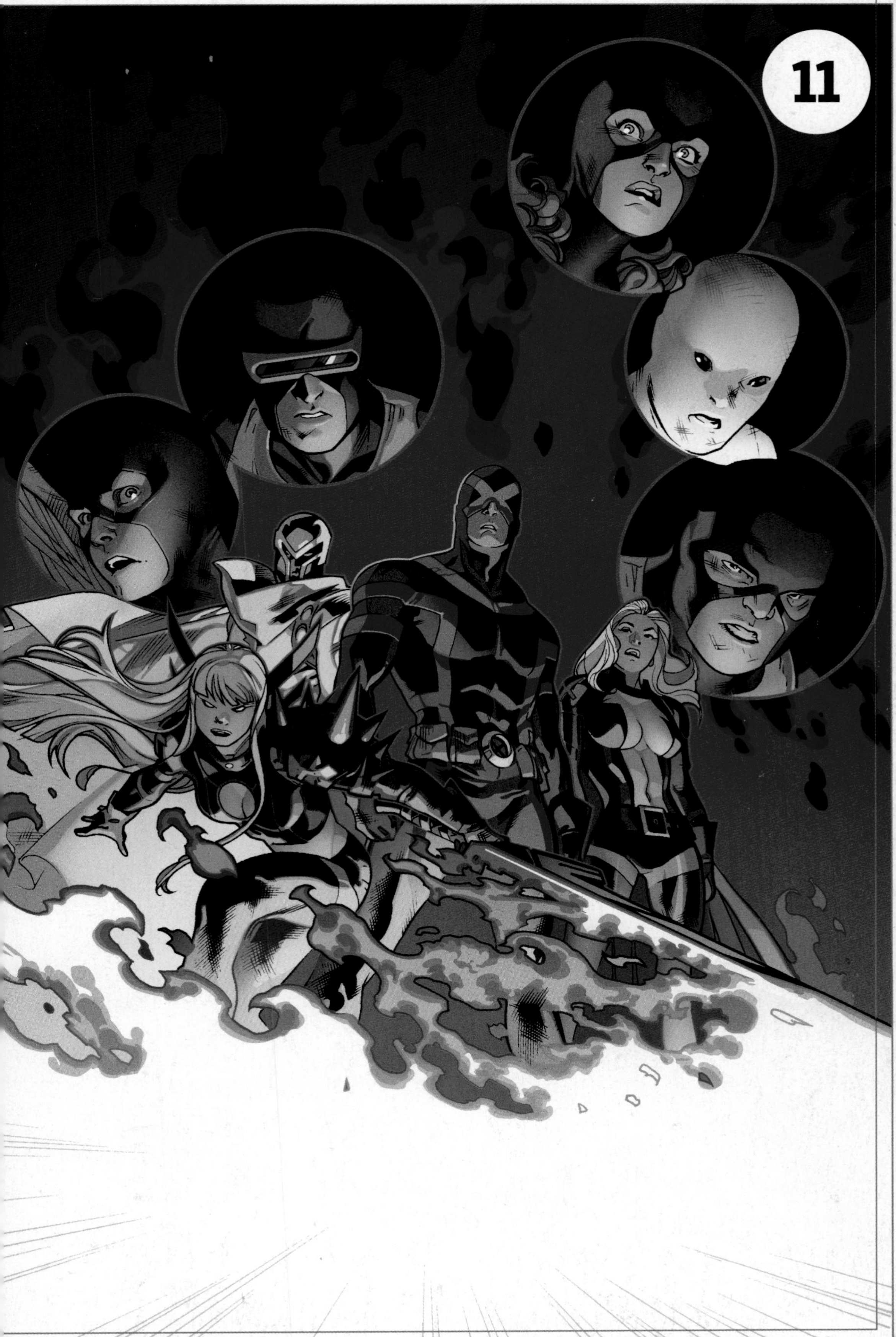
11

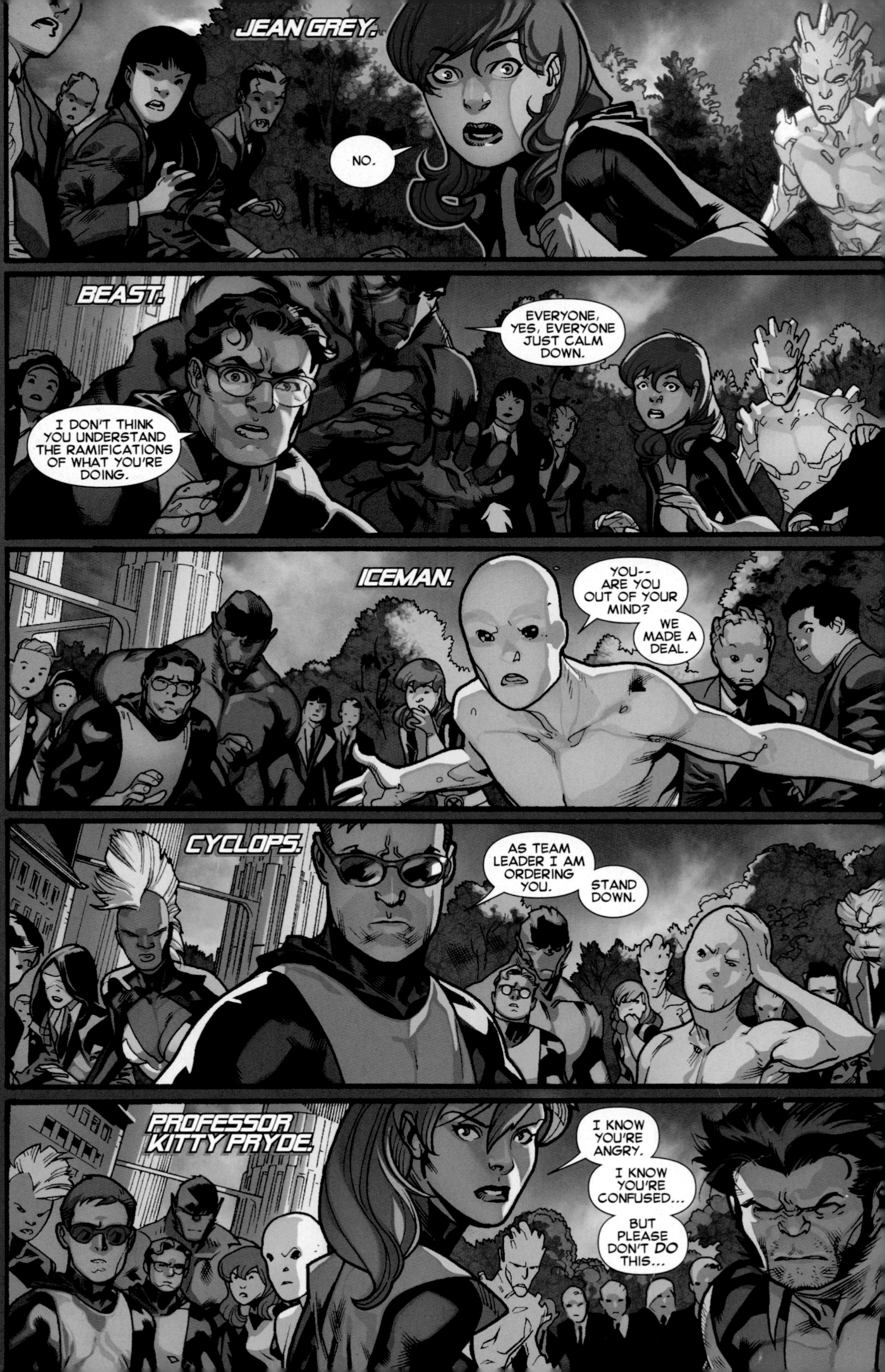
JEAN GREY.
NO.
BEAST.
EVERYONE, YES, EVERYONE JUST CALM DOWN.
I DON'T THINK YOU UNDERSTAND THE RAMIFICATIONS OF WHAT YOU'RE DOING.
ICEMAN.
YOU-- ARE YOU OUT OF YOUR MIND?
WE MADE A DEAL.
CYCLOPS.
AS TEAM LEADER I AM ORDERING YOU.
STAND DOWN.
PROFESSOR KITTY PRYDE.
I KNOW YOU'RE ANGRY.
I KNOW YOU'RE CONFUSED...
BUT PLEASE DON'T DO THIS...

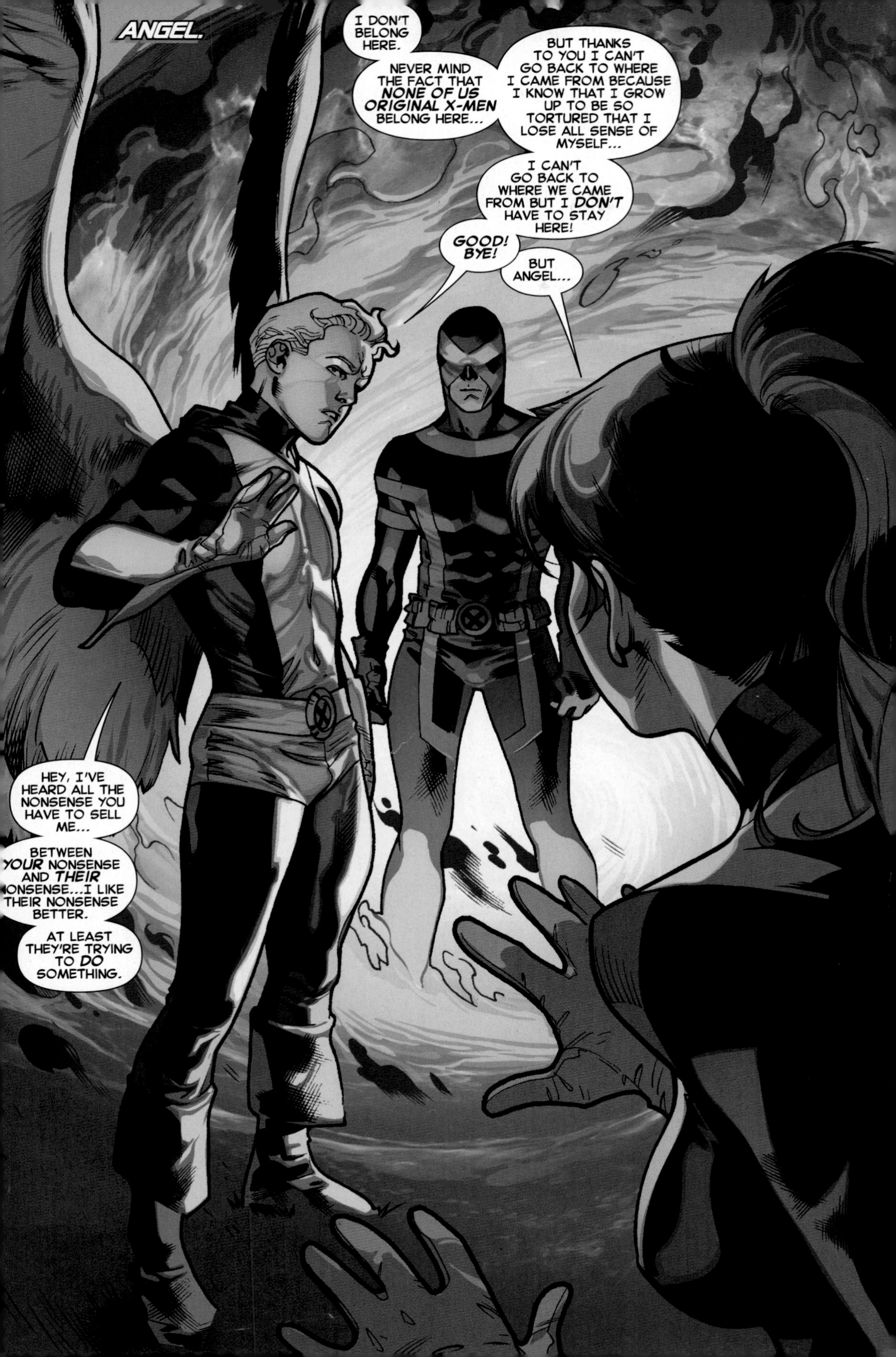
ANGEL.
I DON'T BELONG HERE.
NEVER MIND THE FACT THAT NONE OF US ORIGINAL X-MEN BELONG HERE...
BUT THANKS TO YOU I CAN'T GO BACK TO WHERE I CAME FROM BECAUSE I KNOW THAT I GROW UP TO BE SO TORTURED THAT I LOSE ALL SENSE OF MYSELF...
I CAN'T GO BACK TO WHERE WE CAME FROM BUT I DON'T HAVE TO STAY HERE!
GOOD! BYE!
BUT ANGEL...
HEY, I'VE HEARD ALL THE NONSENSE YOU HAVE TO SELL ME...
BETWEEN YOUR NONSENSE AND THEIR NONSENSE...I LIKE THEIR NONSENSE BETTER.
AT LEAST THEY'RE TRYING TO DO SOMETHING.

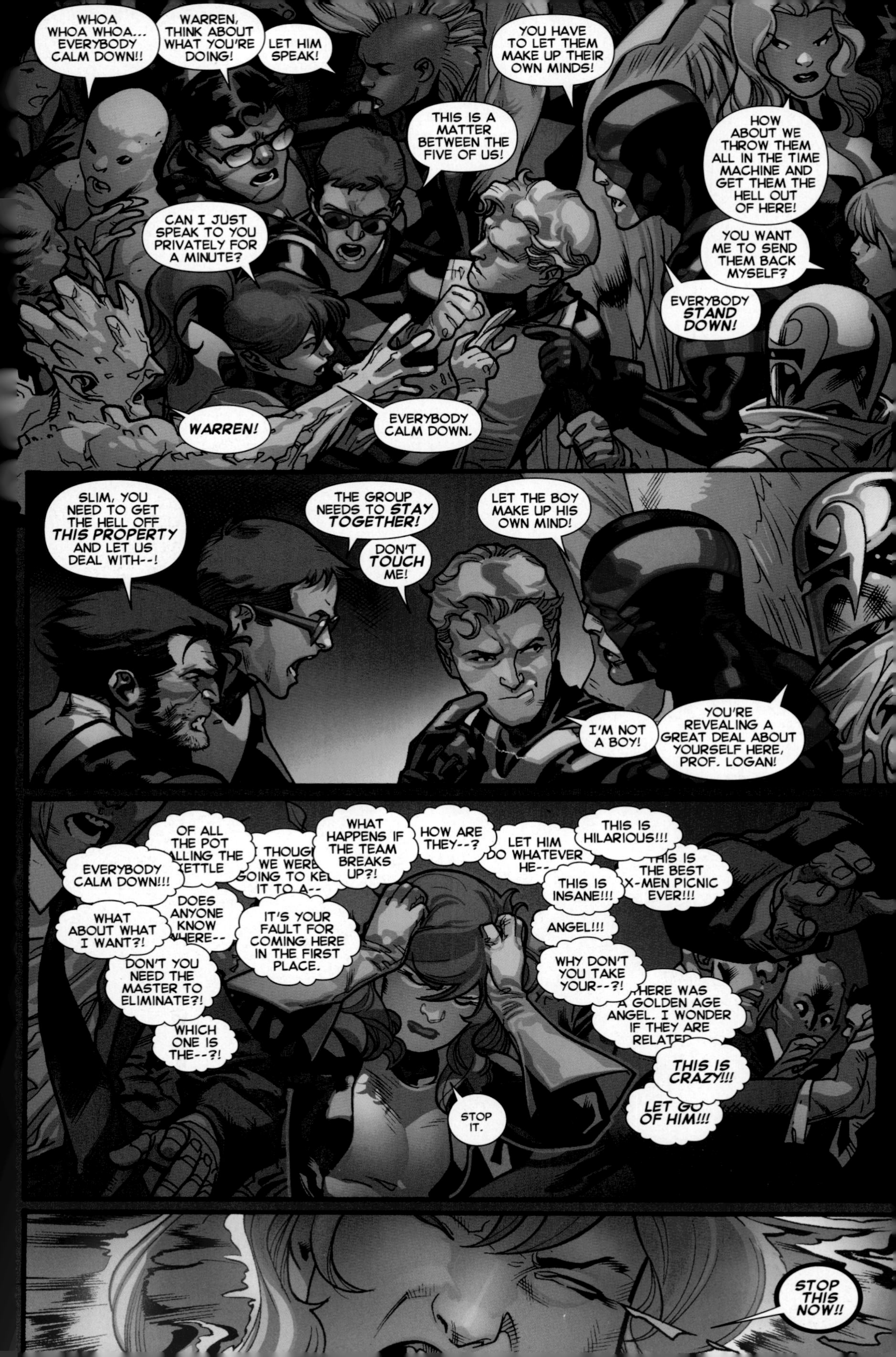

WHOA WHOA WHOA... EVERYBODY CALM DOWN!!
WARREN, THINK ABOUT WHAT YOU'RE DOING!
LET HIM SPEAK!
YOU HAVE TO LET THEM MAKE UP THEIR OWN MINDS!
THIS IS A MATTER BETWEEN THE FIVE OF US!
HOW ABOUT WE THROW THEM ALL IN THE TIME MACHINE AND GET THEM THE HELL OUT OF HERE!
CAN I JUST SPEAK TO YOU PRIVATELY FOR A MINUTE?
YOU WANT ME TO SEND THEM BACK MYSELF?
EVERYBODY STAND DOWN!
WARREN!
EVERYBODY CALM DOWN.
SLIM, YOU NEED TO GET THE HELL OFF THIS PROPERTY AND LET US DEAL WITH--!
THE GROUP NEEDS TO STAY TOGETHER!
DON'T TOUCH ME!
LET THE BOY MAKE UP HIS OWN MIND!
I'M NOT A BOY!
YOU'RE REVEALING A GREAT DEAL ABOUT YOURSELF HERE, PROF. LOGAN!
EVERYBODY CALM DOWN!!!
WHAT ABOUT WHAT I WANT?!
DON'T YOU NEED THE MASTER TO ELIMINATE?!
WHICH ONE IS THE--?!
DOES ANYONE KNOW
IT'S YOUR FAULT FOR COMING HERE IN THE FIRST PLACE.
WHAT HAPPENS IF THE TEAM BREAKS UP?!
HOW ARE THEY--?
THIS IS HILARIOUS!!!
THE BEST X-MEN PICNIC EVER!!!
THIS IS INSANE!!!
ANGEL!!!
WHY DON'T YOU TAKE YOUR--?!
THIS IS CRAZY!!!
STOP IT.
STOP THIS NOW!!

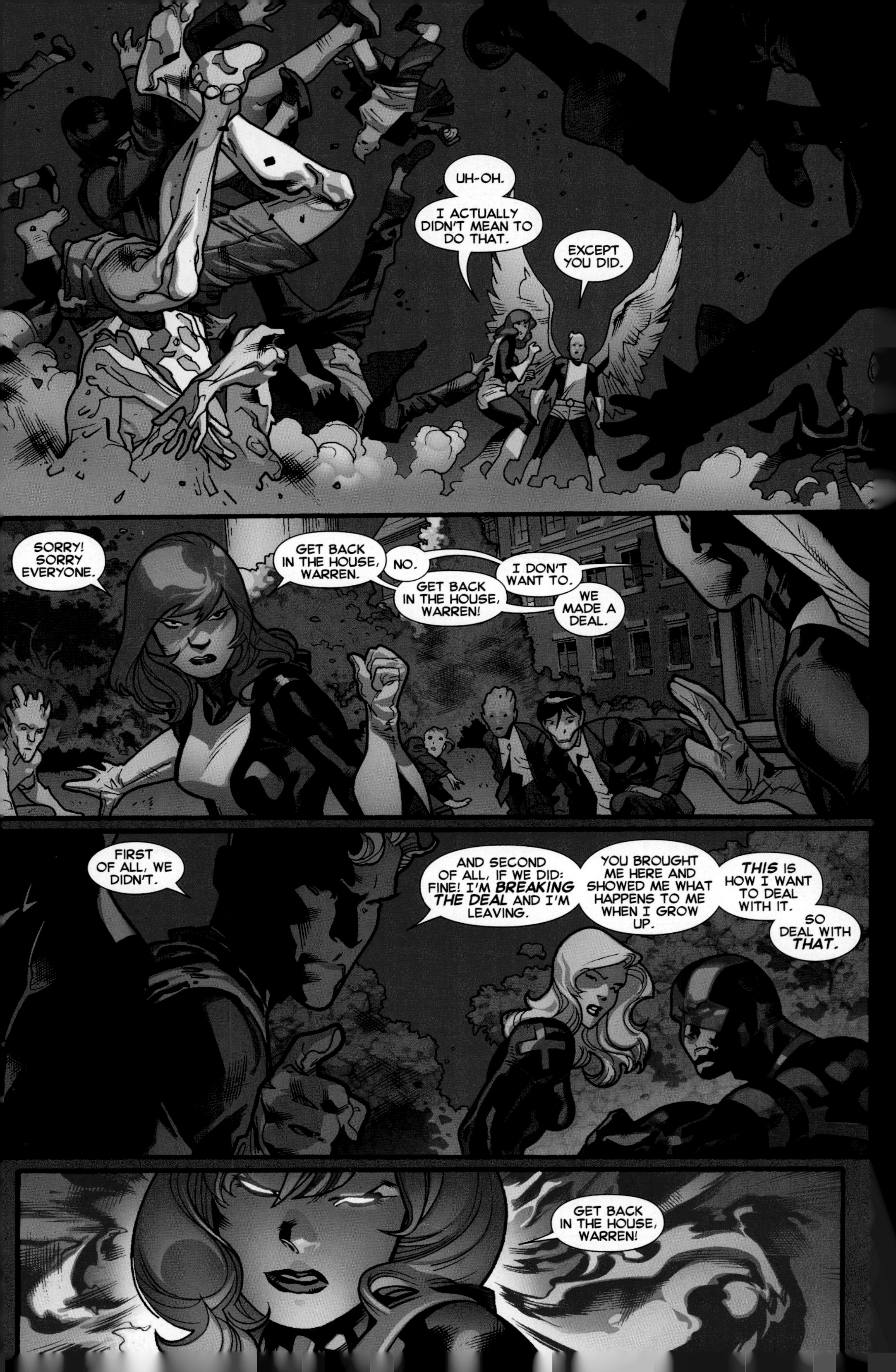

UH-OH.
I ACTUALLY DIDN'T MEAN TO DO THAT.
EXCEPT YOU DID.
SORRY! SORRY EVERYONE.
GET BACK IN THE HOUSE, WARREN.
NO.
GET BACK IN THE HOUSE, WARREN!
I DON'T WANT TO.
WE MADE A DEAL.
FIRST OF ALL, WE DIDN'T.
AND SECOND OF ALL, IF WE DID: FINE! I'M BREAKING THE DEAL AND I'M LEAVING.
YOU BROUGHT ME HERE AND SHOWED ME WHAT HAPPENS TO ME WHEN I GROW UP.
THIS IS HOW I WANT TO DEAL WITH IT.
SO DEAL WITH THAT.
GET BACK IN THE HOUSE, WARREN!

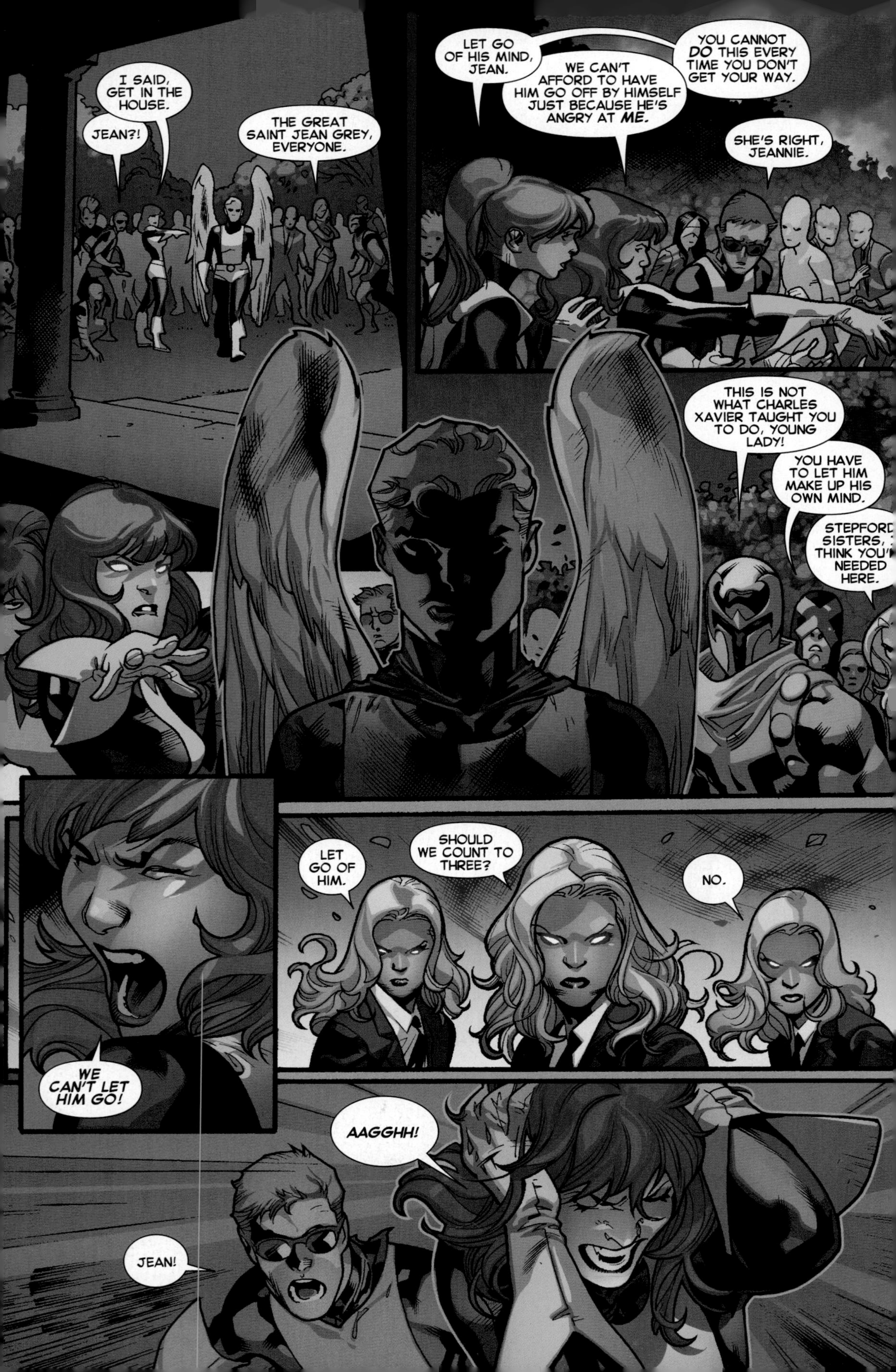
I SAID, GET IN THE HOUSE.
JEAN?!
THE GREAT SAINT JEAN GREY, EVERYONE.
LET GO OF HIS MIND, JEAN.
WE CAN'T AFFORD TO HAVE HIM GO OFF BY HIMSELF JUST BECAUSE HE'S ANGRY AT ME.
YOU CANNOT DO THIS EVERY TIME YOU DON'T GET YOUR WAY.
SHE'S RIGHT, JEANNIE.
THIS IS NOT WHAT CHARLES XAVIER TAUGHT YOU TO DO, YOUNG LADY!
YOU HAVE TO LET HIM MAKE UP HIS OWN MIND.
STEPFORD SISTERS, THINK YOU NEEDED HERE.
WE CAN'T LET HIM GO!
LET GO OF HIM.
SHOULD WE COUNT TO THREE?
NO.
AAGGHH!
JEAN!

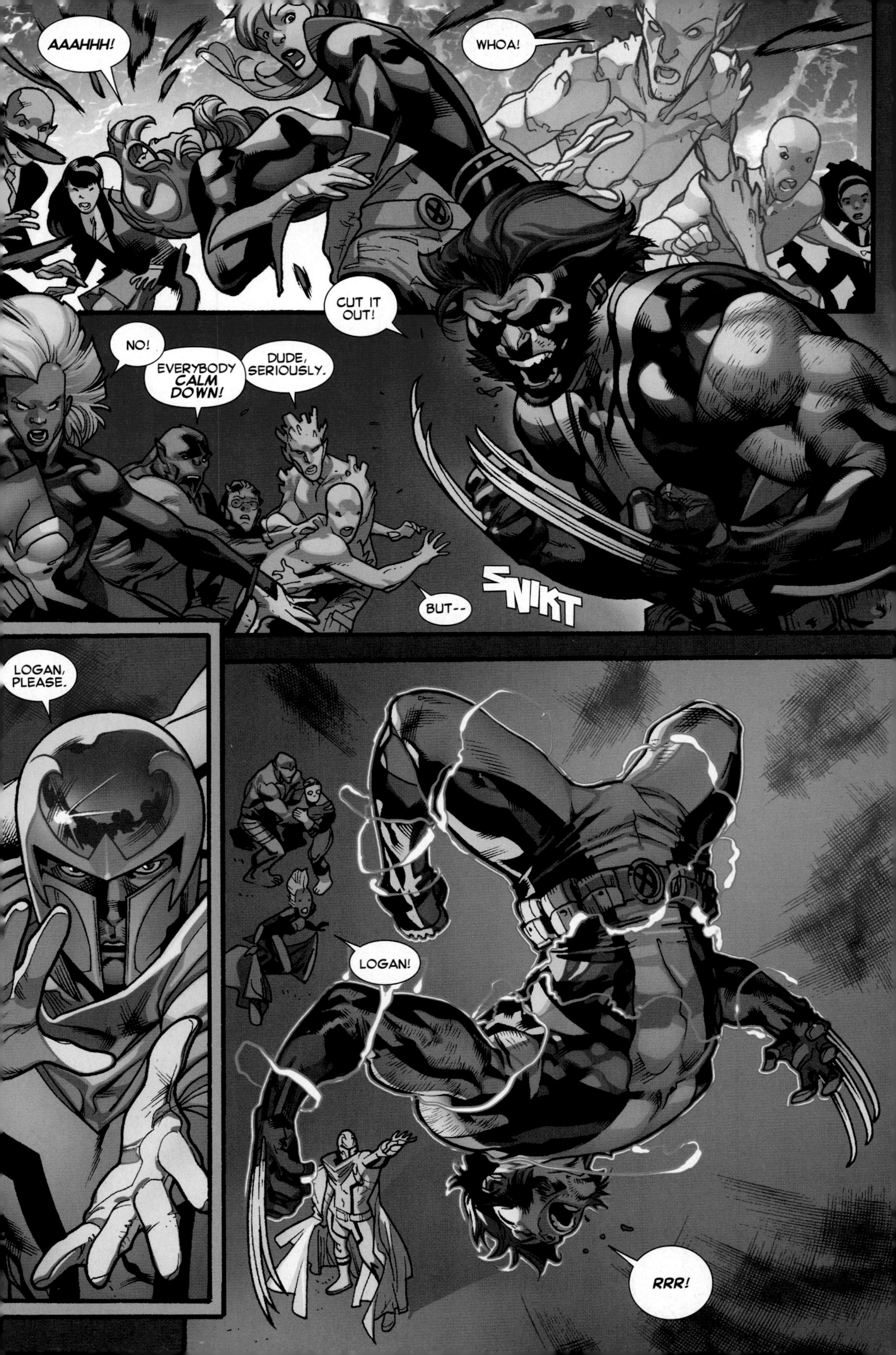
AAAHHH!
WHOA!
CUT IT OUT!
NO!
EVERYBODY CALM DOWN!
DUDE, SERIOUSLY.
BUT--
SNIKT
LOGAN, PLEASE.
LOGAN!
RRR!

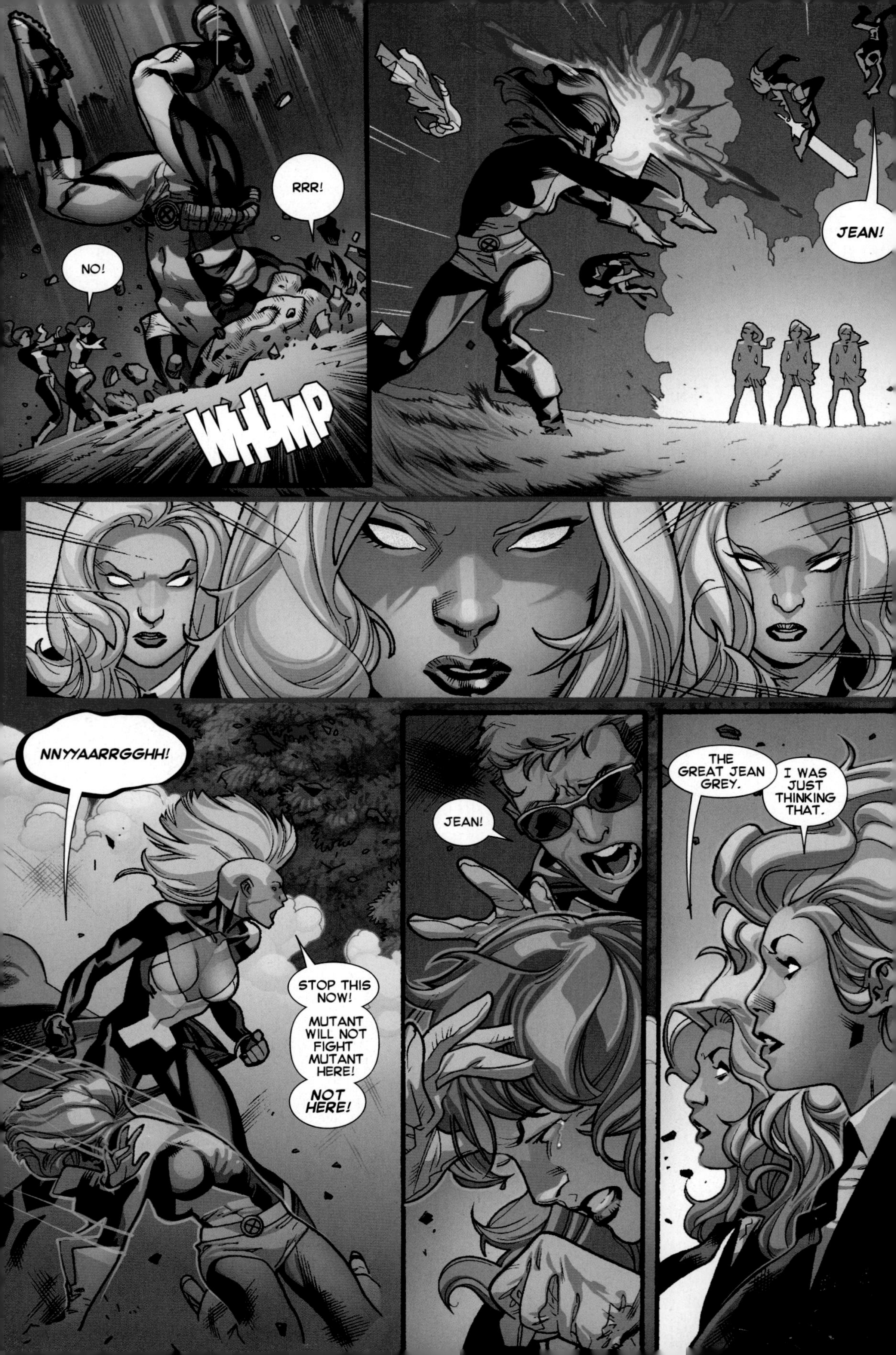
RRR!
NO!
WHUMP
JEAN!
NNYYAARRGGHH!
STOP THIS NOW!
MUTANT WILL NOT FIGHT MUTANT HERE!
NOT HERE!
JEAN!
THE GREAT JEAN GREY.
I WAS JUST THINKING THAT.

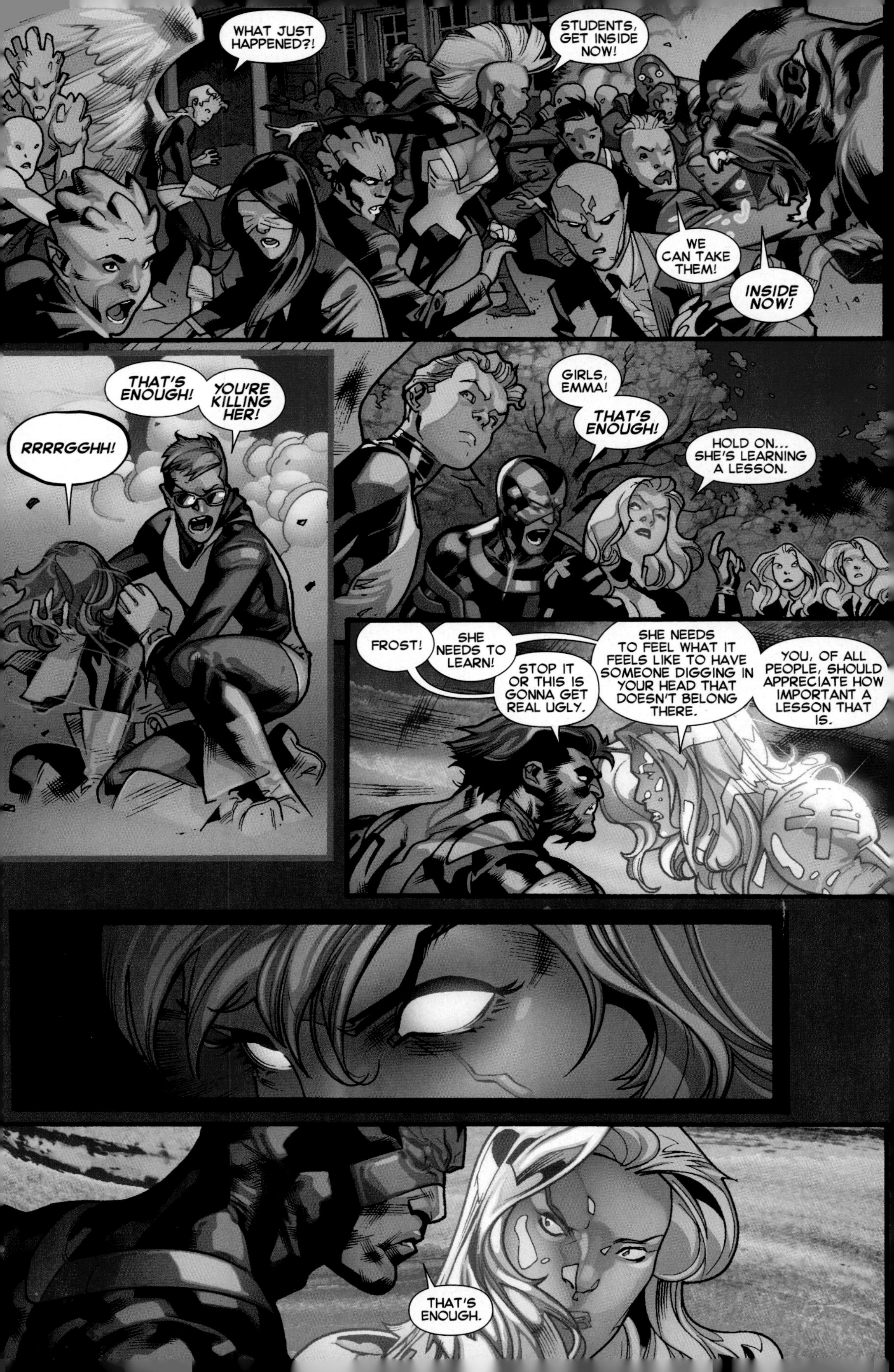
WHAT JUST HAPPENED?!
STUDENTS, GET INSIDE NOW!
WE CAN TAKE THEM!
INSIDE NOW!
THAT'S ENOUGH!
YOU'RE KILLING HER!
RRRRGGHH!
GIRLS, EMMA!
THAT'S ENOUGH!
HOLD ON... SHE'S LEARNING A LESSON.
FROST!
SHE NEEDS TO LEARN!
STOP IT OR THIS IS GONNA GET REAL UGLY.
SHE NEEDS TO FEEL WHAT IT FEELS LIKE TO HAVE SOMEONE DIGGING IN YOUR HEAD THAT DOESN'T BELONG THERE.
YOU, OF ALL PEOPLE, SHOULD APPRECIATE HOW IMPORTANT A LESSON THAT IS.
THAT'S ENOUGH.

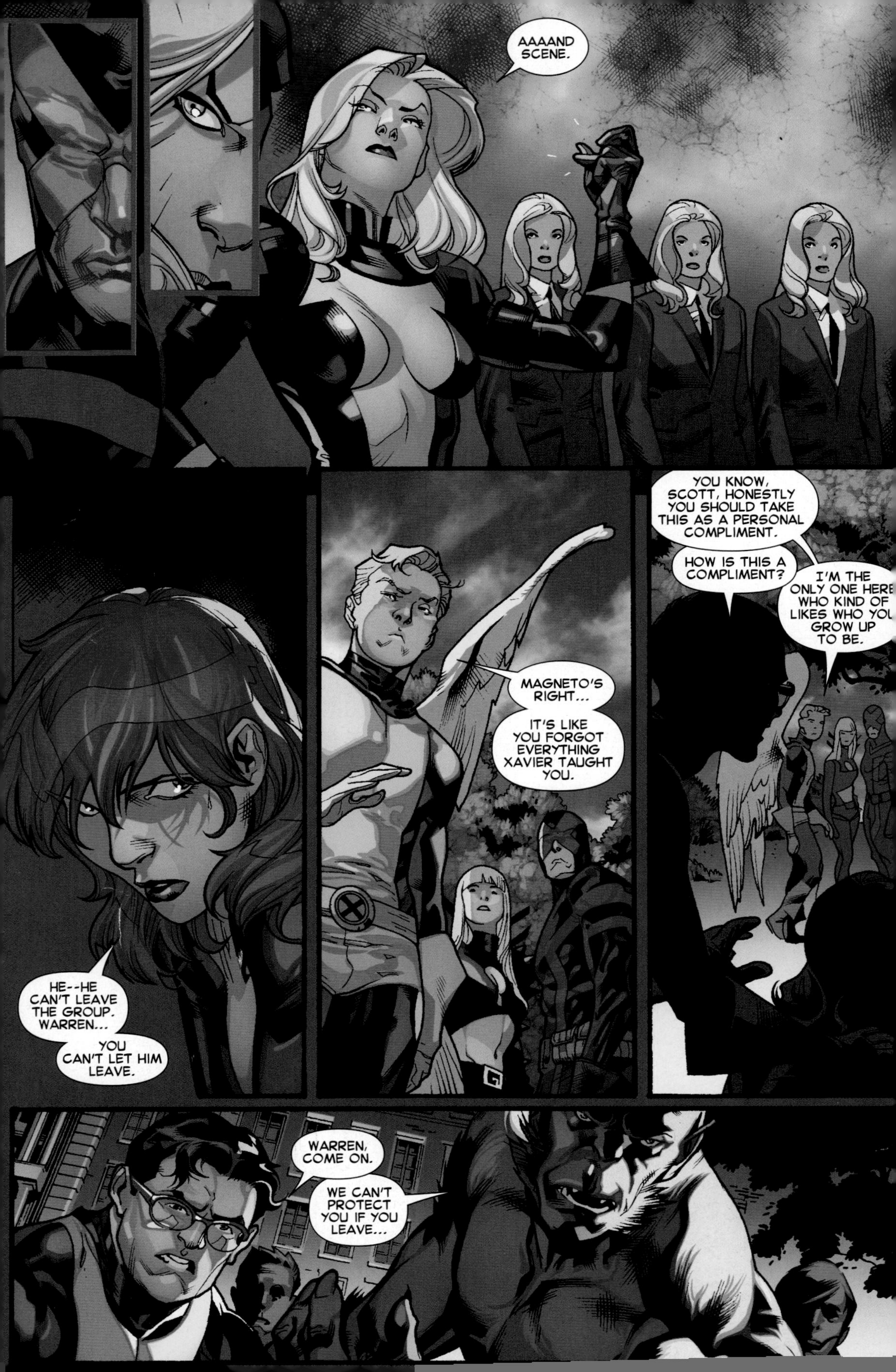
AAAAND SCENE.
YOU KNOW, SCOTT, HONESTLY YOU SHOULD TAKE THIS AS A PERSONAL COMPLIMENT.
HOW IS THIS A COMPLIMENT?
I'M THE ONLY ONE HERE WHO KIND OF LIKES WHO YOU GROW UP TO BE.
MAGNETO'S RIGHT...
IT'S LIKE YOU FORGOT EVERYTHING XAVIER TAUGHT YOU.
HE--HE CAN'T LEAVE THE GROUP. WARREN...
YOU CAN'T LET HIM LEAVE.
WARREN, COME ON.
WE CAN'T PROTECT YOU IF YOU LEAVE...

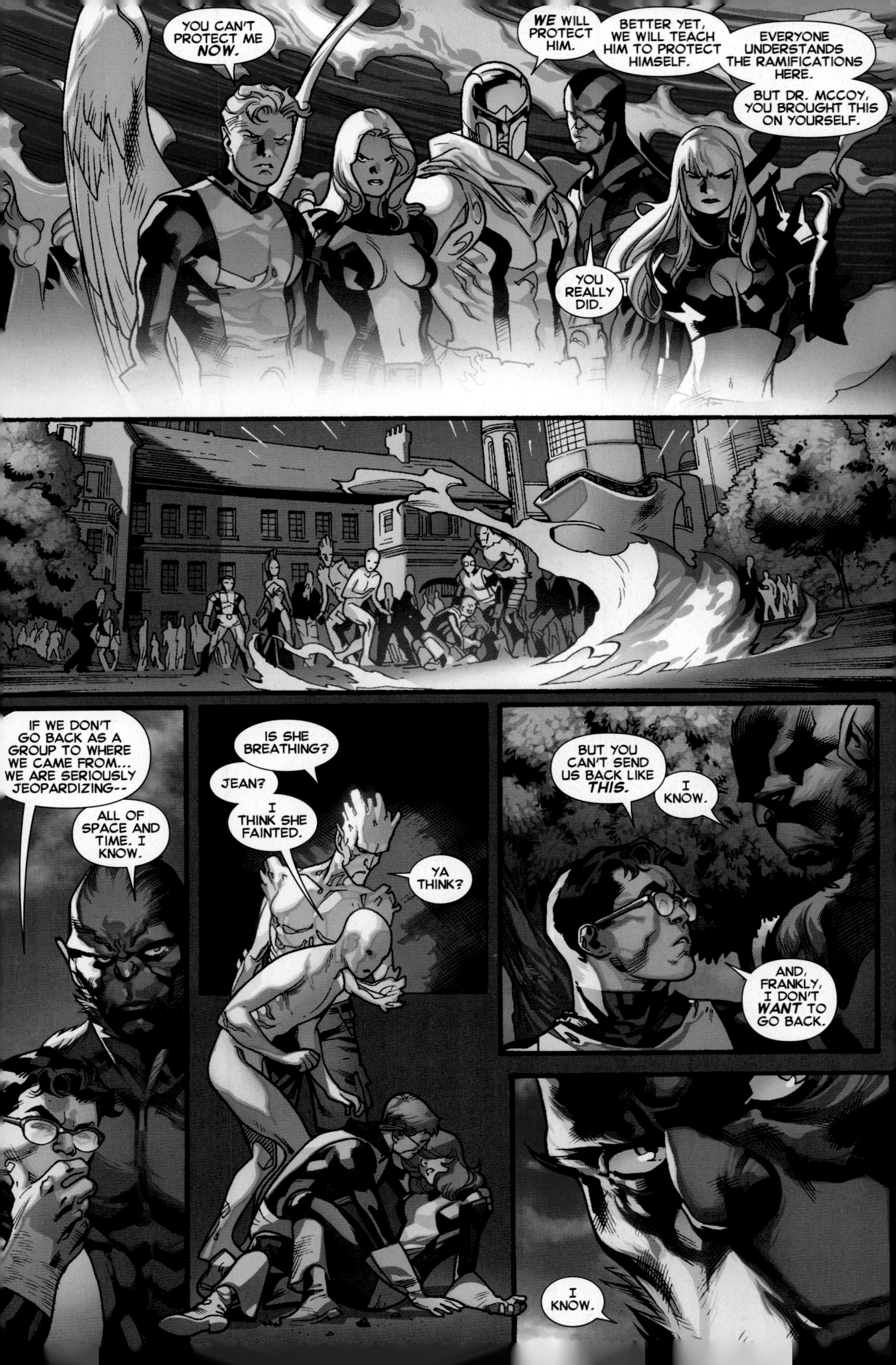
YOU CAN'T PROTECT ME *NOW.*
WE WILL PROTECT HIM.
BETTER YET, WE WILL TEACH HIM TO PROTECT HIMSELF.
EVERYONE UNDERSTANDS THE RAMIFICATIONS HERE.
BUT DR. MCCOY, YOU BROUGHT THIS ON YOURSELF.
YOU REALLY DID.
IF WE DON'T GO BACK AS A GROUP TO WHERE WE CAME FROM... WE ARE SERIOUSLY JEOPARDIZING--
ALL OF SPACE AND TIME. I KNOW.
IS SHE BREATHING?
JEAN?
I THINK SHE FAINTED.
YA THINK?
BUT YOU CAN'T SEND US BACK LIKE *THIS.*
I KNOW.
AND, FRANKLY, I DON'T *WANT* TO GO BACK.
I KNOW.

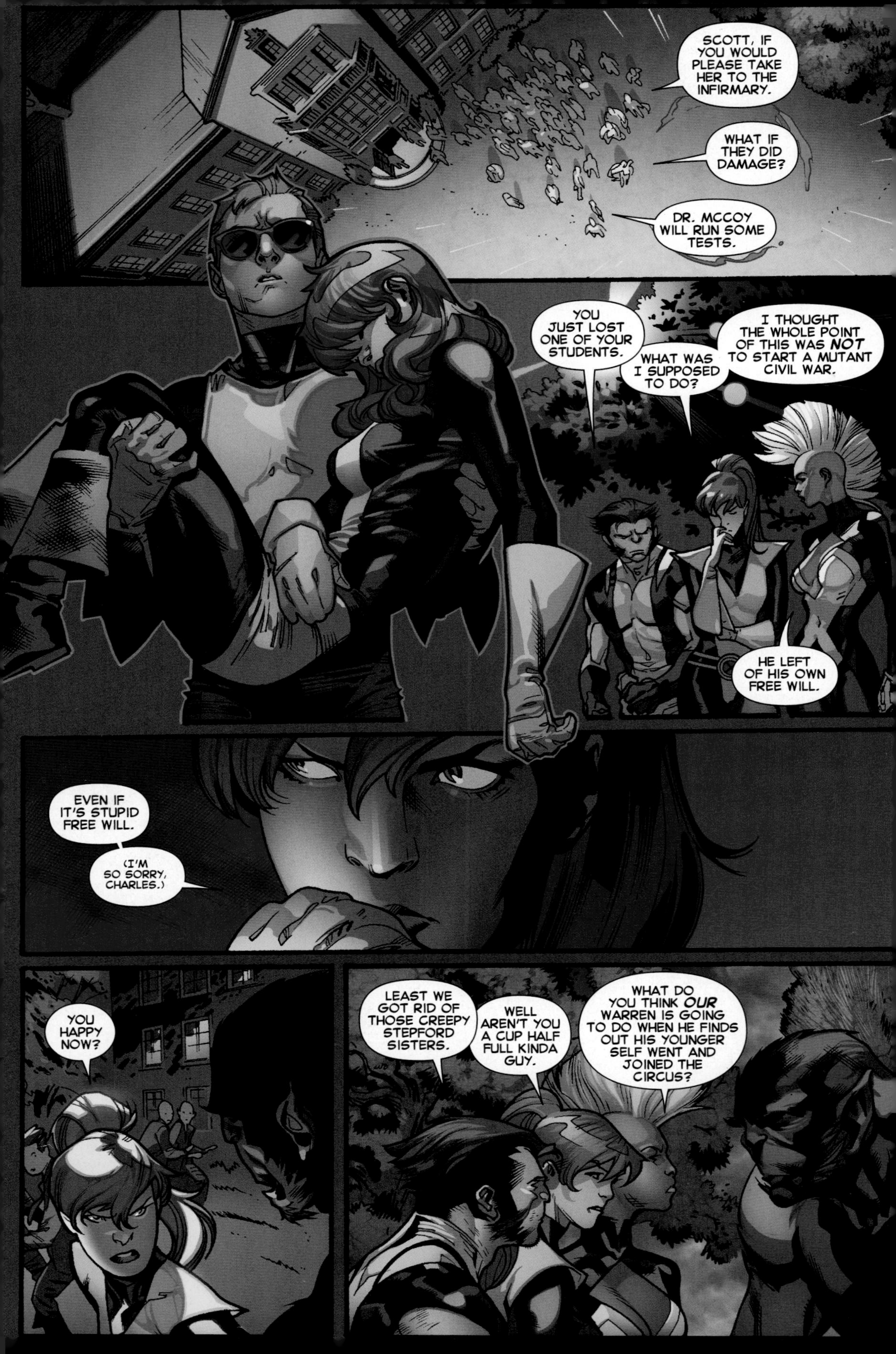
SCOTT, IF YOU WOULD PLEASE TAKE HER TO THE INFIRMARY.
WHAT IF THEY DID DAMAGE?
DR. MCCOY WILL RUN SOME TESTS.
YOU JUST LOST ONE OF YOUR STUDENTS.
WHAT WAS I SUPPOSED TO DO?
I THOUGHT THE WHOLE POINT OF THIS WAS NOT TO START A MUTANT CIVIL WAR.
HE LEFT OF HIS OWN FREE WILL.
EVEN IF IT'S STUPID FREE WILL.
(I'M SO SORRY, CHARLES.)
YOU HAPPY NOW?
LEAST WE GOT RID OF THOSE CREEPY STEPFORD SISTERS.
WELL AREN'T YOU A CUP HALF FULL KINDA GUY.
WHAT DO YOU THINK OUR WARREN IS GOING TO DO WHEN HE FINDS OUT HIS YOUNGER SELF WENT AND JOINED THE CIRCUS?

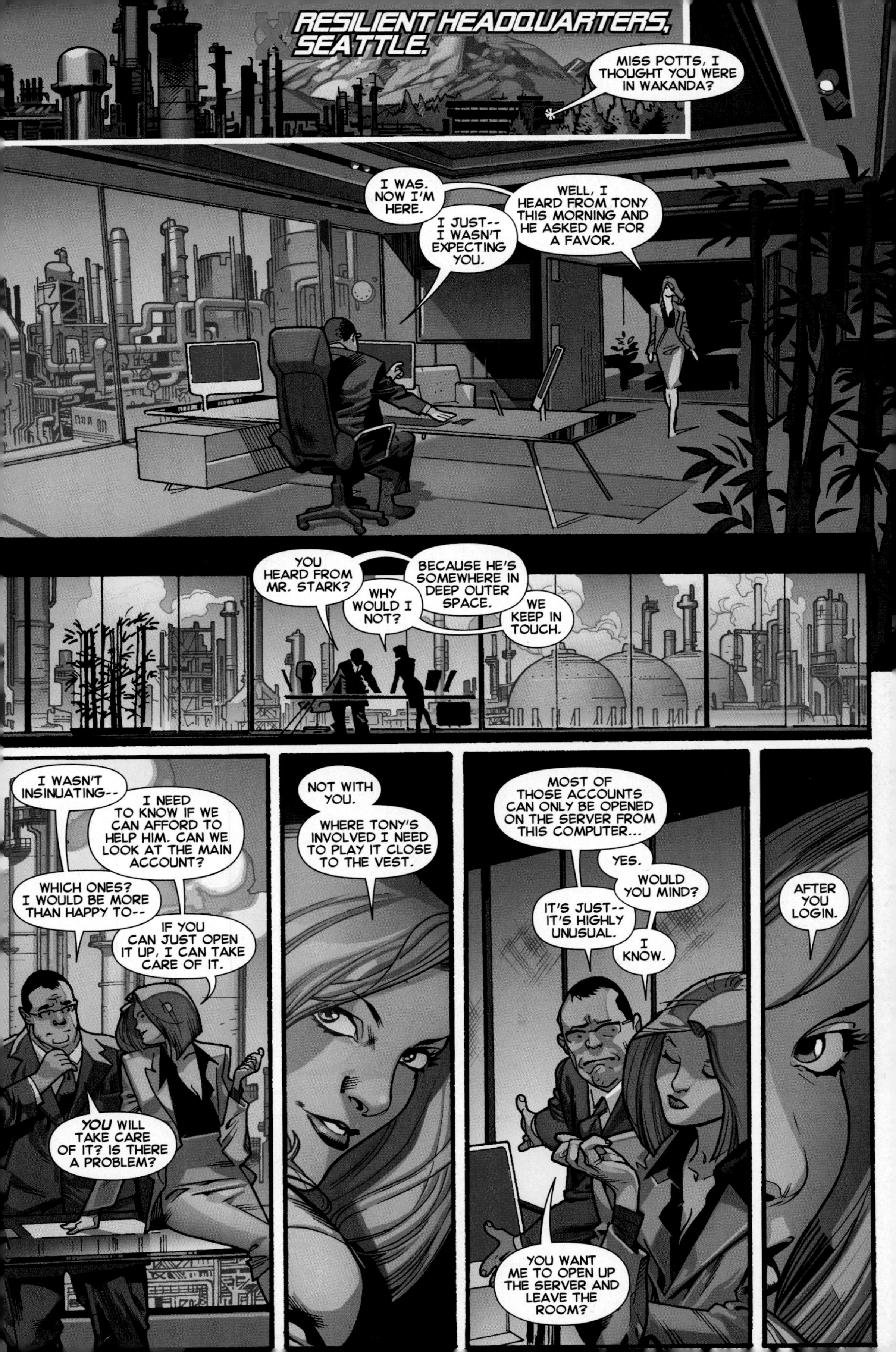
RESILIENT HEADQUARTERS, SEATTLE.
MISS POTTS, I THOUGHT YOU WERE IN WAKANDA?
I WAS. NOW I'M HERE.
I JUST-- I WASN'T EXPECTING YOU.
WELL, I HEARD FROM TONY THIS MORNING AND HE ASKED ME FOR A FAVOR.
YOU HEARD FROM MR. STARK?
WHY WOULD I NOT?
BECAUSE HE'S SOMEWHERE IN DEEP OUTER SPACE.
WE KEEP IN TOUCH.
I WASN'T INSINUATING--
I NEED TO KNOW IF WE CAN AFFORD TO HELP HIM. CAN WE LOOK AT THE MAIN ACCOUNT?
WHICH ONES? I WOULD BE MORE THAN HAPPY TO--
IF YOU CAN JUST OPEN IT UP, I CAN TAKE CARE OF IT.
YOU WILL TAKE CARE OF IT? IS THERE A PROBLEM?
NOT WITH YOU.
WHERE TONY'S INVOLVED I NEED TO PLAY IT CLOSE TO THE VEST.
MOST OF THOSE ACCOUNTS CAN ONLY BE OPENED ON THE SERVER FROM THIS COMPUTER...
YES.
WOULD YOU MIND?
IT'S JUST-- IT'S HIGHLY UNUSUAL.
I KNOW.
YOU WANT ME TO OPEN UP THE SERVER AND LEAVE THE ROOM?
AFTER YOU LOGIN.

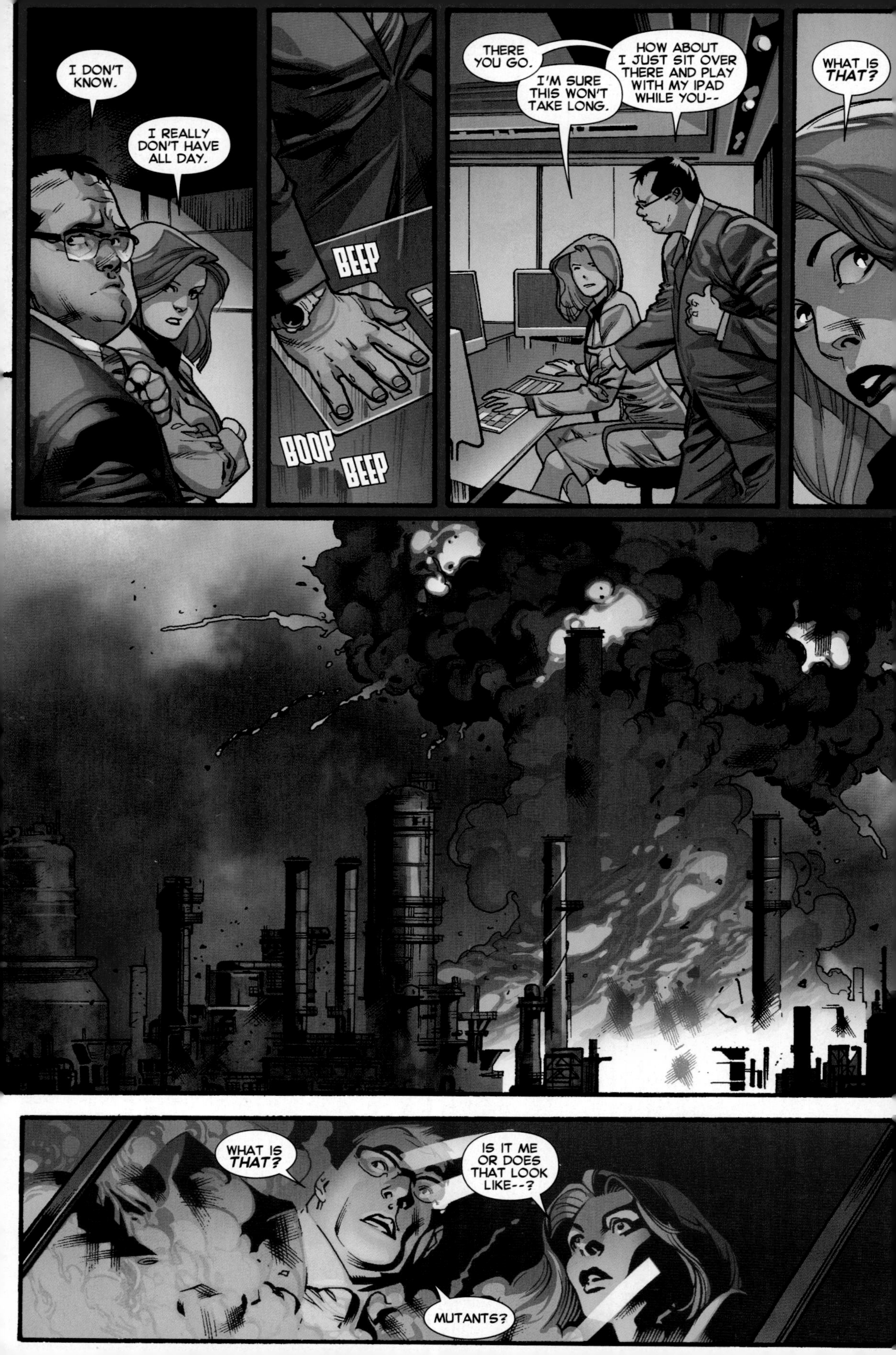
I DON'T KNOW.
I REALLY DON'T HAVE ALL DAY.
BEEP
BOOP
BEEP
THERE YOU GO.
I'M SURE THIS WON'T TAKE LONG.
HOW ABOUT I JUST SIT OVER THERE AND PLAY WITH MY IPAD WHILE YOU--
WHAT IS *THAT?*
WHAT IS *THAT?*
IS IT ME OR DOES THAT LOOK LIKE--?
MUTANTS?

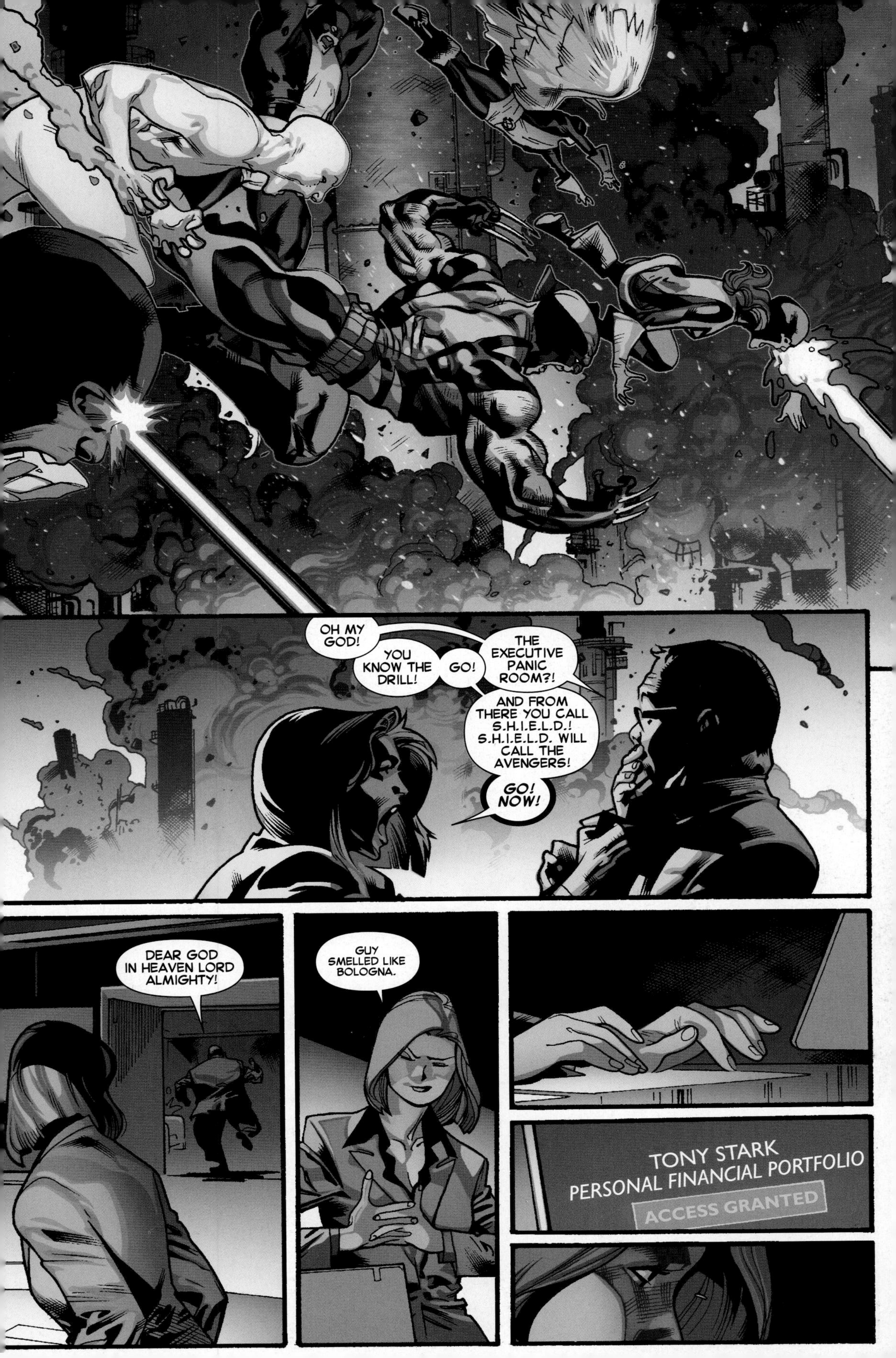

OH MY GOD!
THE EXECUTIVE PANIC ROOM?!
YOU KNOW THE DRILL!
GO!
AND FROM THERE YOU CALL S.H.I.E.L.D.! S.H.I.E.L.D. WILL CALL THE AVENGERS!
GO! NOW!
DEAR GOD IN HEAVEN LORD ALMIGHTY!
GUY SMELLED LIKE BOLOGNA.
TONY STARK
PERSONAL FINANCIAL PORTFOLIO
ACCESS GRANTED

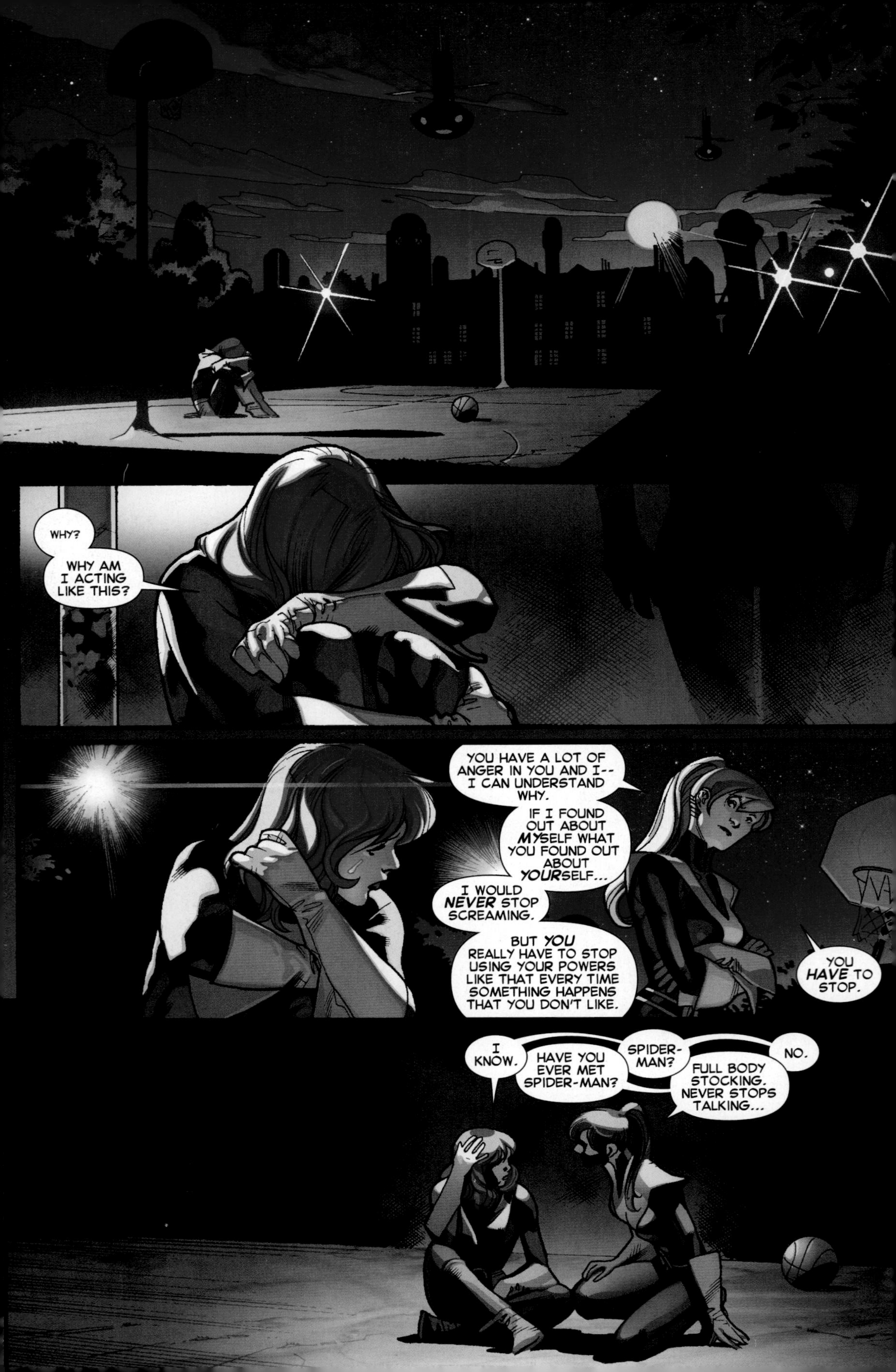
WHY?
WHY AM I ACTING LIKE THIS?
YOU HAVE A LOT OF ANGER IN YOU AND I-- I CAN UNDERSTAND WHY.
IF I FOUND OUT ABOUT **MY**SELF WHAT YOU FOUND OUT ABOUT **YOUR**SELF...
I WOULD **NEVER** STOP SCREAMING.
BUT **YOU** REALLY HAVE TO STOP USING YOUR POWERS LIKE THAT EVERY TIME SOMETHING HAPPENS THAT YOU DON'T LIKE.
YOU **HAVE** TO STOP.
I KNOW.
HAVE YOU EVER MET SPIDER-MAN?
SPIDER-MAN?
NO.
FULL BODY STOCKING. NEVER STOPS TALKING...

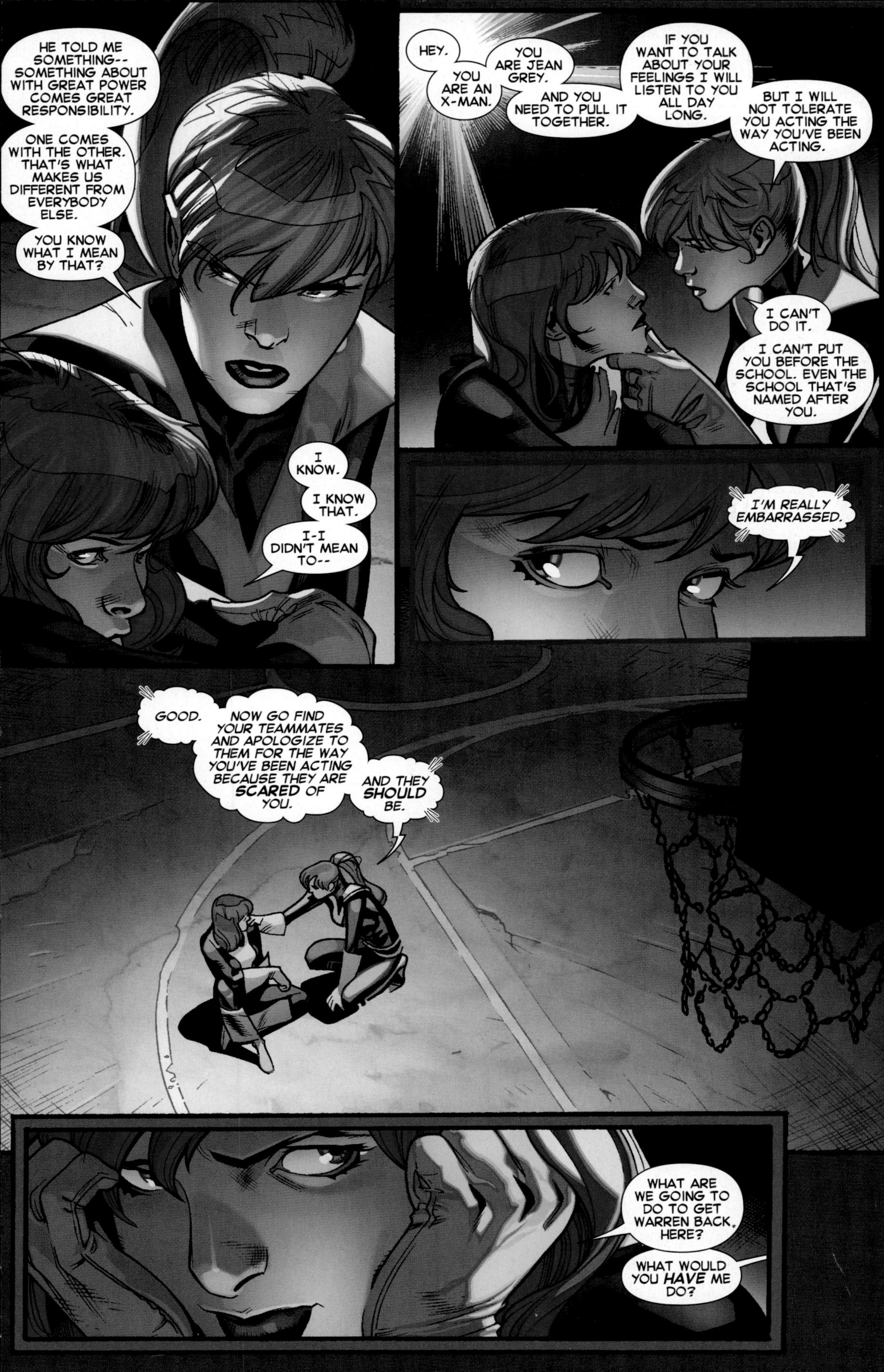
HE TOLD ME SOMETHING-- SOMETHING ABOUT WITH GREAT POWER COMES GREAT RESPONSIBILITY.
ONE COMES WITH THE OTHER. THAT'S WHAT MAKES US DIFFERENT FROM EVERYBODY ELSE.
YOU KNOW WHAT I MEAN BY THAT?
I KNOW.
I KNOW THAT.
I-I DIDN'T MEAN TO--
HEY.
YOU ARE AN X-MAN.
YOU ARE JEAN GREY.
AND YOU NEED TO PULL IT TOGETHER.
IF YOU WANT TO TALK ABOUT YOUR FEELINGS I WILL LISTEN TO YOU ALL DAY LONG.
BUT I WILL NOT TOLERATE YOU ACTING THE WAY YOU'VE BEEN ACTING.
I CAN'T DO IT.
I CAN'T PUT YOU BEFORE THE SCHOOL. EVEN THE SCHOOL THAT'S NAMED AFTER YOU.
I'M REALLY EMBARRASSED.
GOOD.
*NOW GO FIND YOUR TEAMMATES AND APOLOGIZE TO THEM FOR THE WAY YOU'VE BEEN ACTING BECAUSE THEY ARE **SCARED** OF YOU.*
AND THEY **SHOULD** BE.
WHAT ARE WE GOING TO DO TO GET WARREN BACK HERE?
WHAT WOULD YOU ***HAVE*** ME DO?

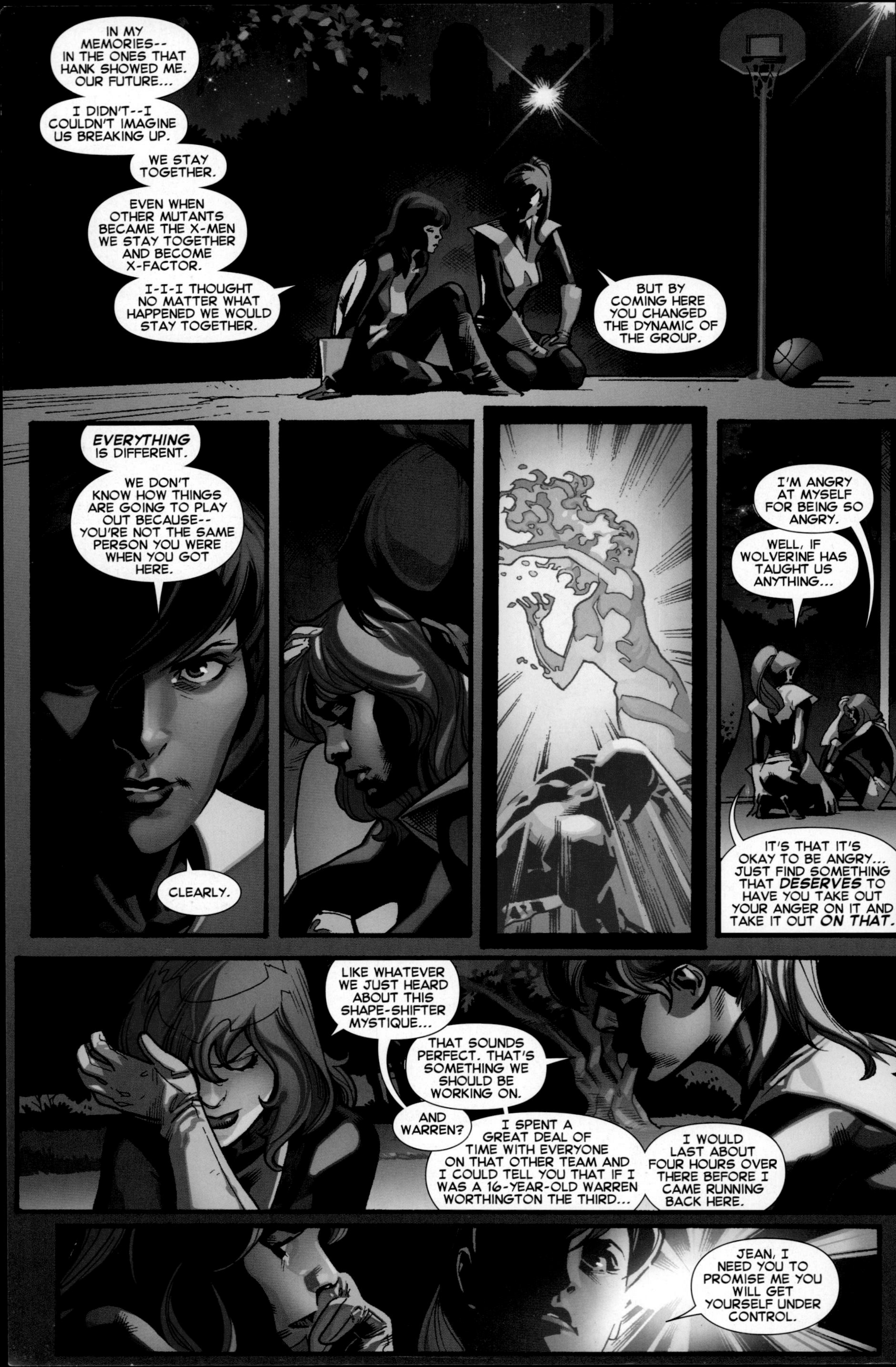
IN MY MEMORIES-- IN THE ONES THAT HANK SHOWED ME. OUR FUTURE...
I DIDN'T--I COULDN'T IMAGINE US BREAKING UP.
WE STAY TOGETHER.
EVEN WHEN OTHER MUTANTS BECAME THE X-MEN WE STAY TOGETHER AND BECOME X-FACTOR.
I-I-I THOUGHT NO MATTER WHAT HAPPENED WE WOULD STAY TOGETHER.
BUT BY COMING HERE YOU CHANGED THE DYNAMIC OF THE GROUP.
EVERYTHING IS DIFFERENT.
WE DON'T KNOW HOW THINGS ARE GOING TO PLAY OUT BECAUSE-- YOU'RE NOT THE SAME PERSON YOU WERE WHEN YOU GOT HERE.
CLEARLY.
I'M ANGRY AT MYSELF FOR BEING SO ANGRY.
WELL, IF WOLVERINE HAS TAUGHT US ANYTHING...
IT'S THAT IT'S OKAY TO BE ANGRY... JUST FIND SOMETHING THAT DESERVES TO HAVE YOU TAKE OUT YOUR ANGER ON IT AND TAKE IT OUT ON THAT.
LIKE WHATEVER WE JUST HEARD ABOUT THIS SHAPE-SHIFTER MYSTIQUE...
THAT SOUNDS PERFECT. THAT'S SOMETHING WE SHOULD BE WORKING ON.
AND WARREN?
I SPENT A GREAT DEAL OF TIME WITH EVERYONE ON THAT OTHER TEAM AND I COULD TELL YOU THAT IF I WAS A 16-YEAR-OLD WARREN WORTHINGTON THE THIRD...
I WOULD LAST ABOUT FOUR HOURS OVER THERE BEFORE I CAME RUNNING BACK HERE.
JEAN, I NEED YOU TO PROMISE ME YOU WILL GET YOURSELF UNDER CONTROL.

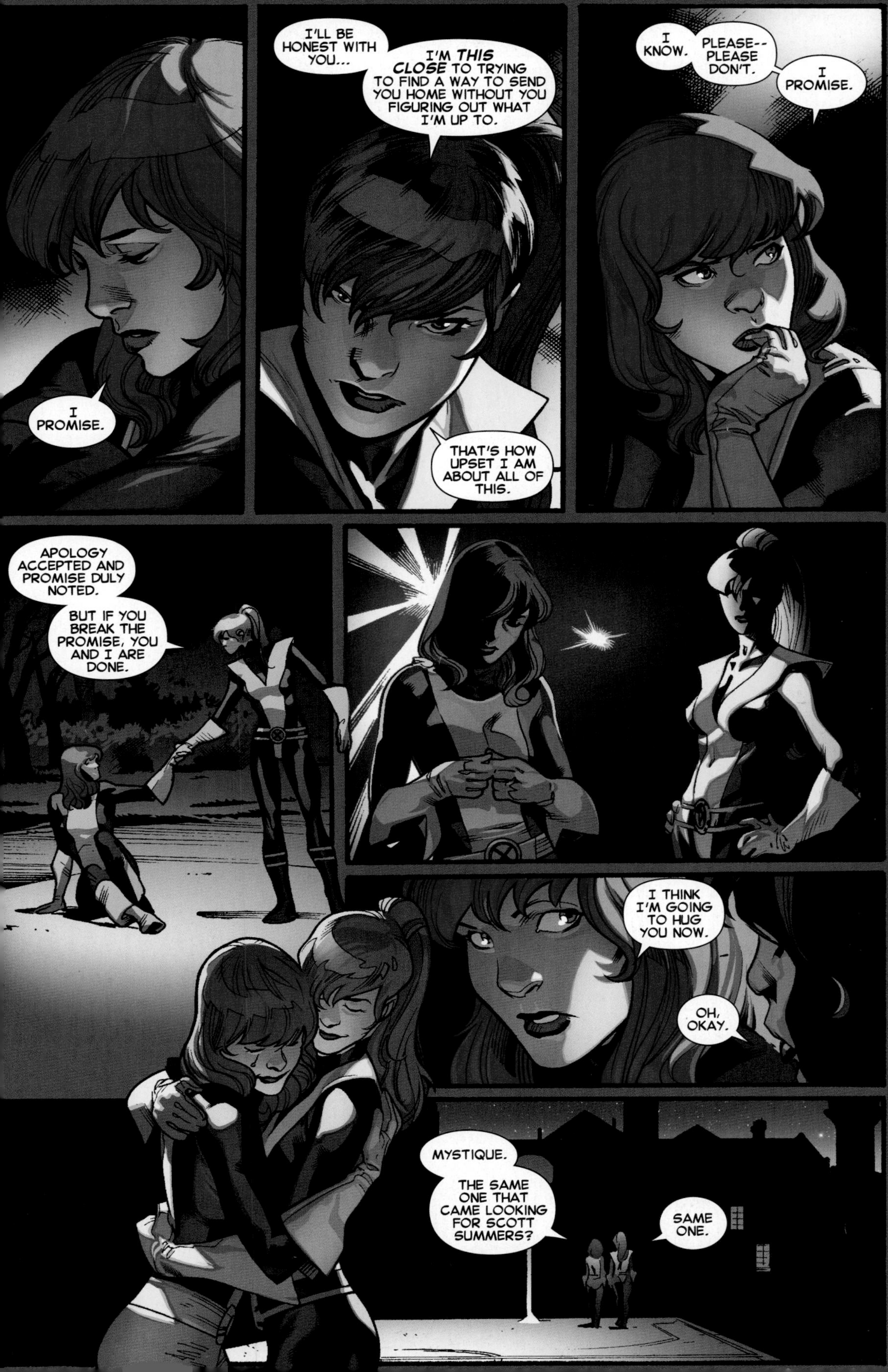
I PROMISE.
I'LL BE HONEST WITH YOU...
I'M *THIS CLOSE* TO TRYING TO FIND A WAY TO SEND YOU HOME WITHOUT YOU FIGURING OUT WHAT I'M UP TO.
THAT'S HOW UPSET I AM ABOUT ALL OF THIS.
I KNOW.
PLEASE-- PLEASE DON'T.
I PROMISE.
APOLOGY ACCEPTED AND PROMISE DULY NOTED.
BUT IF YOU BREAK THE PROMISE, YOU AND I ARE DONE.
I THINK I'M GOING TO HUG YOU NOW.
OH, OKAY.
MYSTIQUE.
THE SAME ONE THAT CAME LOOKING FOR SCOTT SUMMERS?
SAME ONE.

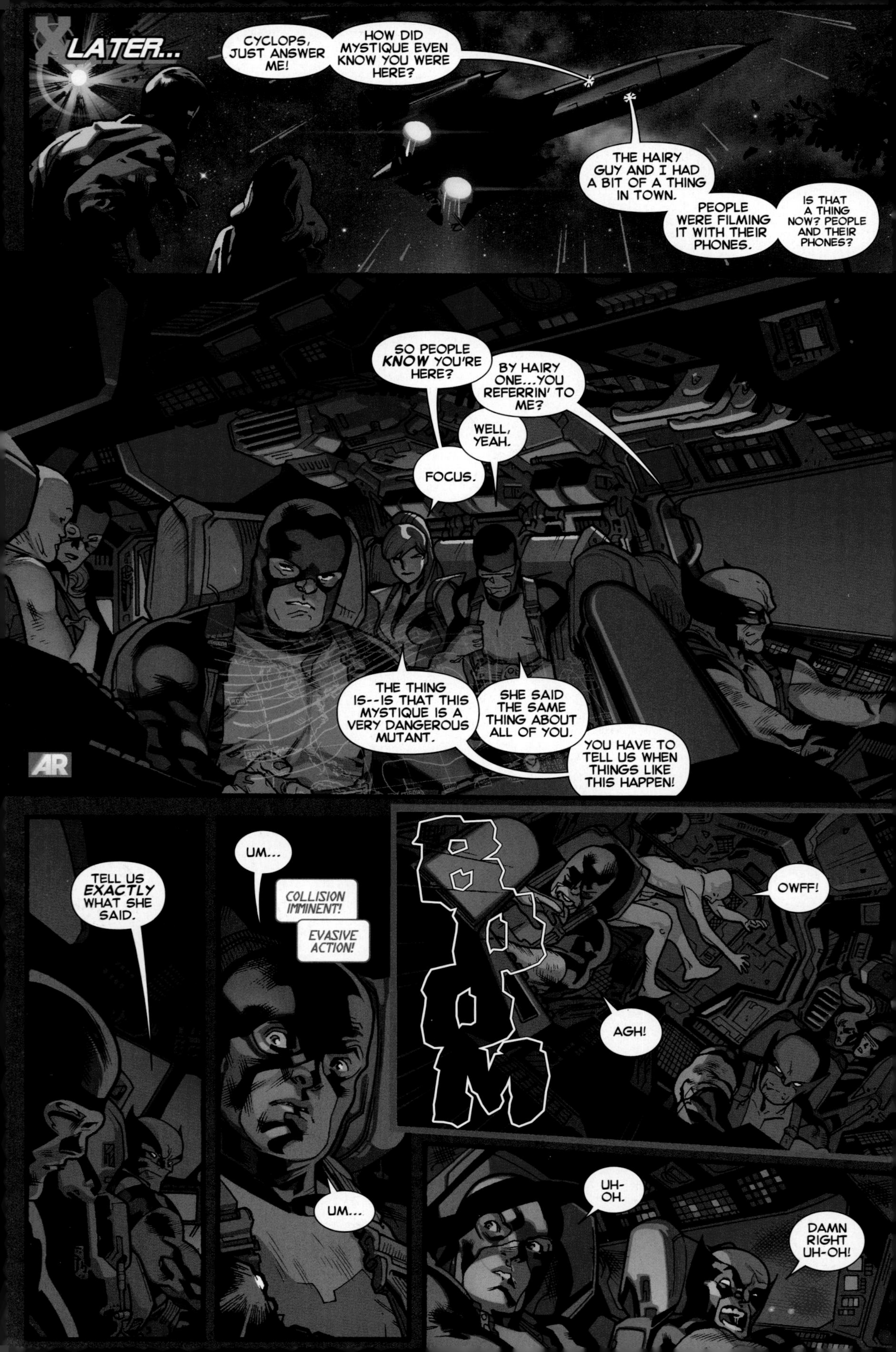
LATER...
CYCLOPS, JUST ANSWER ME!
HOW DID MYSTIQUE EVEN KNOW YOU WERE HERE?
THE HAIRY GUY AND I HAD A BIT OF A THING IN TOWN.
PEOPLE WERE FILMING IT WITH THEIR PHONES.
IS THAT A THING NOW? PEOPLE AND THEIR PHONES?
SO PEOPLE KNOW YOU'RE HERE?
BY HAIRY ONE...YOU REFERRIN' TO ME?
WELL, YEAH.
FOCUS.
THE THING IS--IS THAT THIS MYSTIQUE IS A VERY DANGEROUS MUTANT.
SHE SAID THE SAME THING ABOUT ALL OF YOU.
YOU HAVE TO TELL US WHEN THINGS LIKE THIS HAPPEN!
TELL US EXACTLY WHAT SHE SAID.
UM...
COLLISION IMMINENT!
EVASIVE ACTION!
UM...
BOOM
OWFF!
AGH!
UH-OH.
DAMN RIGHT UH-OH!

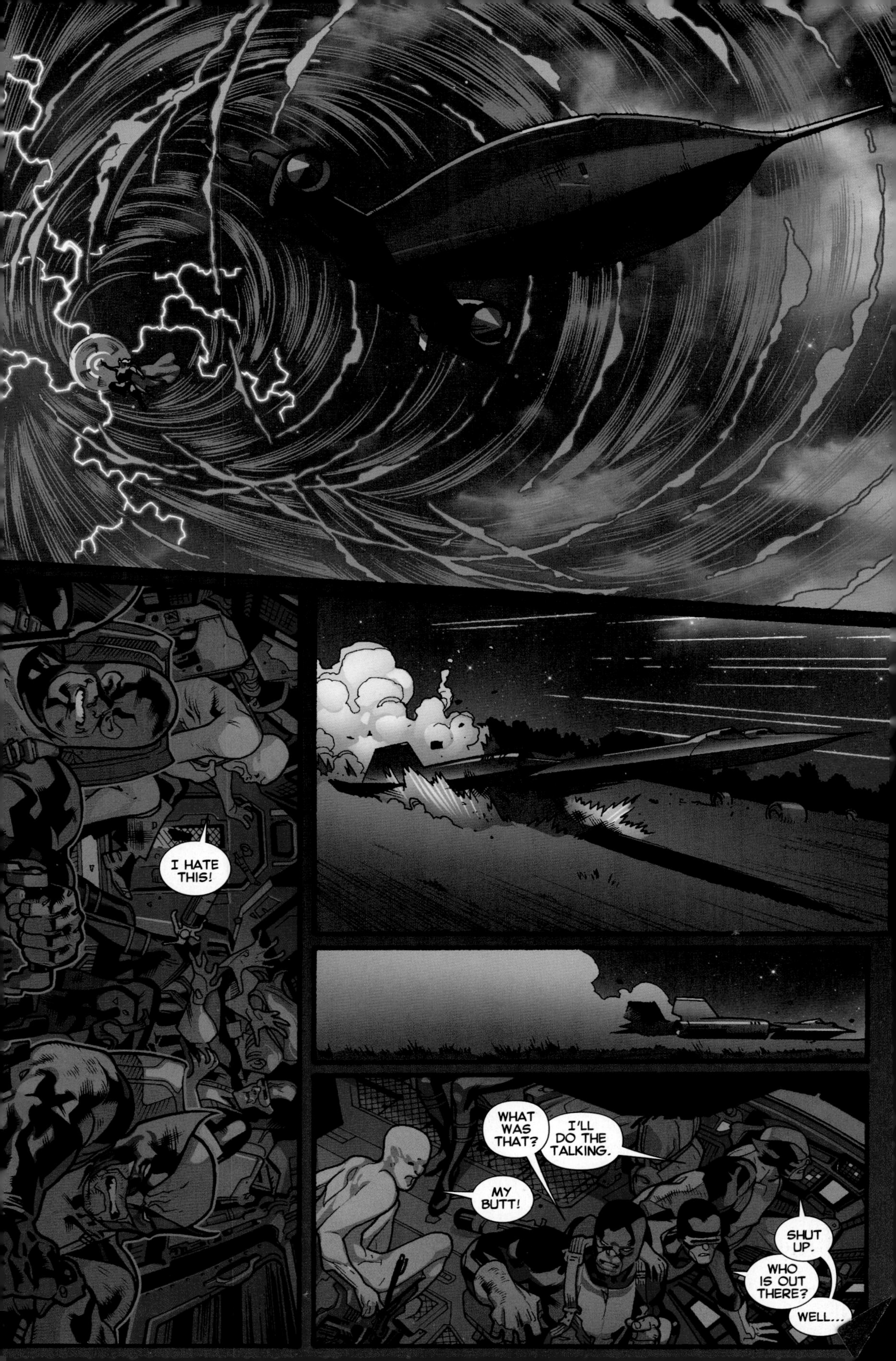
I HATE THIS!
WHAT WAS THAT?
I'LL DO THE TALKING.
MY BUTT!
SHUT UP.
WHO IS OUT THERE?
WELL...

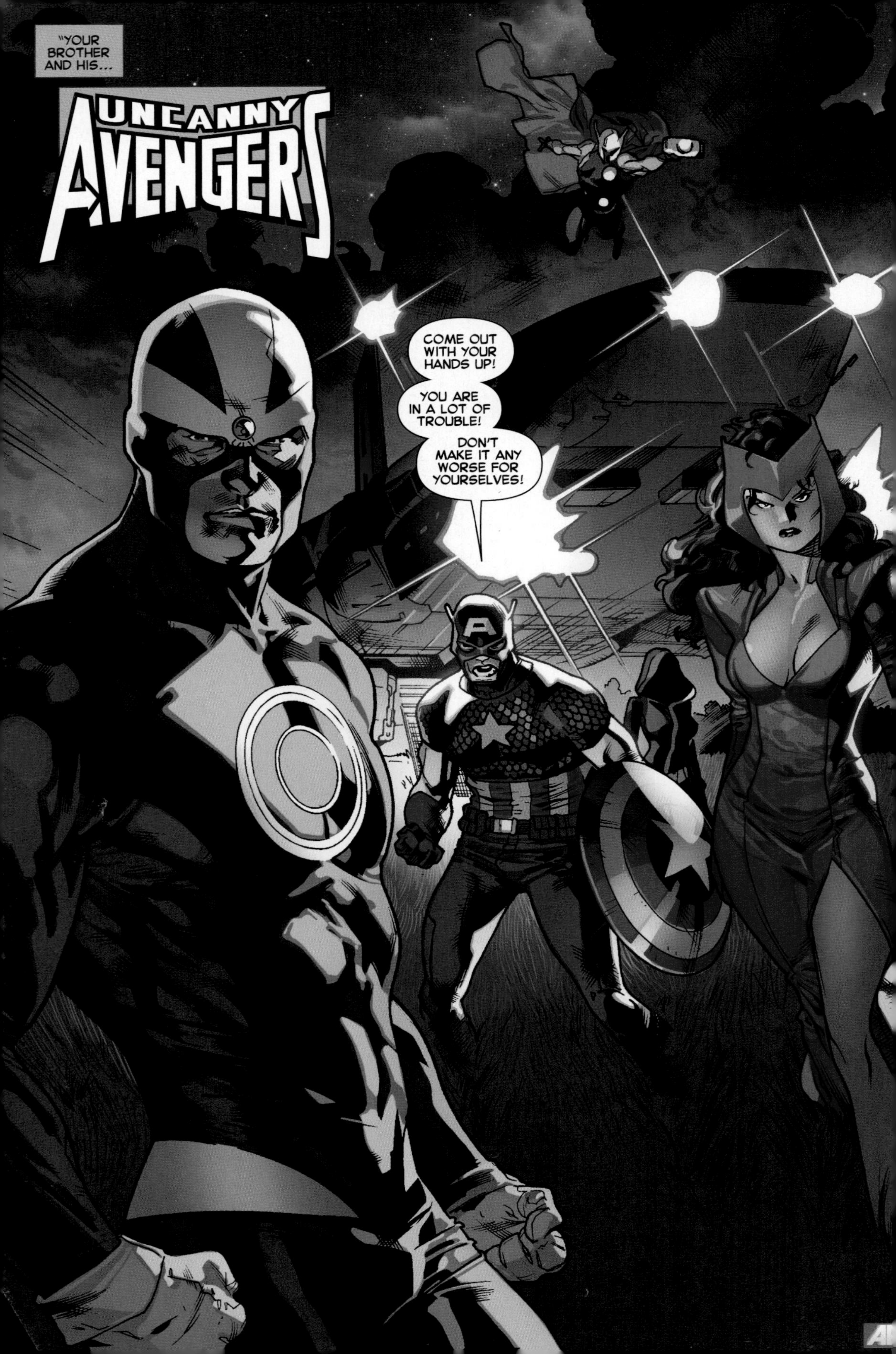
"YOUR BROTHER AND HIS...
UNCANNY AVENGERS
COME OUT WITH YOUR HANDS UP!
YOU ARE IN A LOT OF TROUBLE!
DON'T MAKE IT ANY WORSE FOR YOURSELVES!

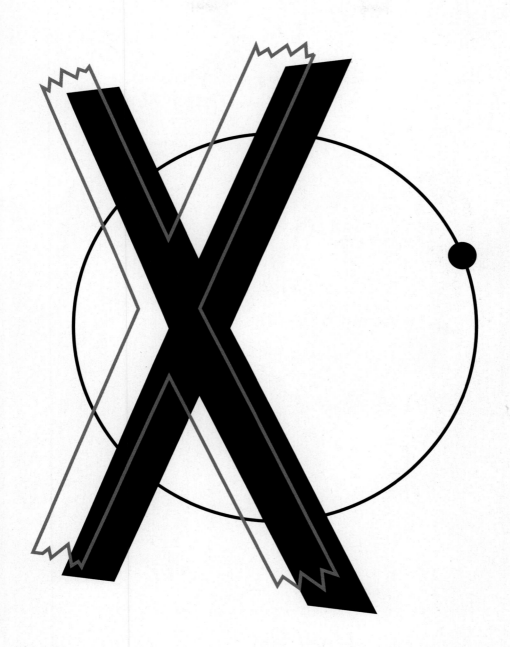

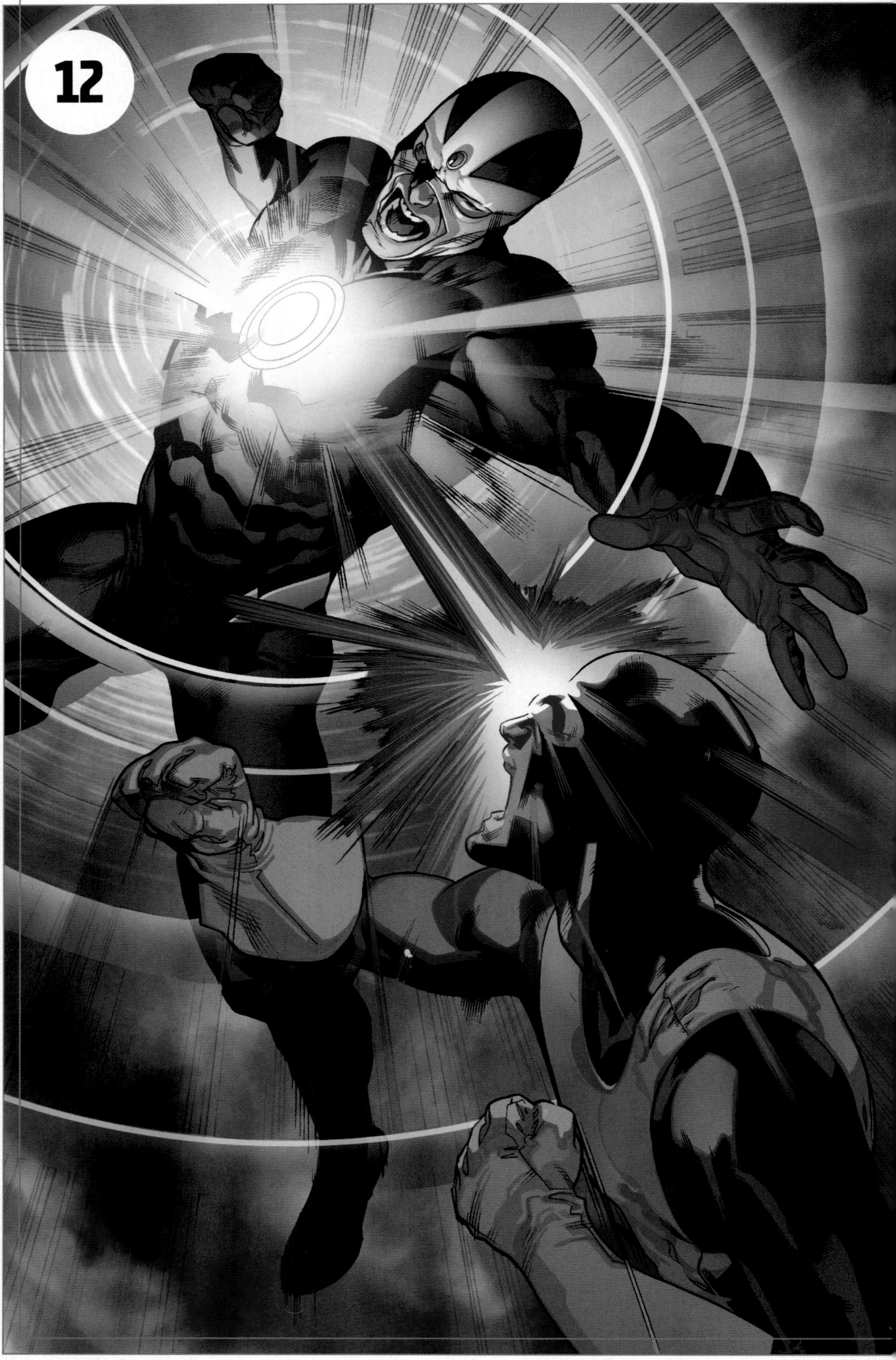
12

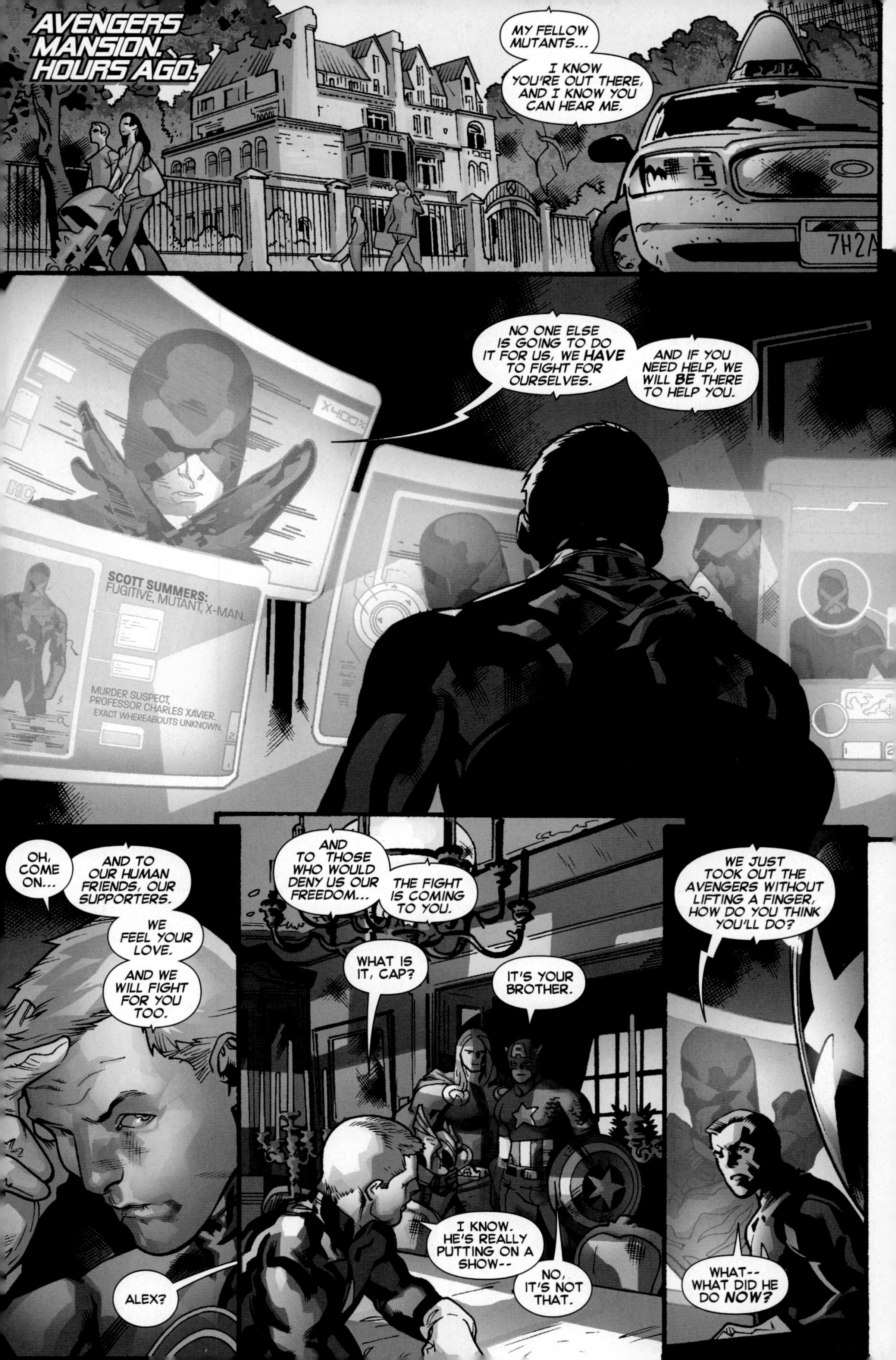
AVENGERS MANSION. HOURS AGO.
MY FELLOW MUTANTS...
I KNOW YOU'RE OUT THERE, AND I KNOW YOU CAN HEAR ME.
7H2A
NO ONE ELSE IS GOING TO DO IT FOR US, WE HAVE TO FIGHT FOR OURSELVES.
AND IF YOU NEED HELP, WE WILL BE THERE TO HELP YOU.
X400%
SCOTT SUMMERS: FUGITIVE, MUTANT, X-MAN.
MURDER SUSPECT, PROFESSOR CHARLES XAVIER. EXACT WHEREABOUTS UNKNOWN.
OH, COME ON...
AND TO OUR HUMAN FRIENDS, OUR SUPPORTERS.
WE FEEL YOUR LOVE.
AND WE WILL FIGHT FOR YOU TOO.
ALEX?
AND TO THOSE WHO WOULD DENY US OUR FREEDOM...
THE FIGHT IS COMING TO YOU.
WHAT IS IT, CAP?
IT'S YOUR BROTHER.
I KNOW. HE'S REALLY PUTTING ON A SHOW--
NO, IT'S NOT THAT.
WE JUST TOOK OUT THE AVENGERS WITHOUT LIFTING A FINGER, HOW DO YOU THINK YOU'LL DO?
WHAT-- WHAT DID HE DO NOW?

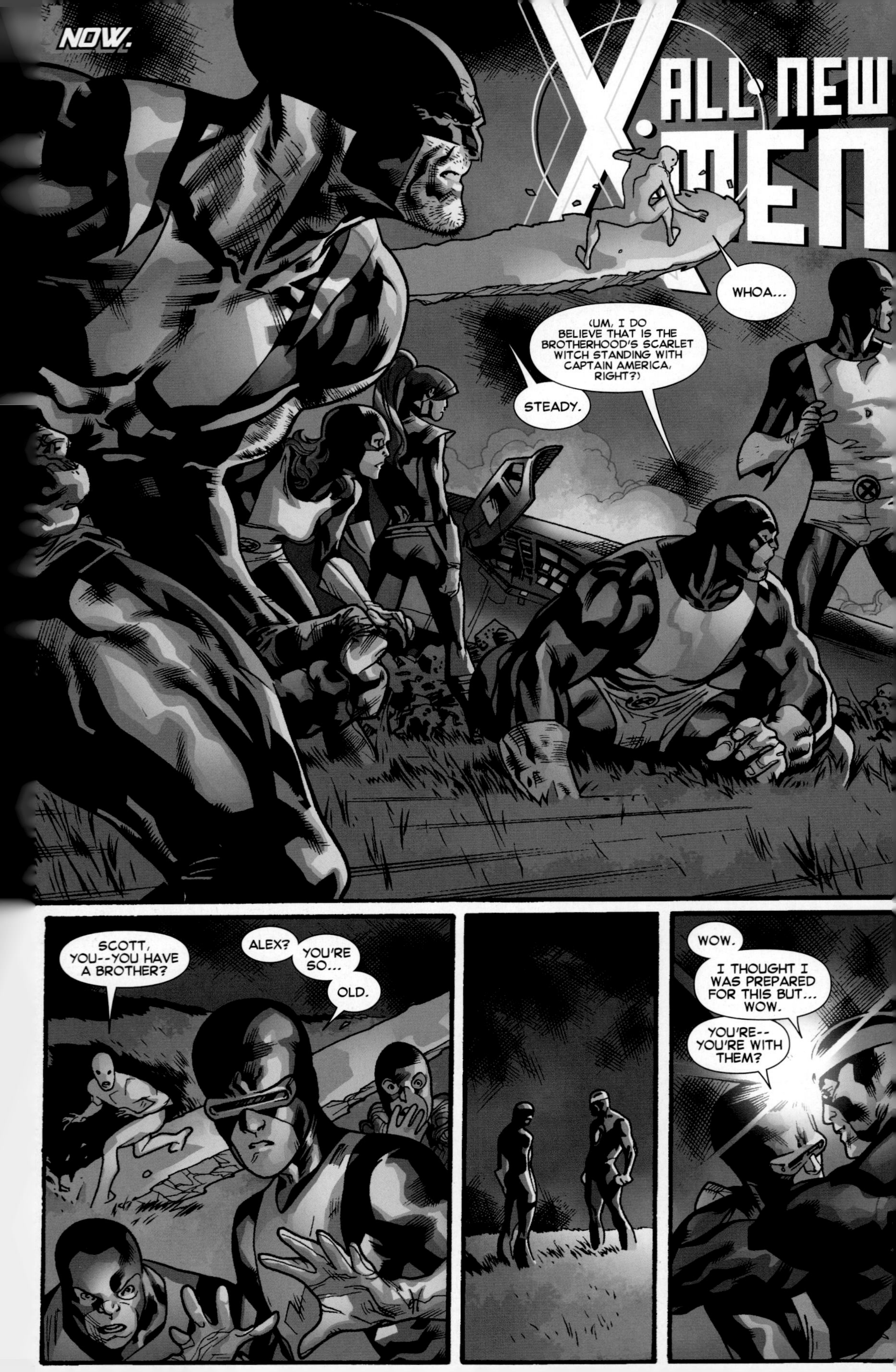
NOW.
ALL-NEW X-MEN
WHOA...
(UM, I DO BELIEVE THAT IS THE BROTHERHOOD'S SCARLET WITCH STANDING WITH CAPTAIN AMERICA, RIGHT?)
STEADY.
SCOTT, YOU--YOU HAVE A BROTHER?
ALEX?
YOU'RE SO...
OLD.
WOW.
I THOUGHT I WAS PREPARED FOR THIS BUT... WOW.
YOU'RE--YOU'RE WITH THEM?

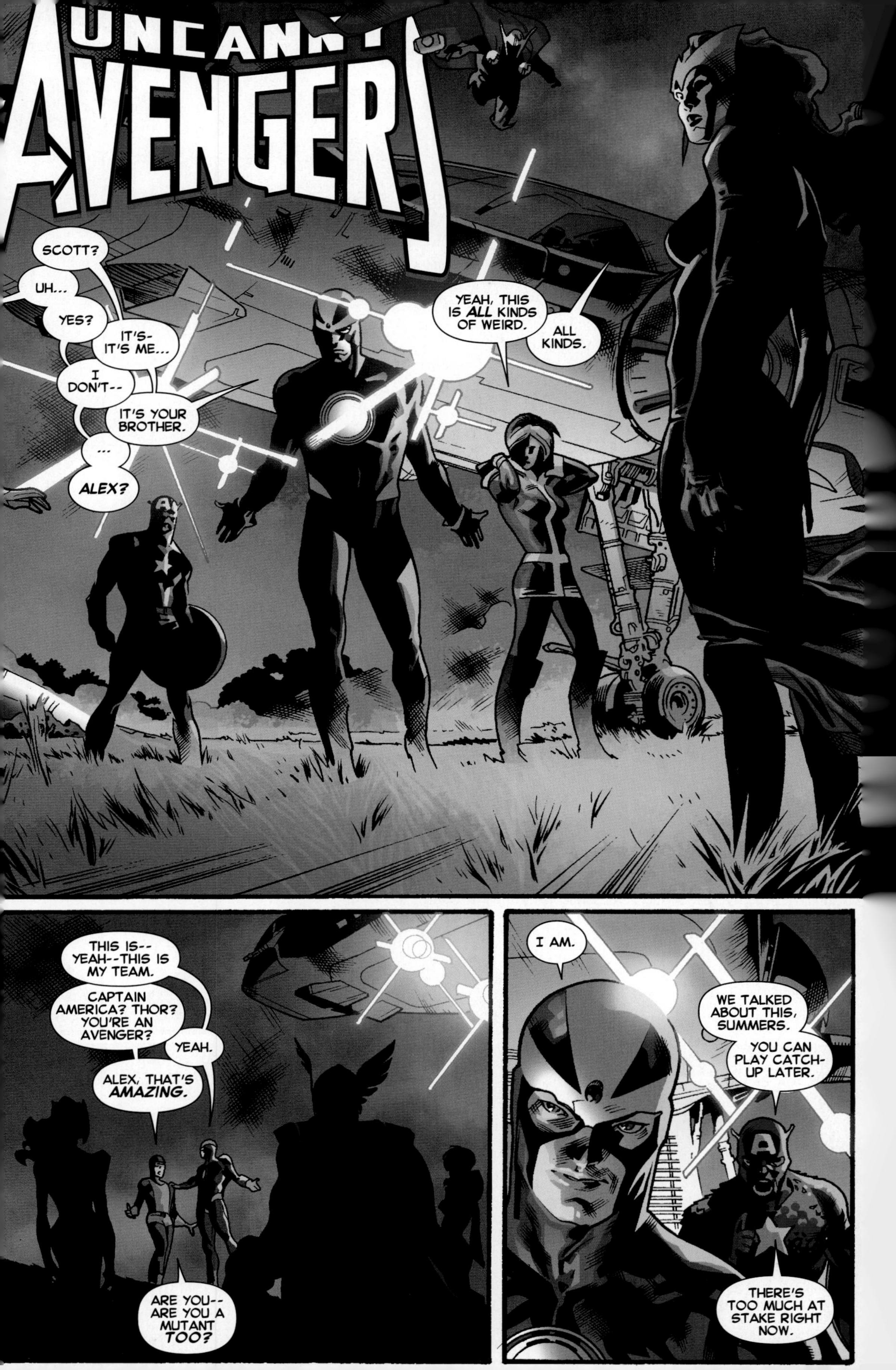
UNCANNY AVENGERS
SCOTT?
UH...
YES?
IT'S-- IT'S ME...
I DON'T--
IT'S YOUR BROTHER.
...
ALEX?
YEAH, THIS IS ALL KINDS OF WEIRD.
ALL KINDS.
THIS IS-- YEAH--THIS IS MY TEAM.
CAPTAIN AMERICA? THOR? YOU'RE AN AVENGER?
YEAH.
ALEX, THAT'S AMAZING.
ARE YOU-- ARE YOU A MUTANT TOO?
I AM.
WE TALKED ABOUT THIS, SUMMERS.
YOU CAN PLAY CATCH-UP LATER.
THERE'S TOO MUCH AT STAKE RIGHT NOW.

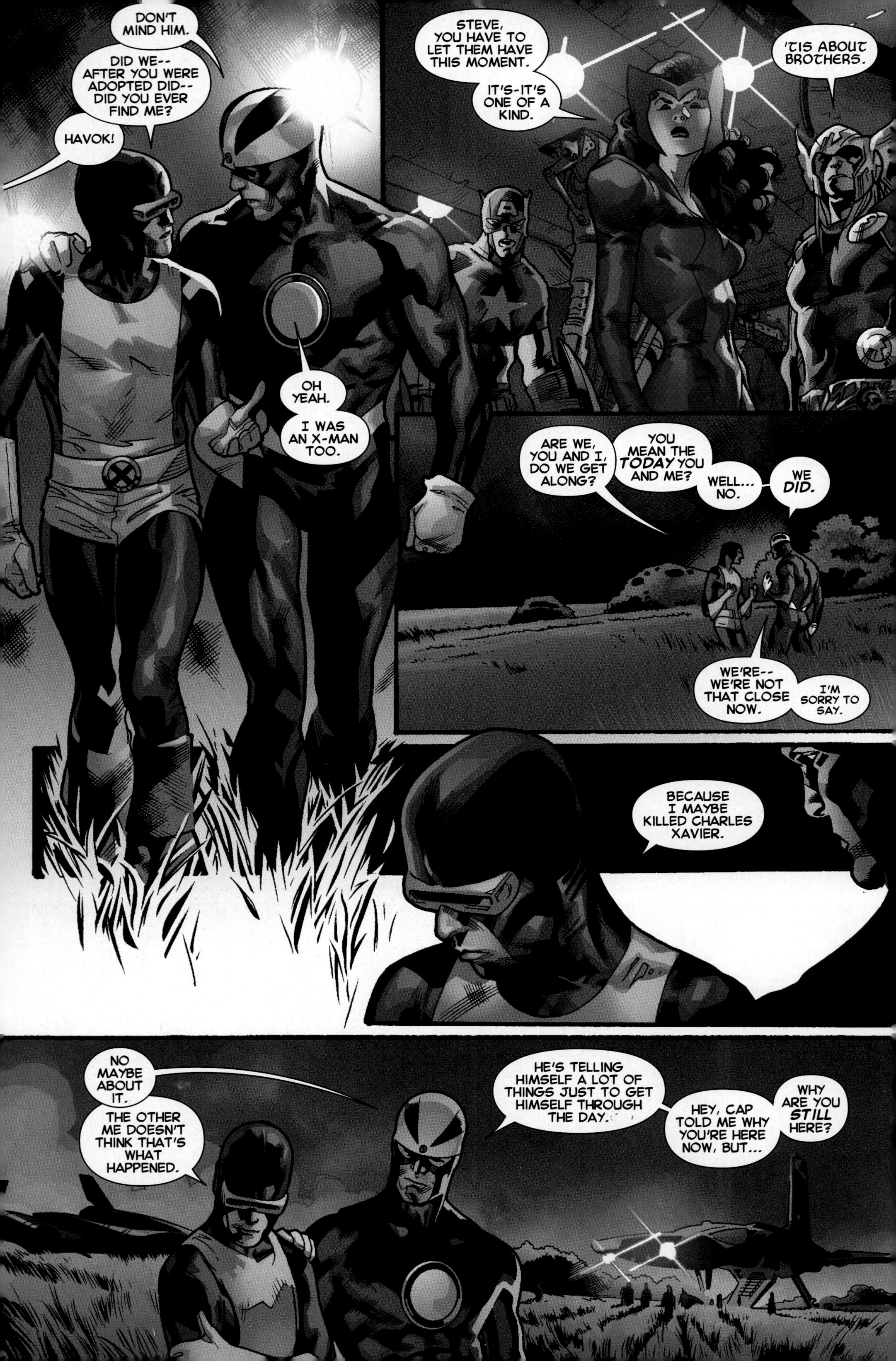

DON'T MIND HIM.
DID WE-- AFTER YOU WERE ADOPTED DID-- DID YOU EVER FIND ME?
HAVOK!
OH YEAH.
I WAS AN X-MAN TOO.
STEVE, YOU HAVE TO LET THEM HAVE THIS MOMENT.
IT'S-IT'S ONE OF A KIND.
'TIS ABOUT BROTHERS.
ARE WE, YOU AND I, DO WE GET ALONG?
YOU MEAN THE TODAY YOU AND ME?
WELL... NO.
WE DID.
WE'RE-- WE'RE NOT THAT CLOSE NOW.
I'M SORRY TO SAY.
BECAUSE I MAYBE KILLED CHARLES XAVIER.
NO MAYBE ABOUT IT.
THE OTHER ME DOESN'T THINK THAT'S WHAT HAPPENED.
HE'S TELLING HIMSELF A LOT OF THINGS JUST TO GET HIMSELF THROUGH THE DAY.
HEY, CAP TOLD ME WHY YOU'RE HERE NOW, BUT...
WHY ARE YOU STILL HERE?

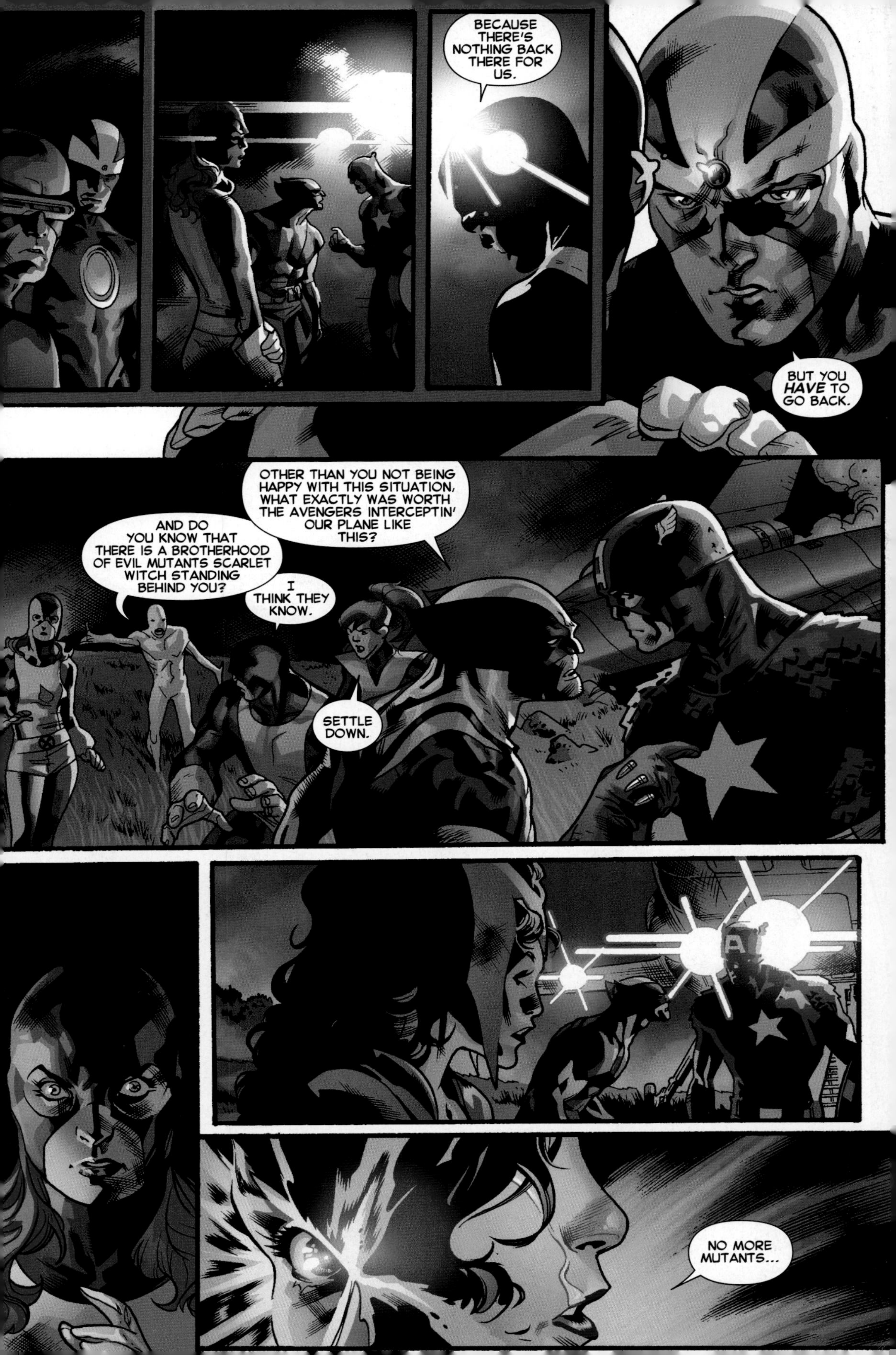
BECAUSE THERE'S NOTHING BACK THERE FOR US.
BUT YOU HAVE TO GO BACK.
OTHER THAN YOU NOT BEING HAPPY WITH THIS SITUATION, WHAT EXACTLY WAS WORTH THE AVENGERS INTERCEPTIN' OUR PLANE LIKE THIS?
AND DO YOU KNOW THAT THERE IS A BROTHERHOOD OF EVIL MUTANTS SCARLET WITCH STANDING BEHIND YOU?
I THINK THEY KNOW.
SETTLE DOWN.
NO MORE MUTANTS...

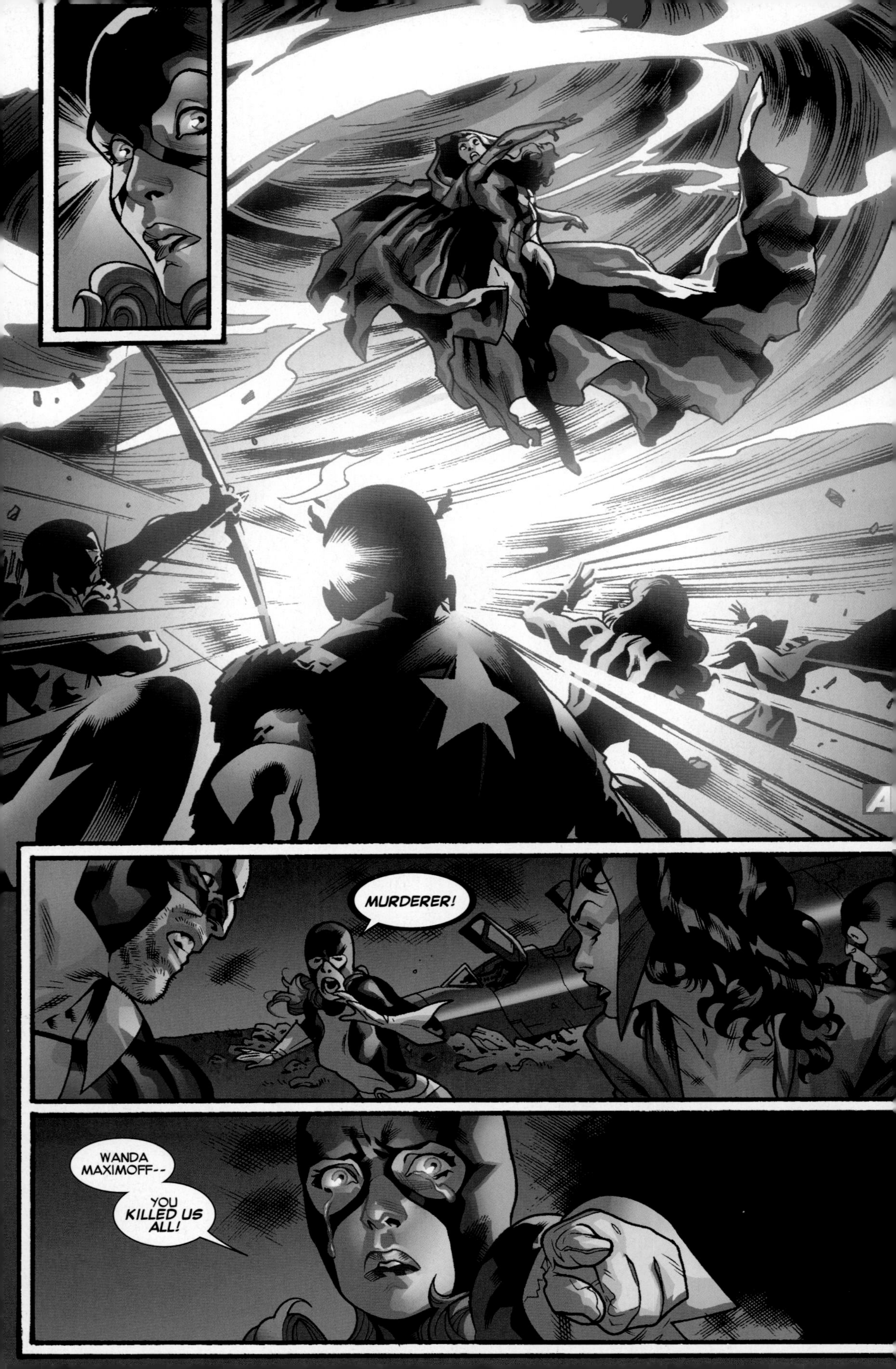
MURDERER!
WANDA MAXIMOFF--
YOU KILLED US ALL!

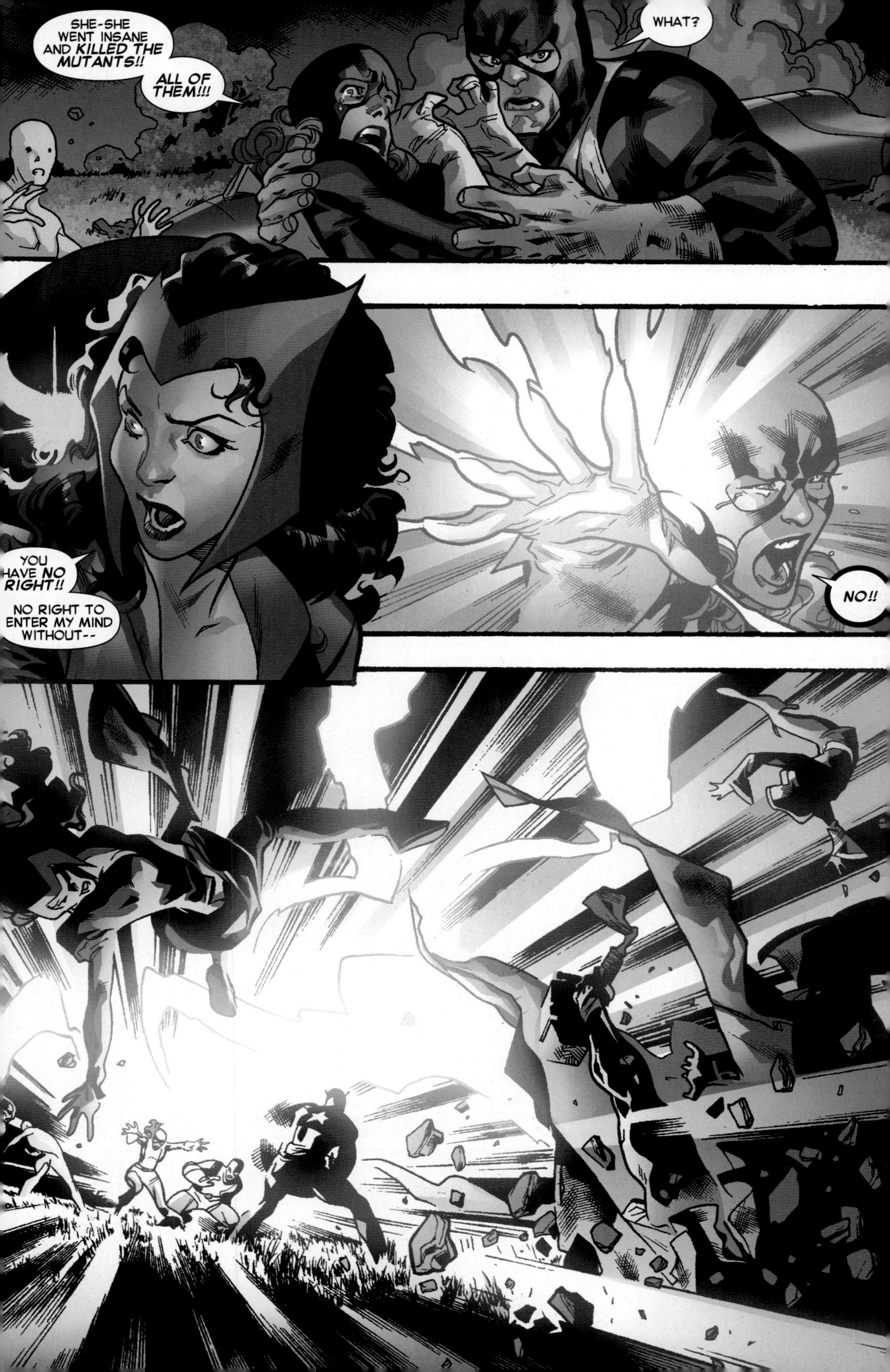
SHE-SHE WENT INSANE AND KILLED THE MUTANTS!!
ALL OF THEM!!!
WHAT?
YOU HAVE NO RIGHT!!
NO RIGHT TO ENTER MY MIND WITHOUT--
NO!!

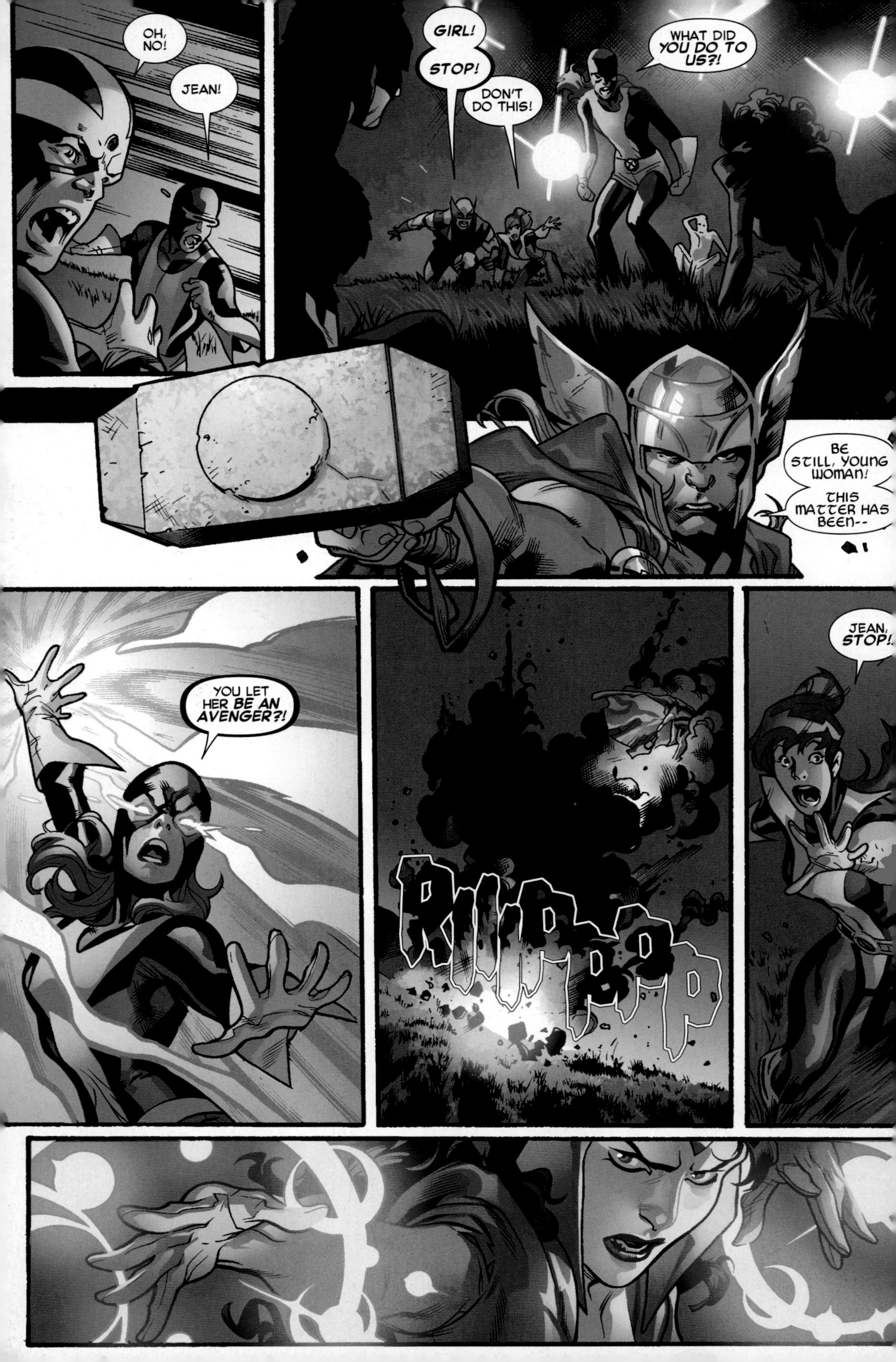
OH, NO!
JEAN!
GIRL!
STOP!
DON'T DO THIS!
WHAT DID YOU DO TO US?!
BE STILL, YOUNG WOMAN!
THIS MATTER HAS BEEN--
YOU LET HER BE AN AVENGER?!
JEAN, STOP!

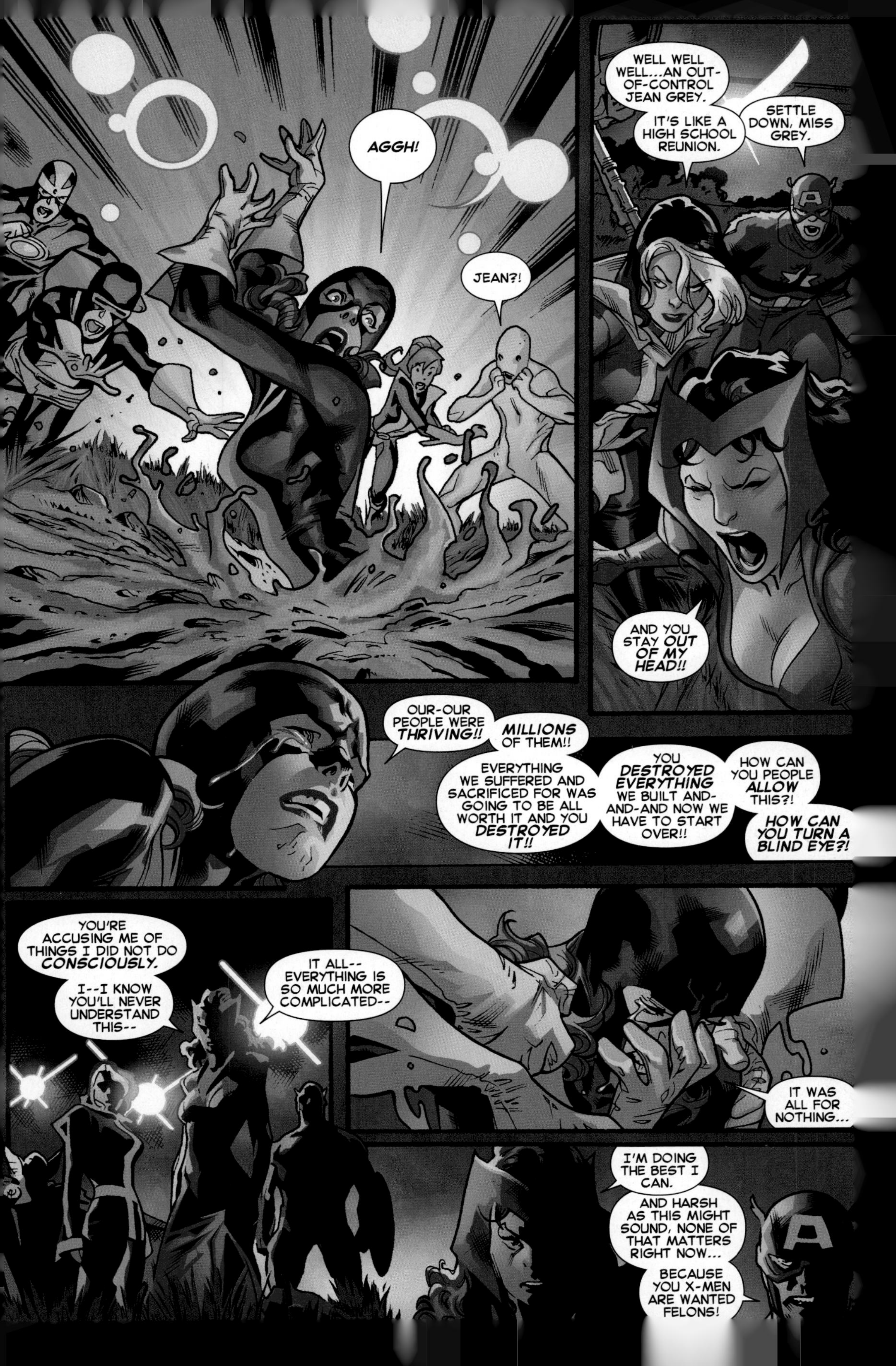
AGGH!
JEAN?!
WELL WELL WELL...AN OUT-OF-CONTROL JEAN GREY.
IT'S LIKE A HIGH SCHOOL REUNION.
SETTLE DOWN, MISS GREY.
AND YOU STAY OUT OF MY HEAD!!
OUR-OUR PEOPLE WERE THRIVING!!
MILLIONS OF THEM!!
EVERYTHING WE SUFFERED AND SACRIFICED FOR WAS GOING TO BE ALL WORTH IT AND YOU DESTROYED IT!!
YOU DESTROYED EVERYTHING WE BUILT AND-AND-AND NOW WE HAVE TO START OVER!!
HOW CAN YOU PEOPLE ALLOW THIS?!
HOW CAN YOU TURN A BLIND EYE?!
YOU'RE ACCUSING ME OF THINGS I DID NOT DO CONSCIOUSLY.
I--I KNOW YOU'LL NEVER UNDERSTAND THIS--
IT ALL--EVERYTHING IS SO MUCH MORE COMPLICATED--
IT WAS ALL FOR NOTHING...
I'M DOING THE BEST I CAN.
AND HARSH AS THIS MIGHT SOUND, NONE OF THAT MATTERS RIGHT NOW...
BECAUSE YOU X-MEN ARE WANTED FELONS!

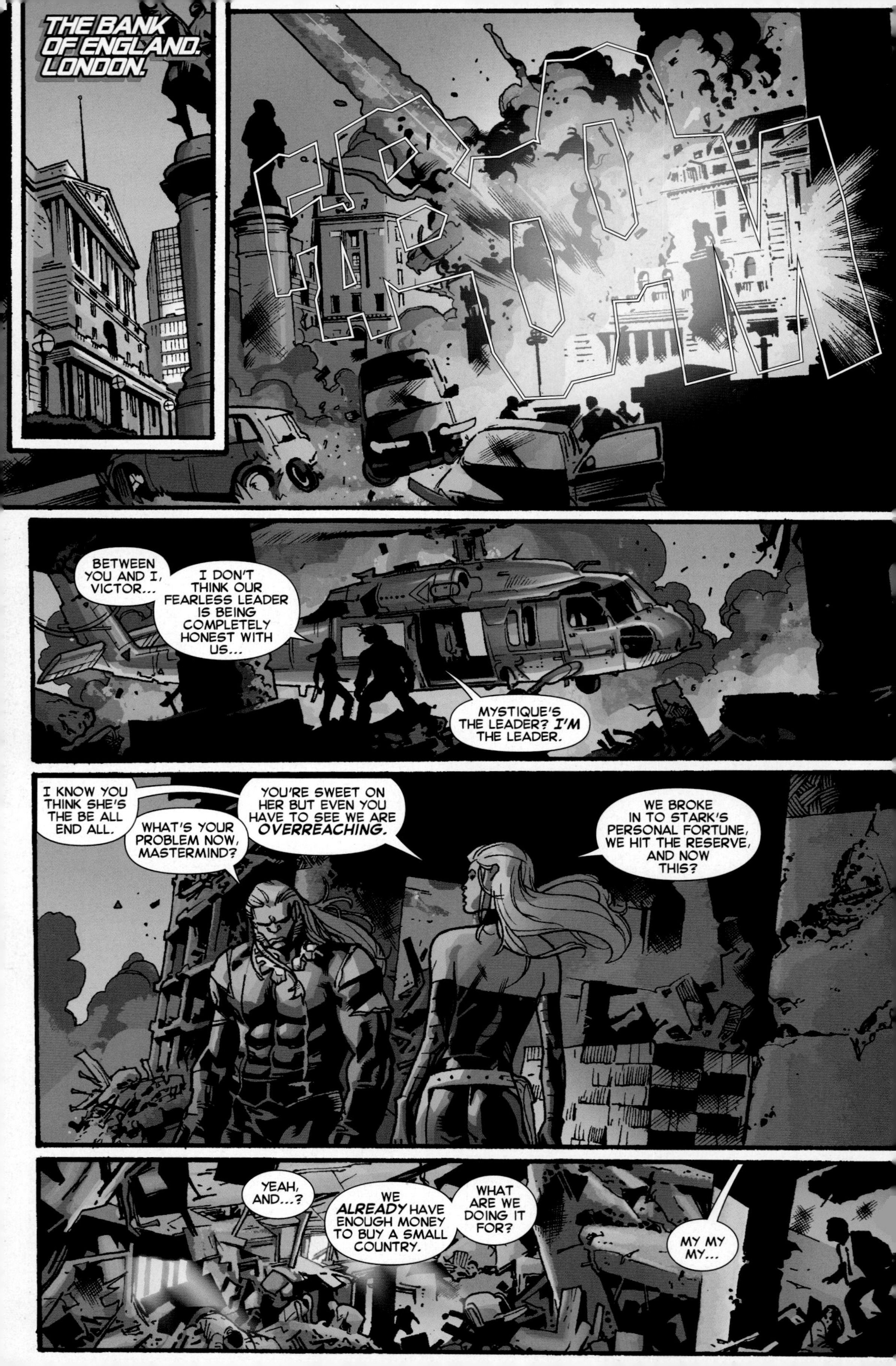
THE BANK OF ENGLAND. LONDON.
KA-BOOM
BETWEEN YOU AND I, VICTOR...
I DON'T THINK OUR FEARLESS LEADER IS BEING COMPLETELY HONEST WITH US...
MYSTIQUE'S THE LEADER? *I'M* THE LEADER.
I KNOW YOU THINK SHE'S THE BE ALL END ALL.
WHAT'S YOUR PROBLEM NOW, MASTERMIND?
YOU'RE SWEET ON HER BUT EVEN YOU HAVE TO SEE WE ARE *OVERREACHING.*
WE BROKE IN TO STARK'S PERSONAL FORTUNE, WE HIT THE RESERVE, AND NOW THIS?
YEAH, AND...?
WE *ALREADY* HAVE ENOUGH MONEY TO BUY A SMALL COUNTRY.
WHAT ARE WE DOING IT FOR?
MY MY MY...

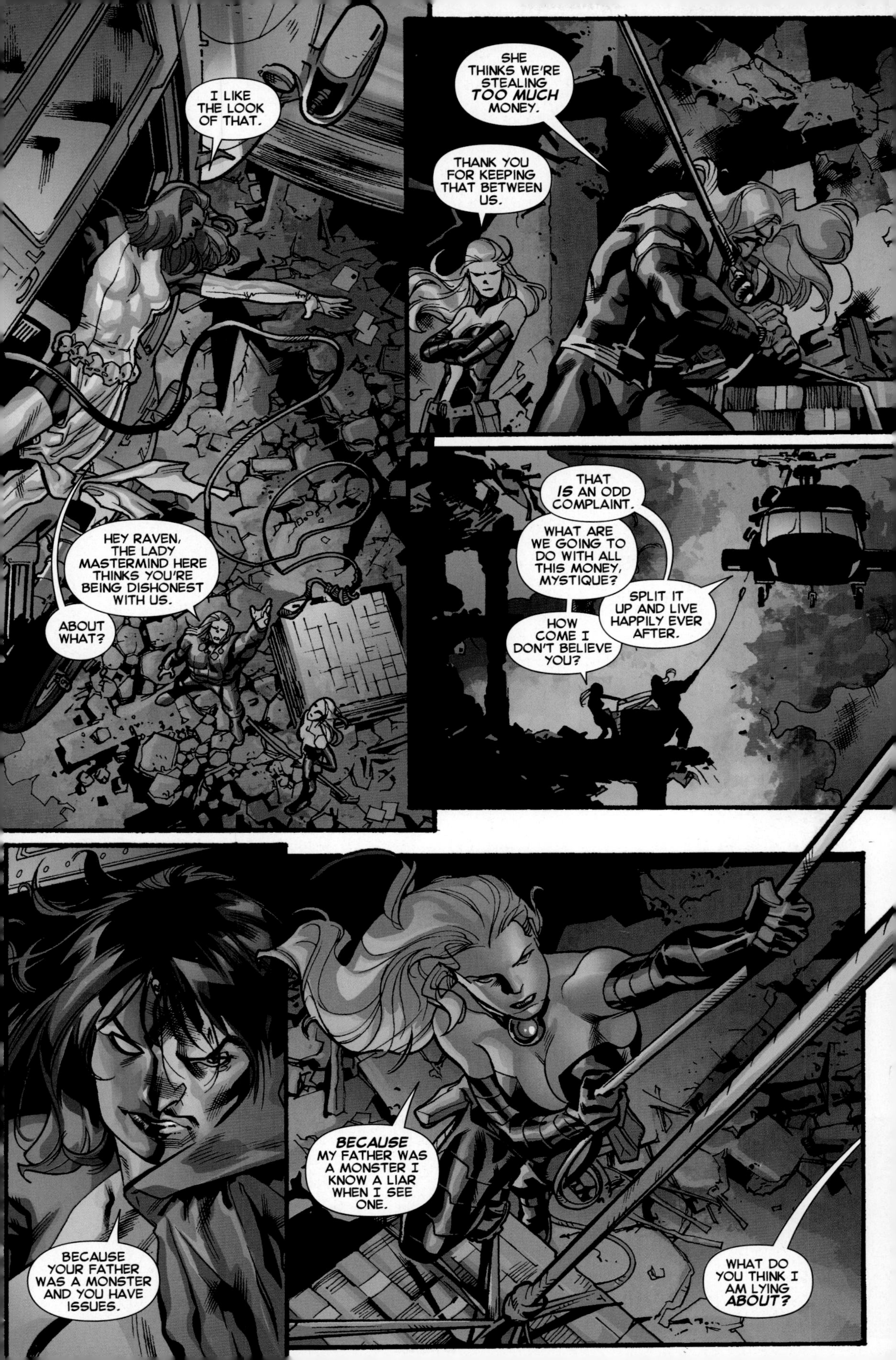

I LIKE THE LOOK OF THAT.
HEY RAVEN, THE LADY MASTERMIND HERE THINKS YOU'RE BEING DISHONEST WITH US.
ABOUT WHAT?
SHE THINKS WE'RE STEALING TOO MUCH MONEY.
THANK YOU FOR KEEPING THAT BETWEEN US.
THAT IS AN ODD COMPLAINT.
WHAT ARE WE GOING TO DO WITH ALL THIS MONEY, MYSTIQUE?
SPLIT IT UP AND LIVE HAPPILY EVER AFTER.
HOW COME I DON'T BELIEVE YOU?
BECAUSE YOUR FATHER WAS A MONSTER AND YOU HAVE ISSUES.
BECAUSE MY FATHER WAS A MONSTER I KNOW A LIAR WHEN I SEE ONE.
WHAT DO YOU THINK I AM LYING ABOUT?

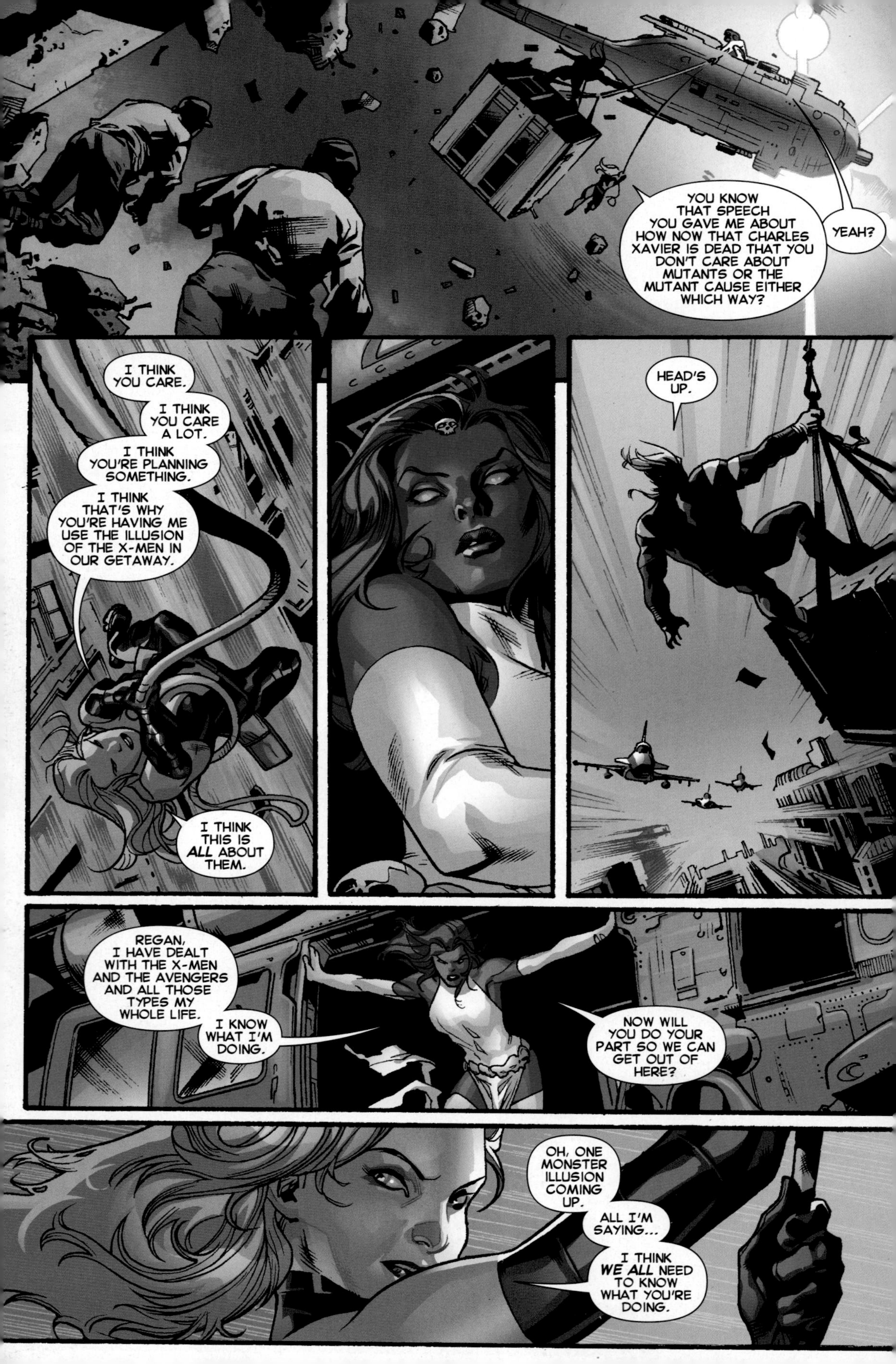
YOU KNOW THAT SPEECH YOU GAVE ME ABOUT HOW NOW THAT CHARLES XAVIER IS DEAD THAT YOU DON'T CARE ABOUT MUTANTS OR THE MUTANT CAUSE EITHER WHICH WAY?
YEAH?
I THINK YOU CARE.
I THINK YOU CARE A LOT.
I THINK YOU'RE PLANNING SOMETHING.
I THINK THAT'S WHY YOU'RE HAVING ME USE THE ILLUSION OF THE X-MEN IN OUR GETAWAY.
I THINK THIS IS ALL ABOUT THEM.
HEAD'S UP.
REGAN, I HAVE DEALT WITH THE X-MEN AND THE AVENGERS AND ALL THOSE TYPES MY WHOLE LIFE.
I KNOW WHAT I'M DOING.
NOW WILL YOU DO YOUR PART SO WE CAN GET OUT OF HERE?
OH, ONE MONSTER ILLUSION COMING UP.
ALL I'M SAYING...
I THINK WE ALL NEED TO KNOW WHAT YOU'RE DOING.

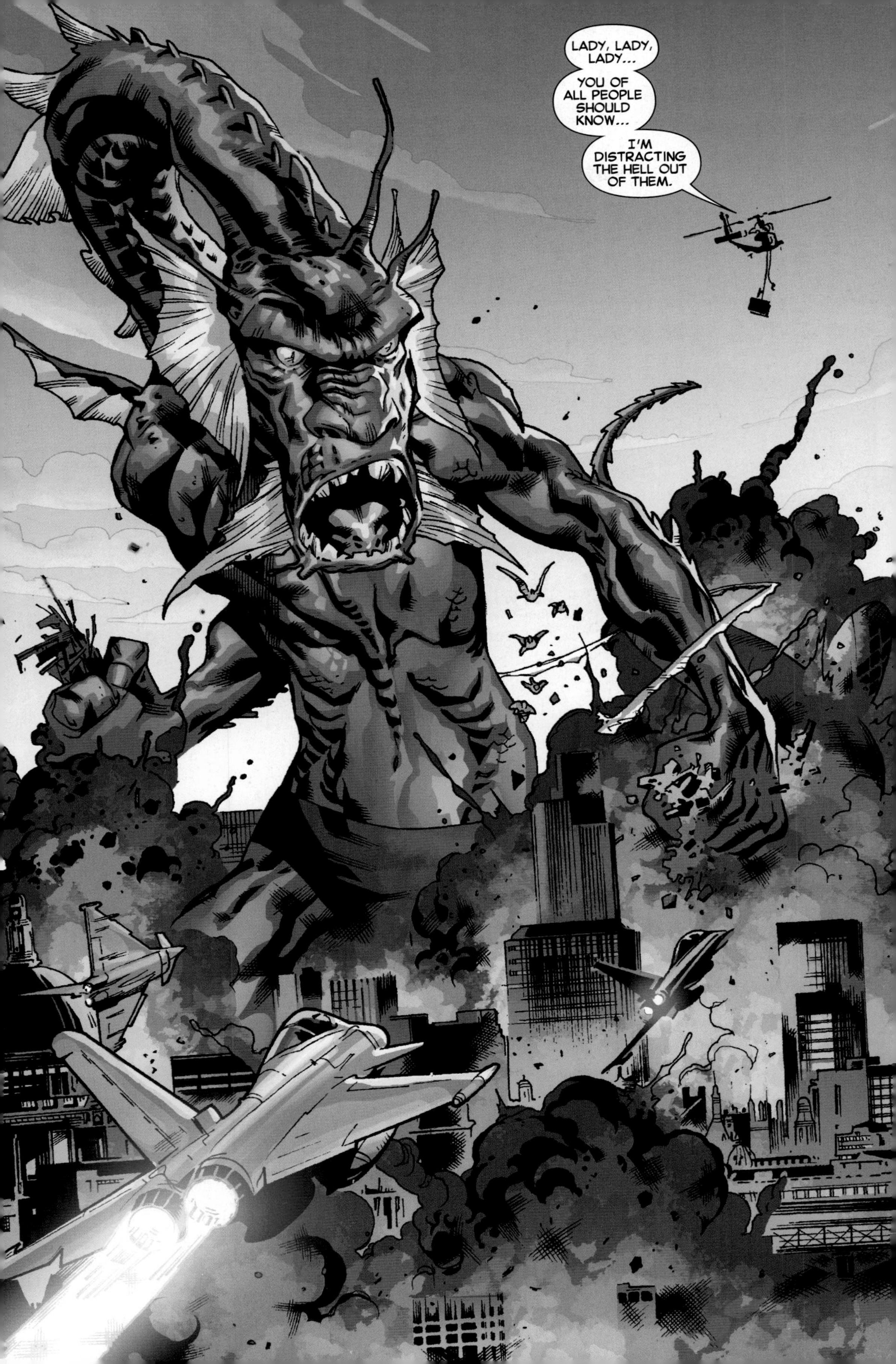
LADY, LADY, LADY...
YOU OF ALL PEOPLE SHOULD KNOW...
I'M DISTRACTING THE HELL OUT OF THEM.

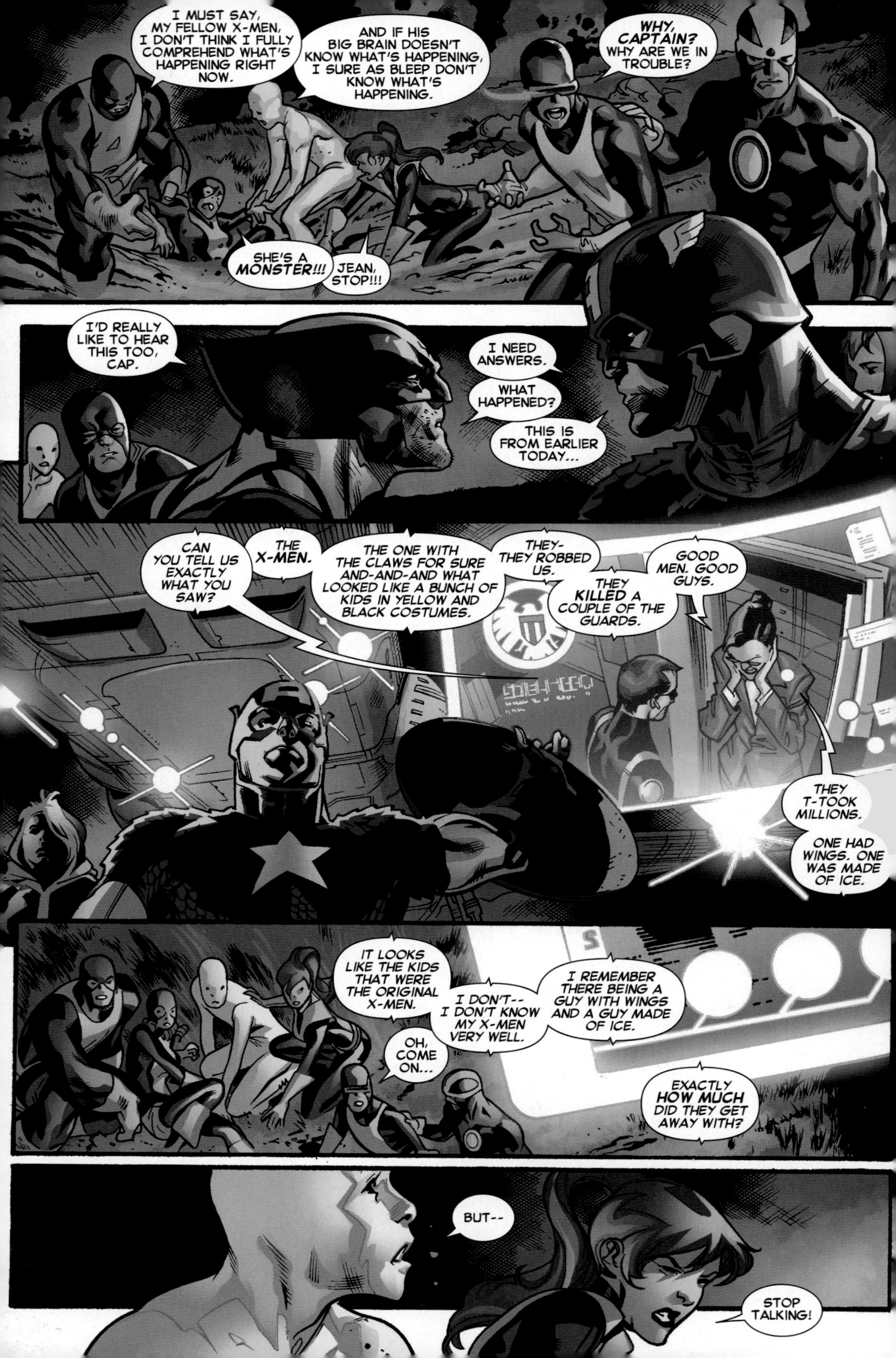
I MUST SAY, MY FELLOW X-MEN, I DON'T THINK I FULLY COMPREHEND WHAT'S HAPPENING RIGHT NOW.
AND IF HIS BIG BRAIN DOESN'T KNOW WHAT'S HAPPENING, I SURE AS BLEEP DON'T KNOW WHAT'S HAPPENING.
WHY, CAPTAIN? WHY ARE WE IN TROUBLE?
SHE'S A MONSTER!!!
JEAN, STOP!!!
I'D REALLY LIKE TO HEAR THIS TOO, CAP.
I NEED ANSWERS.
WHAT HAPPENED?
THIS IS FROM EARLIER TODAY...
CAN YOU TELL US EXACTLY WHAT YOU SAW?
THE X-MEN.
THE ONE WITH THE CLAWS FOR SURE AND-AND-AND WHAT LOOKED LIKE A BUNCH OF KIDS IN YELLOW AND BLACK COSTUMES.
THEY- THEY ROBBED US.
THEY KILLED A COUPLE OF THE GUARDS.
GOOD MEN. GOOD GUYS.
THEY T-TOOK MILLIONS.
ONE HAD WINGS. ONE WAS MADE OF ICE.
IT LOOKS LIKE THE KIDS THAT WERE THE ORIGINAL X-MEN.
I DON'T-- I DON'T KNOW MY X-MEN VERY WELL.
I REMEMBER THERE BEING A GUY WITH WINGS AND A GUY MADE OF ICE.
OH, COME ON...
EXACTLY HOW MUCH DID THEY GET AWAY WITH?
BUT--
STOP TALKING!

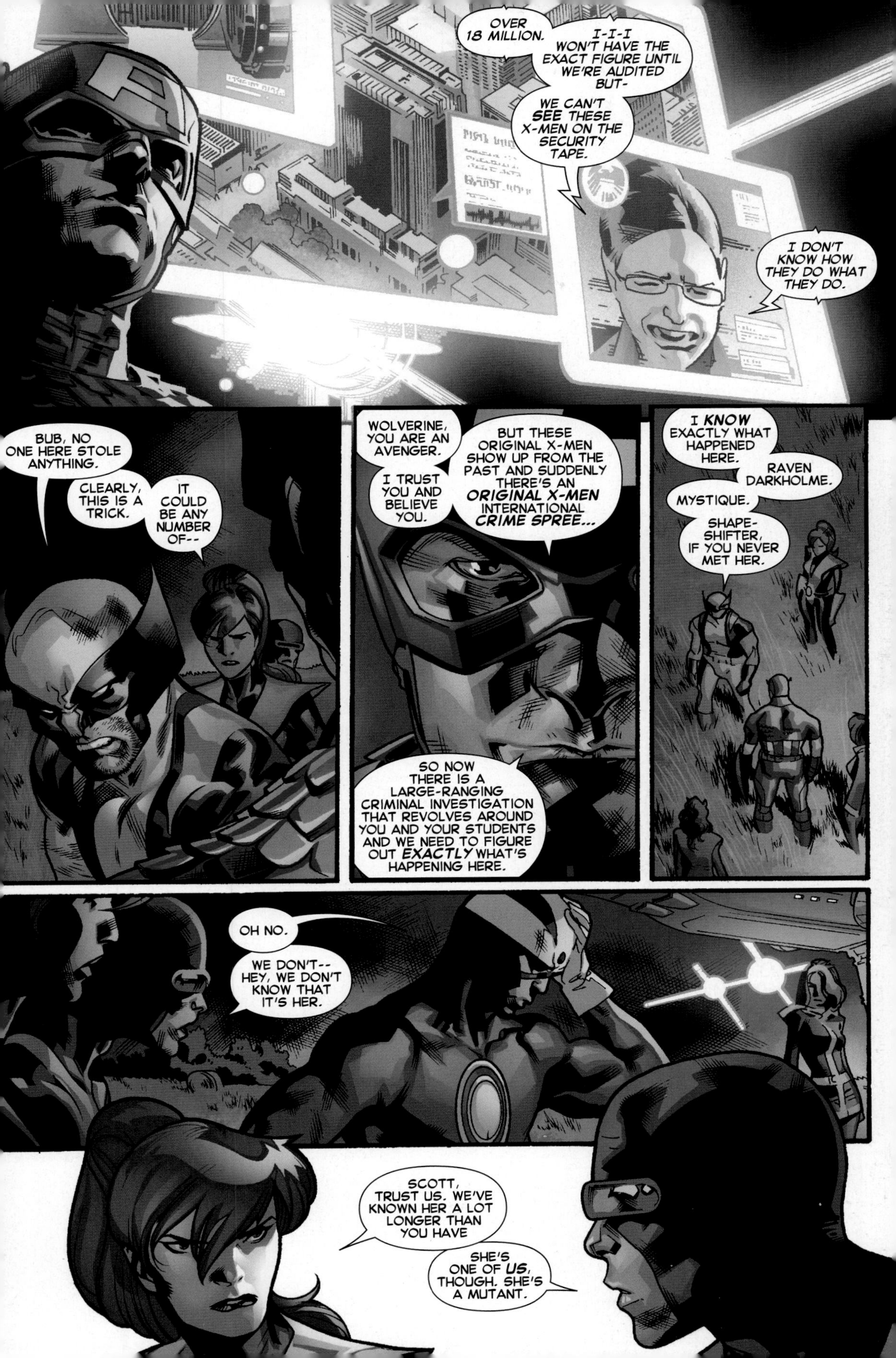
OVER 18 MILLION.
I-I-I WON'T HAVE THE EXACT FIGURE UNTIL WE'RE AUDITED BUT-
WE CAN'T SEE THESE X-MEN ON THE SECURITY TAPE.
I DON'T KNOW HOW THEY DO WHAT THEY DO.
BUB, NO ONE HERE STOLE ANYTHING.
CLEARLY, THIS IS A TRICK.
IT COULD BE ANY NUMBER OF--
WOLVERINE, YOU ARE AN AVENGER.
I TRUST YOU AND BELIEVE YOU.
BUT THESE ORIGINAL X-MEN SHOW UP FROM THE PAST AND SUDDENLY THERE'S AN ORIGINAL X-MEN INTERNATIONAL CRIME SPREE...
SO NOW THERE IS A LARGE-RANGING CRIMINAL INVESTIGATION THAT REVOLVES AROUND YOU AND YOUR STUDENTS AND WE NEED TO FIGURE OUT EXACTLY WHAT'S HAPPENING HERE.
I KNOW EXACTLY WHAT HAPPENED HERE.
RAVEN DARKHOLME.
MYSTIQUE.
SHAPE-SHIFTER, IF YOU NEVER MET HER.
OH NO.
WE DON'T-- HEY, WE DON'T KNOW THAT IT'S HER.
SCOTT, TRUST US. WE'VE KNOWN HER A LOT LONGER THAN YOU HAVE
SHE'S ONE OF US, THOUGH. SHE'S A MUTANT.

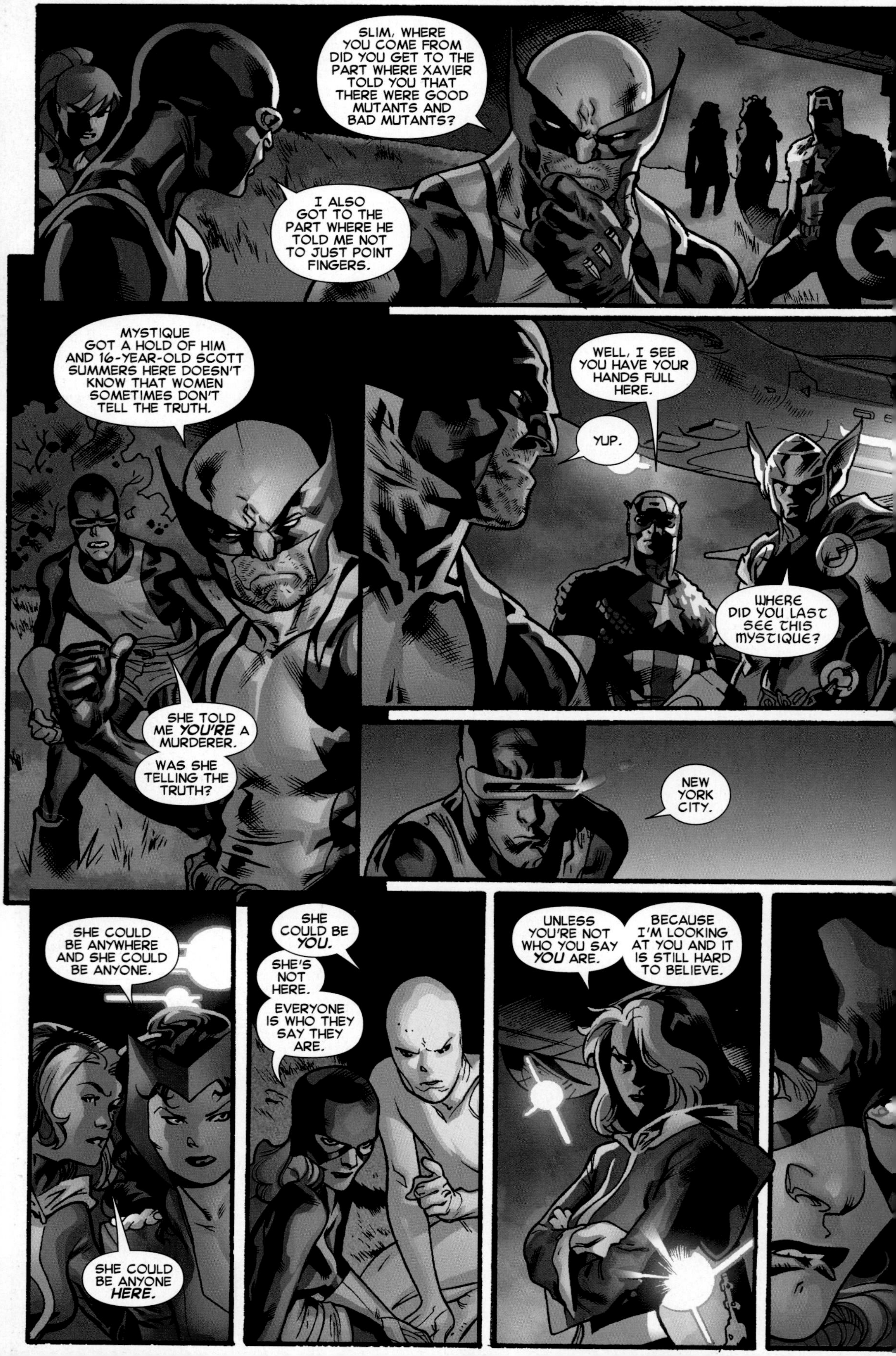
SLIM, WHERE YOU COME FROM DID YOU GET TO THE PART WHERE XAVIER TOLD YOU THAT THERE WERE GOOD MUTANTS AND BAD MUTANTS?
I ALSO GOT TO THE PART WHERE HE TOLD ME NOT TO JUST POINT FINGERS.
MYSTIQUE GOT A HOLD OF HIM AND 16-YEAR-OLD SCOTT SUMMERS HERE DOESN'T KNOW THAT WOMEN SOMETIMES DON'T TELL THE TRUTH.
SHE TOLD ME YOU'RE A MURDERER.
WAS SHE TELLING THE TRUTH?
WELL, I SEE YOU HAVE YOUR HANDS FULL HERE.
YUP.
WHERE DID YOU LAST SEE THIS MYSTIQUE?
NEW YORK CITY.
SHE COULD BE ANYWHERE AND SHE COULD BE ANYONE.
SHE COULD BE ANYONE HERE.
SHE COULD BE YOU.
SHE'S NOT HERE.
EVERYONE IS WHO THEY SAY THEY ARE.
UNLESS YOU'RE NOT WHO YOU SAY YOU ARE.
BECAUSE I'M LOOKING AT YOU AND IT IS STILL HARD TO BELIEVE.

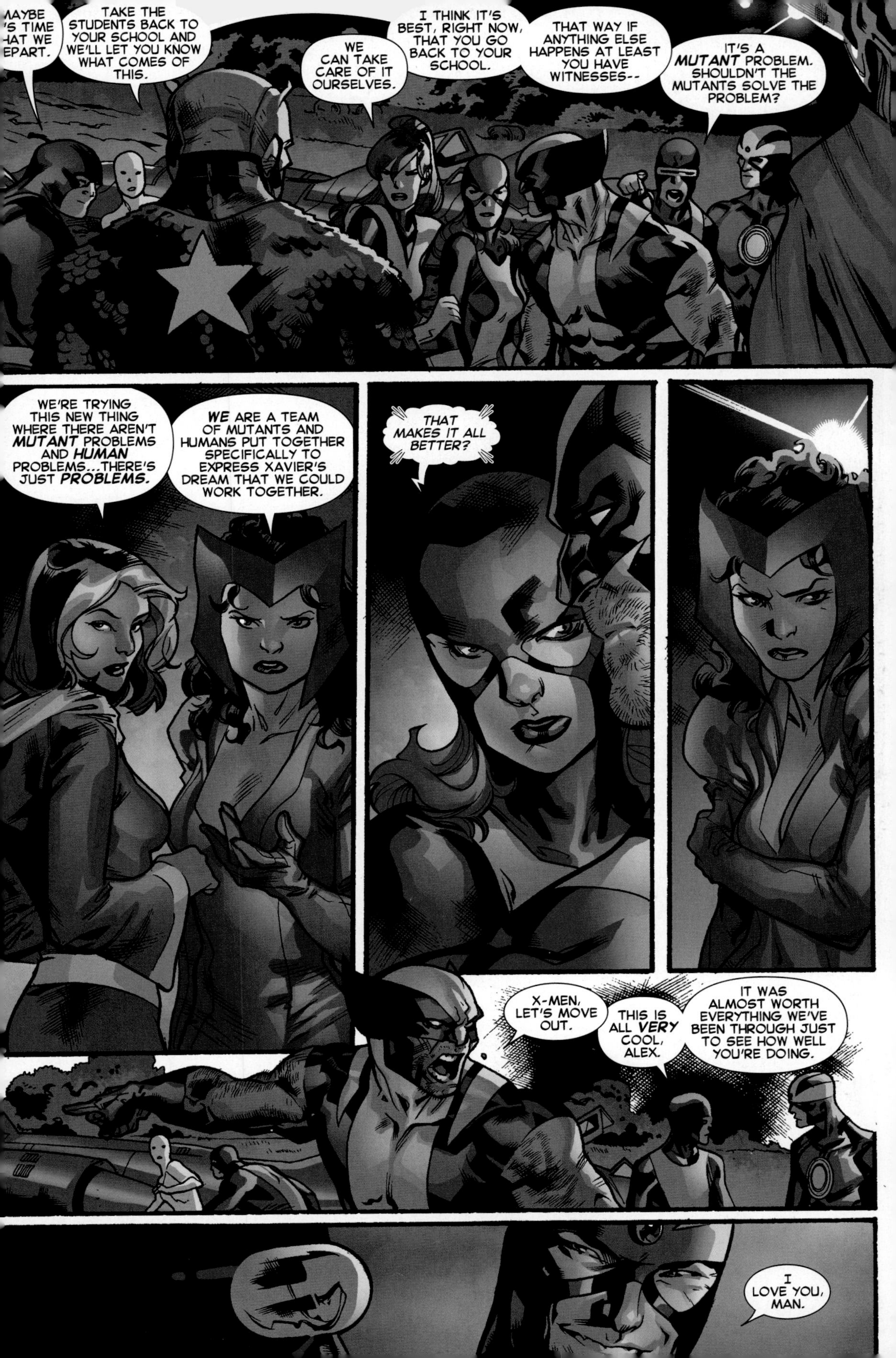
MAYBE 'S TIME HAT WE EPART.
TAKE THE STUDENTS BACK TO YOUR SCHOOL AND WE'LL LET YOU KNOW WHAT COMES OF THIS.
WE CAN TAKE CARE OF IT OURSELVES.
I THINK IT'S BEST, RIGHT NOW, THAT YOU GO BACK TO YOUR SCHOOL.
THAT WAY IF ANYTHING ELSE HAPPENS AT LEAST YOU HAVE WITNESSES--
IT'S A MUTANT PROBLEM. SHOULDN'T THE MUTANTS SOLVE THE PROBLEM?
WE'RE TRYING THIS NEW THING WHERE THERE AREN'T MUTANT PROBLEMS AND HUMAN PROBLEMS...THERE'S JUST PROBLEMS.
WE ARE A TEAM OF MUTANTS AND HUMANS PUT TOGETHER SPECIFICALLY TO EXPRESS XAVIER'S DREAM THAT WE COULD WORK TOGETHER.
THAT MAKES IT ALL BETTER?
X-MEN, LET'S MOVE OUT.
THIS IS ALL VERY COOL, ALEX.
IT WAS ALMOST WORTH EVERYTHING WE'VE BEEN THROUGH JUST TO SEE HOW WELL YOU'RE DOING.
I LOVE YOU, MAN.

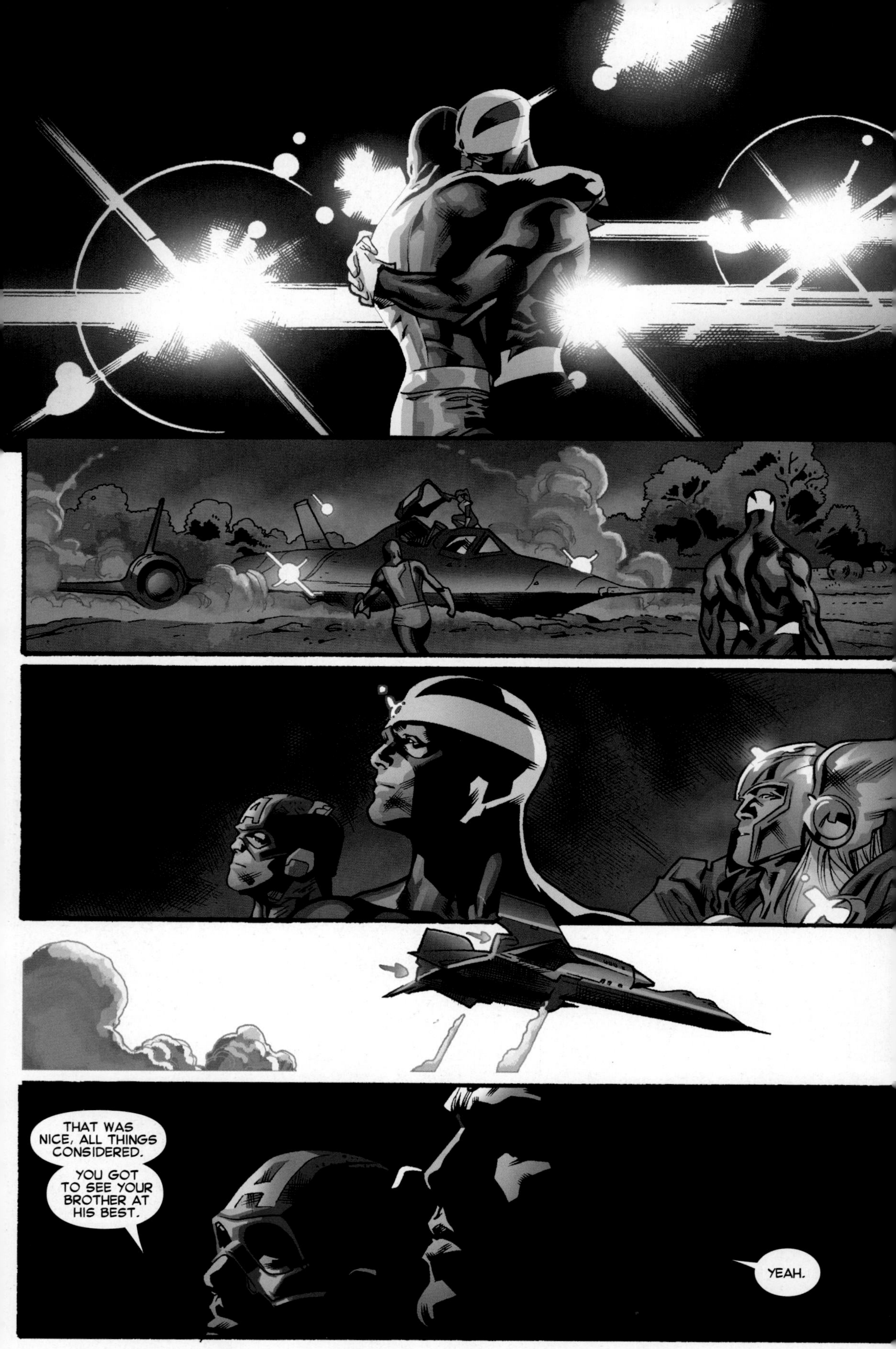
THAT WAS NICE, ALL THINGS CONSIDERED.
YOU GOT TO SEE YOUR BROTHER AT HIS BEST.
YEAH.

THAT WAS A RATHER UNNERVING INTERACTION.

HEAD DUE EAST.

WE'RE NOT GOING BACK TO THE SCHOOL?

NOPE.

WON'T CAPTAIN AMERICA BE PERTURBED?

WE HAVE AN UNDERSTANDING.

I DO WHATEVER I WANT AND HE UNDERSTANDS.

THE SCARLET WITCH D-D-DECIMATED THE MUTANT RACE AND YOU DIDN'T *DO ANYTHING* ABOUT IT?

WHAT DID WE SAY ABOUT DIGGING INTO PEOPLE'S HEADS?

I *WASN'T* DIGGING.

SHE WAS *SCREAMING* IT OUT THERE. MENTALLY. LIKE IT'S *ALL* SHE THINKS ABOUT.

IS IT *TRUE?*

IT WAS OUR WORST MOMENT AS A PEOPLE.

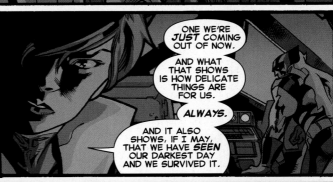

ONE WE'RE *JUST* COMING OUT OF NOW.

AND WHAT THAT SHOWS IS HOW DELICATE THINGS ARE FOR US.

ALWAYS.

AND IT ALSO SHOWS, IF I MAY, THAT WE HAVE *SEEN* OUR DARKEST DAY AND WE SURVIVED IT.

AND SCARLET WITCH IS JUST ALLOWED TO WALK AROUND?

IT'S COMPLICATED, McCOY.

DOESN'T SEEM LIKE IT WOULD BE.

WELL, YOU WEREN'T THERE.

AND NEITHER OF *US* SHOULD TALK.

WHAT DOES *THAT* MEAN?

NOW, FINALLY, IT IS OUR TIME!

NEW MUTANTS ARE POPPING UP *ALL OVER THE WORLD.*

AND *SHE* GETS TO BE AN AVENGER.

WELL, MASTER WOLVERINE, ARE YOU GOING TO TELL ME WHERE I'M FLYING TO?

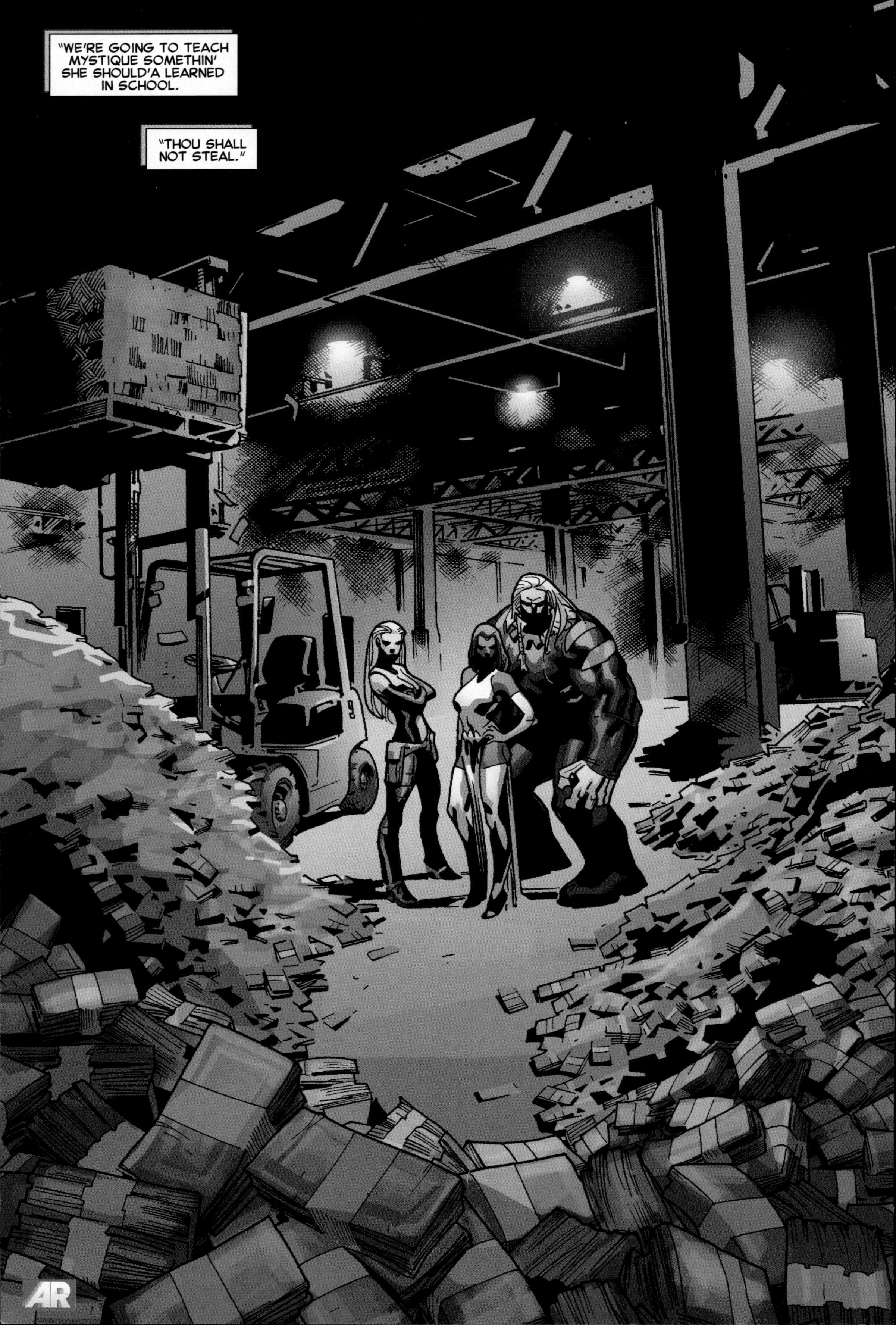
"WE'RE GOING TO TEACH MYSTIQUE SOMETHIN' SHE SHOULD'A LEARNED IN SCHOOL.
"THOU SHALL NOT STEAL."

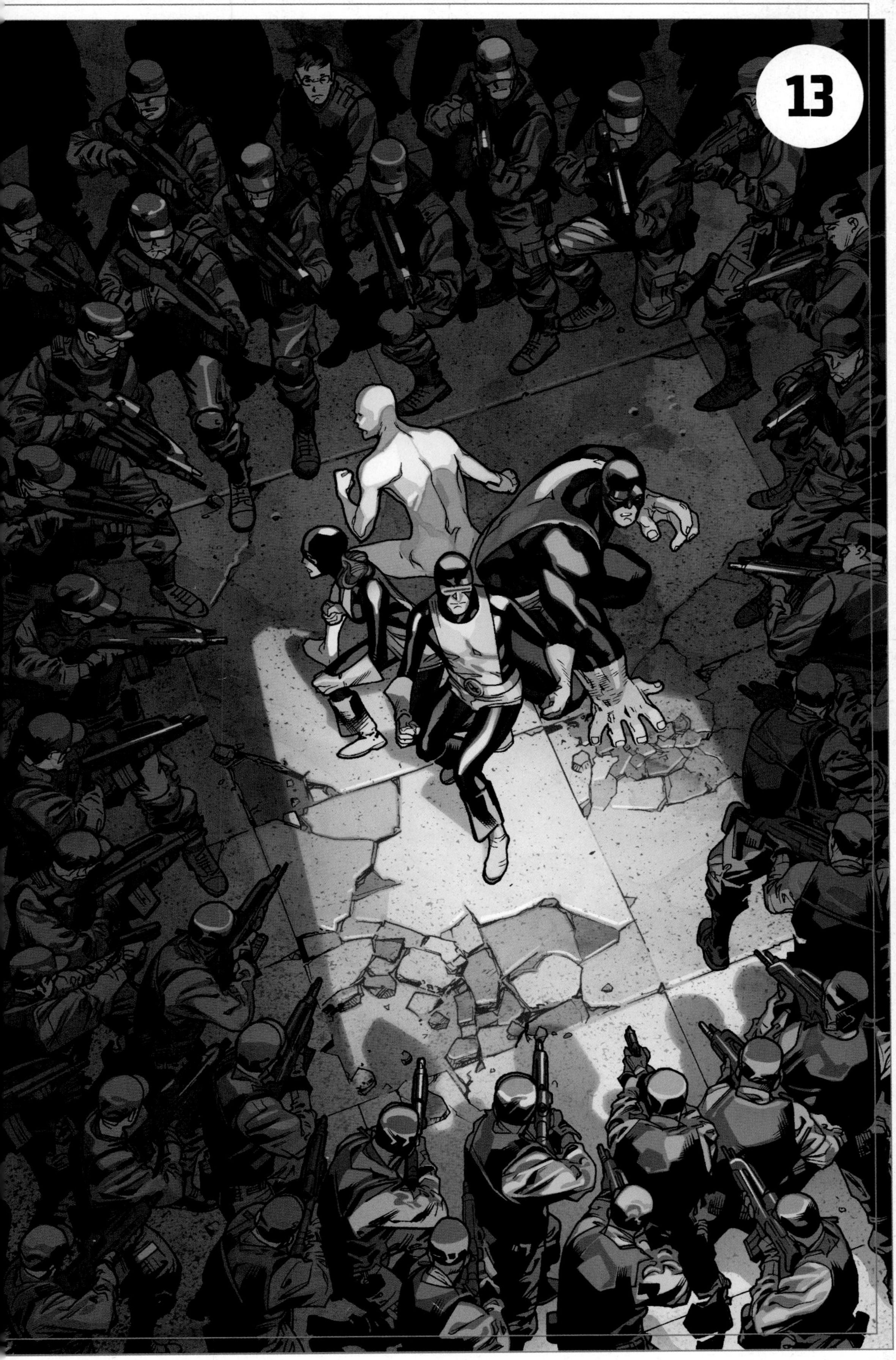
13

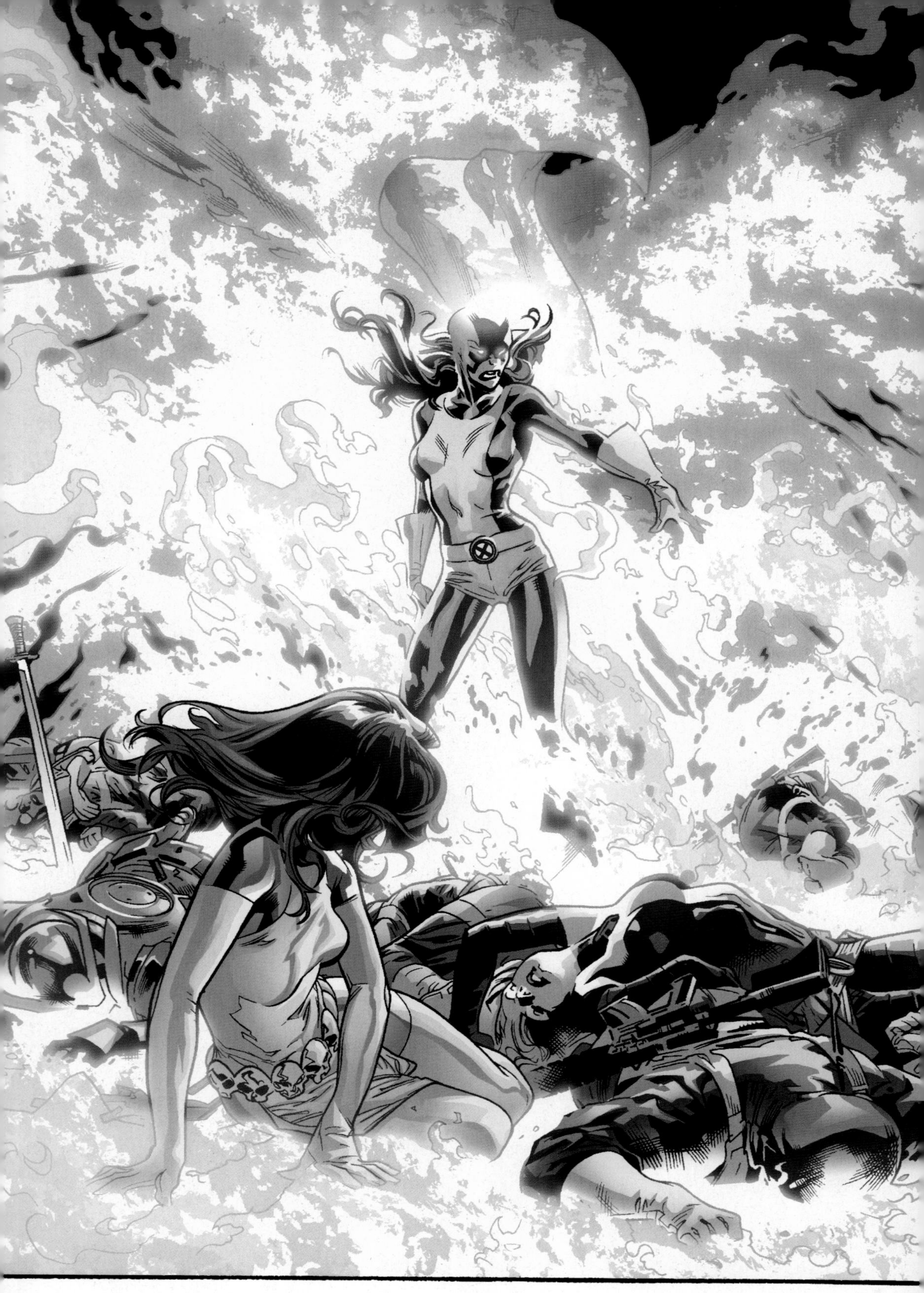

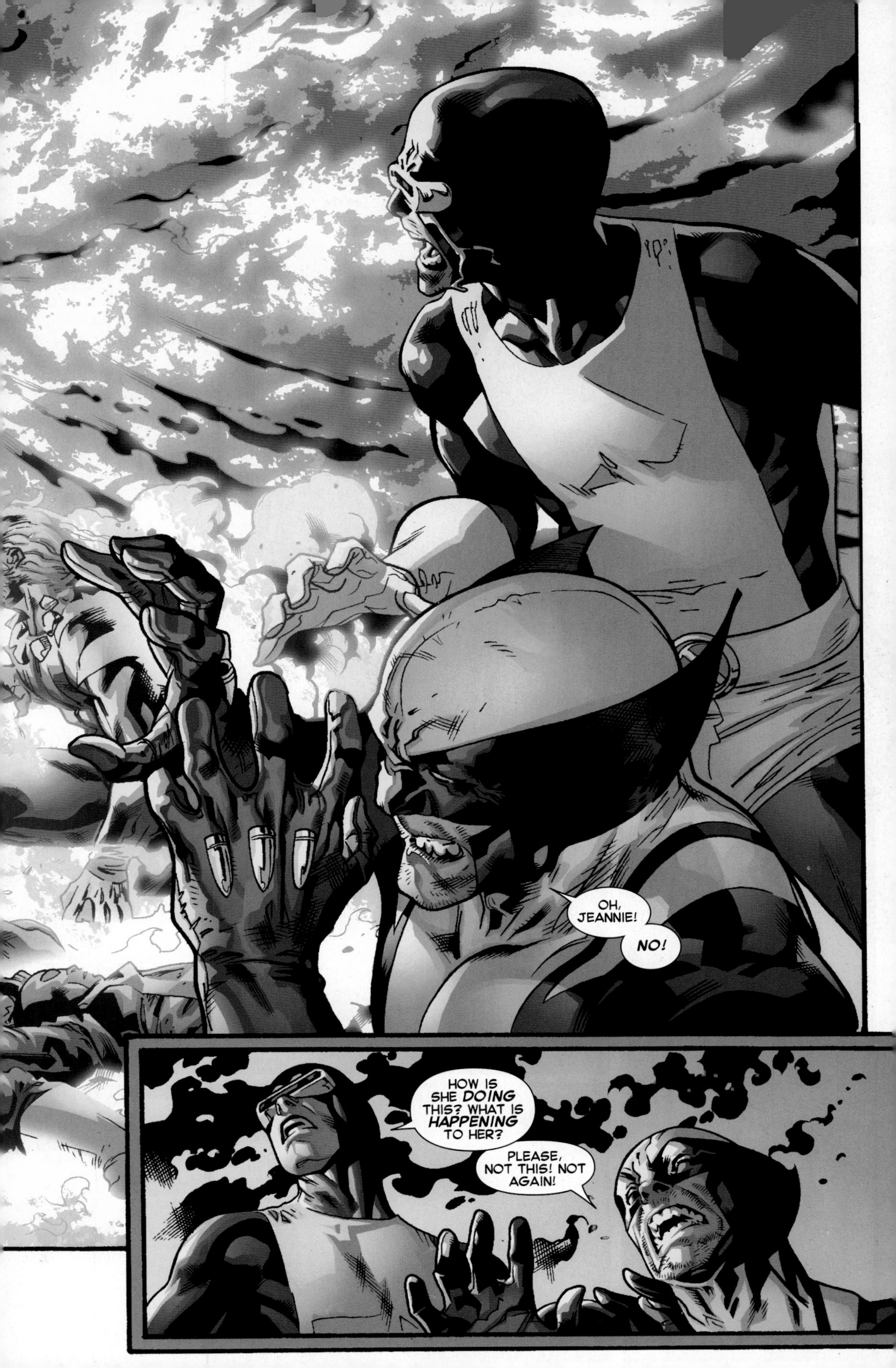
OH, JEANNIE!
NO!
HOW IS SHE DOING THIS? WHAT IS HAPPENING TO HER?
PLEASE, NOT THIS! NOT AGAIN!

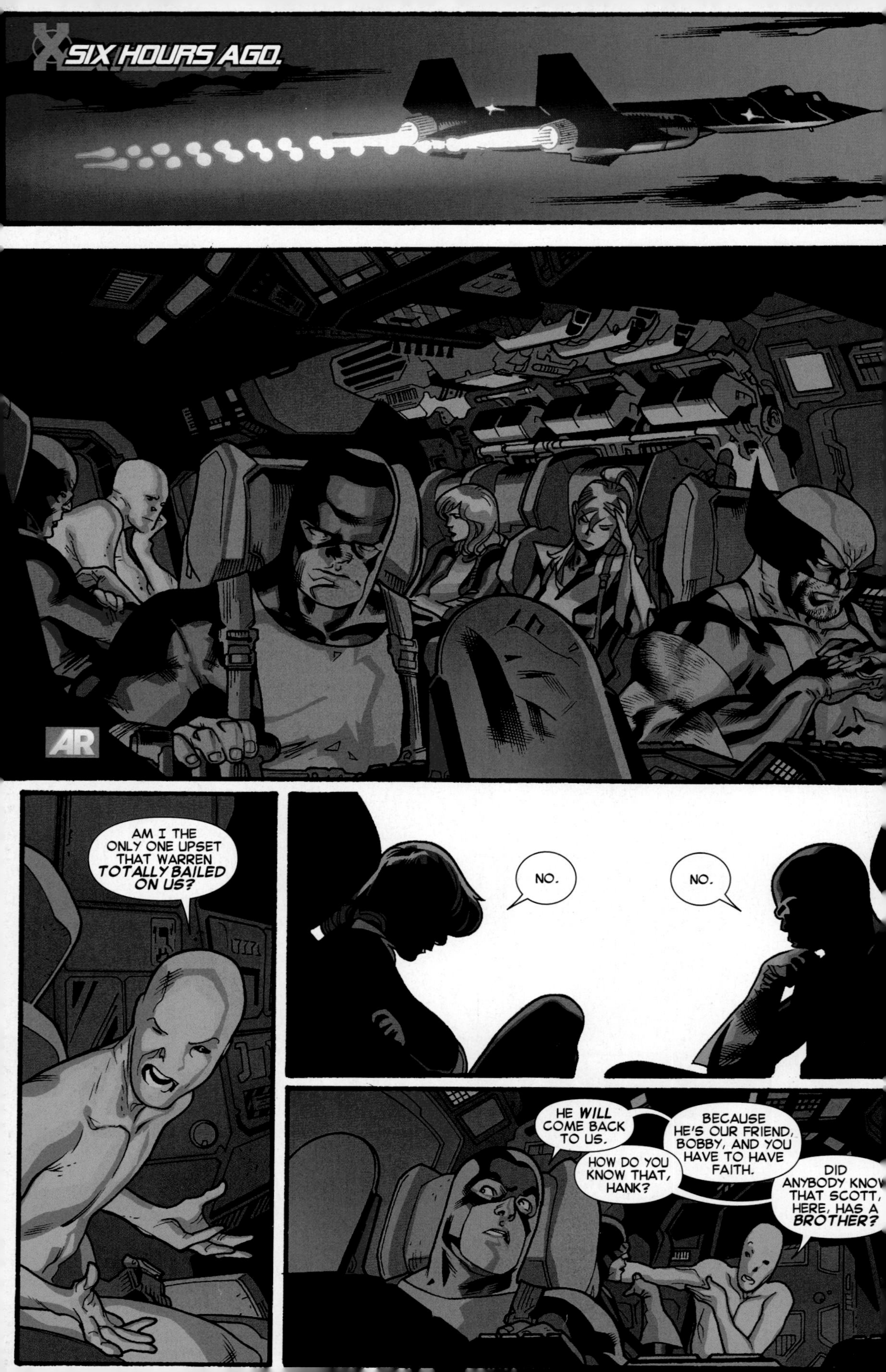
SIX HOURS AGO.
AM I THE ONLY ONE UPSET THAT WARREN TOTALLY BAILED ON US?
NO.
NO.
HE WILL COME BACK TO US.
HOW DO YOU KNOW THAT, HANK?
BECAUSE HE'S OUR FRIEND, BOBBY, AND YOU HAVE TO HAVE FAITH.
DID ANYBODY KNOW THAT SCOTT, HERE, HAS A BROTHER?

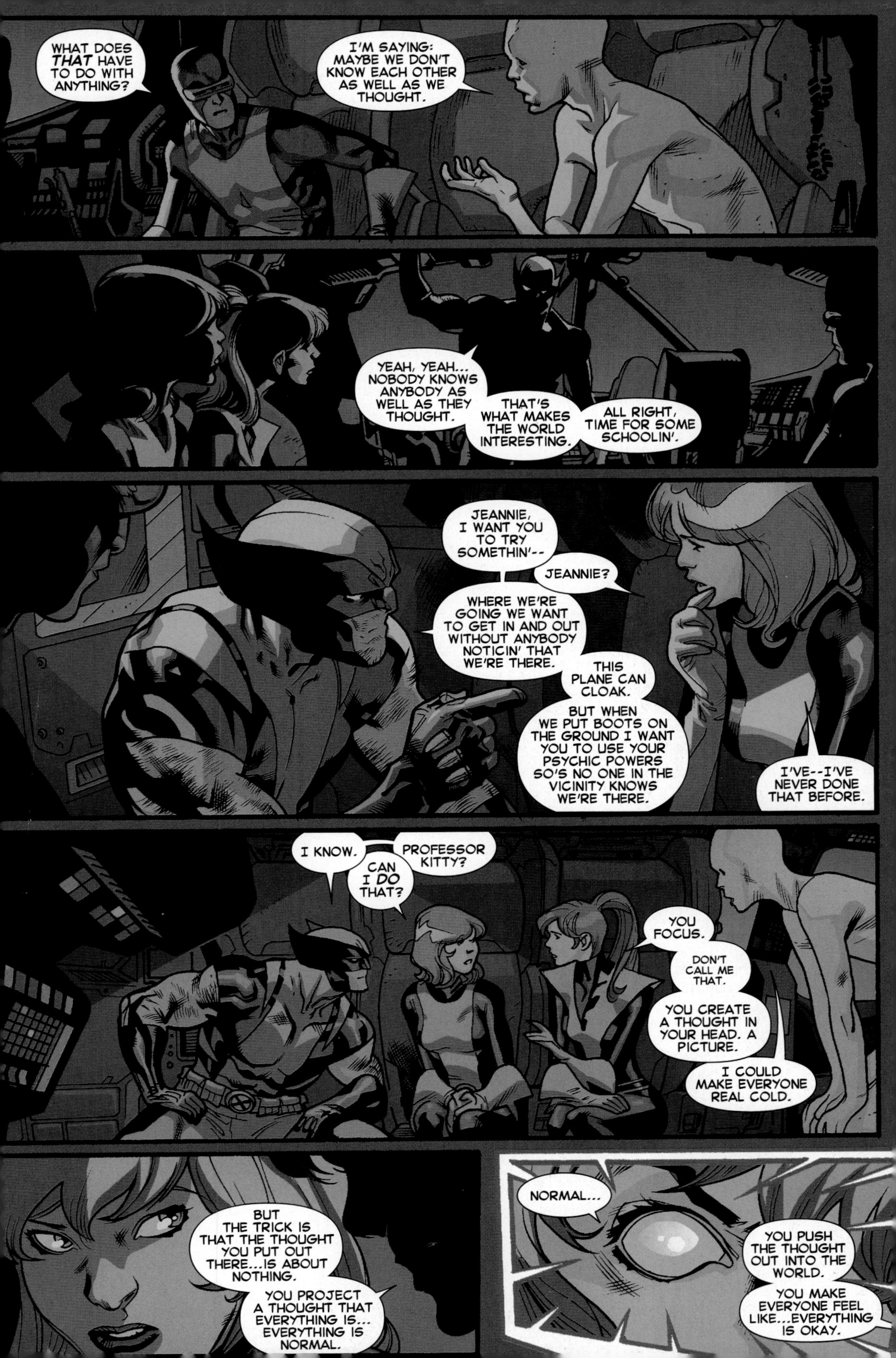
WHAT DOES THAT HAVE TO DO WITH ANYTHING?
I'M SAYING: MAYBE WE DON'T KNOW EACH OTHER AS WELL AS WE THOUGHT.
YEAH, YEAH... NOBODY KNOWS ANYBODY AS WELL AS THEY THOUGHT.
THAT'S WHAT MAKES THE WORLD INTERESTING.
ALL RIGHT, TIME FOR SOME SCHOOLIN'.
JEANNIE, I WANT YOU TO TRY SOMETHIN'--
JEANNIE?
WHERE WE'RE GOING WE WANT TO GET IN AND OUT WITHOUT ANYBODY NOTICIN' THAT WE'RE THERE.
THIS PLANE CAN CLOAK.
BUT WHEN WE PUT BOOTS ON THE GROUND I WANT YOU TO USE YOUR PSYCHIC POWERS SO'S NO ONE IN THE VICINITY KNOWS WE'RE THERE.
I'VE--I'VE NEVER DONE THAT BEFORE.
I KNOW.
PROFESSOR KITTY?
CAN I DO THAT?
YOU FOCUS.
DON'T CALL ME THAT.
YOU CREATE A THOUGHT IN YOUR HEAD. A PICTURE.
I COULD MAKE EVERYONE REAL COLD.
BUT THE TRICK IS THAT THE THOUGHT YOU PUT OUT THERE...IS ABOUT NOTHING.
YOU PROJECT A THOUGHT THAT EVERYTHING IS... EVERYTHING IS NORMAL.
NORMAL...
YOU PUSH THE THOUGHT OUT INTO THE WORLD.
YOU MAKE EVERYONE FEEL LIKE...EVERYTHING IS OKAY.

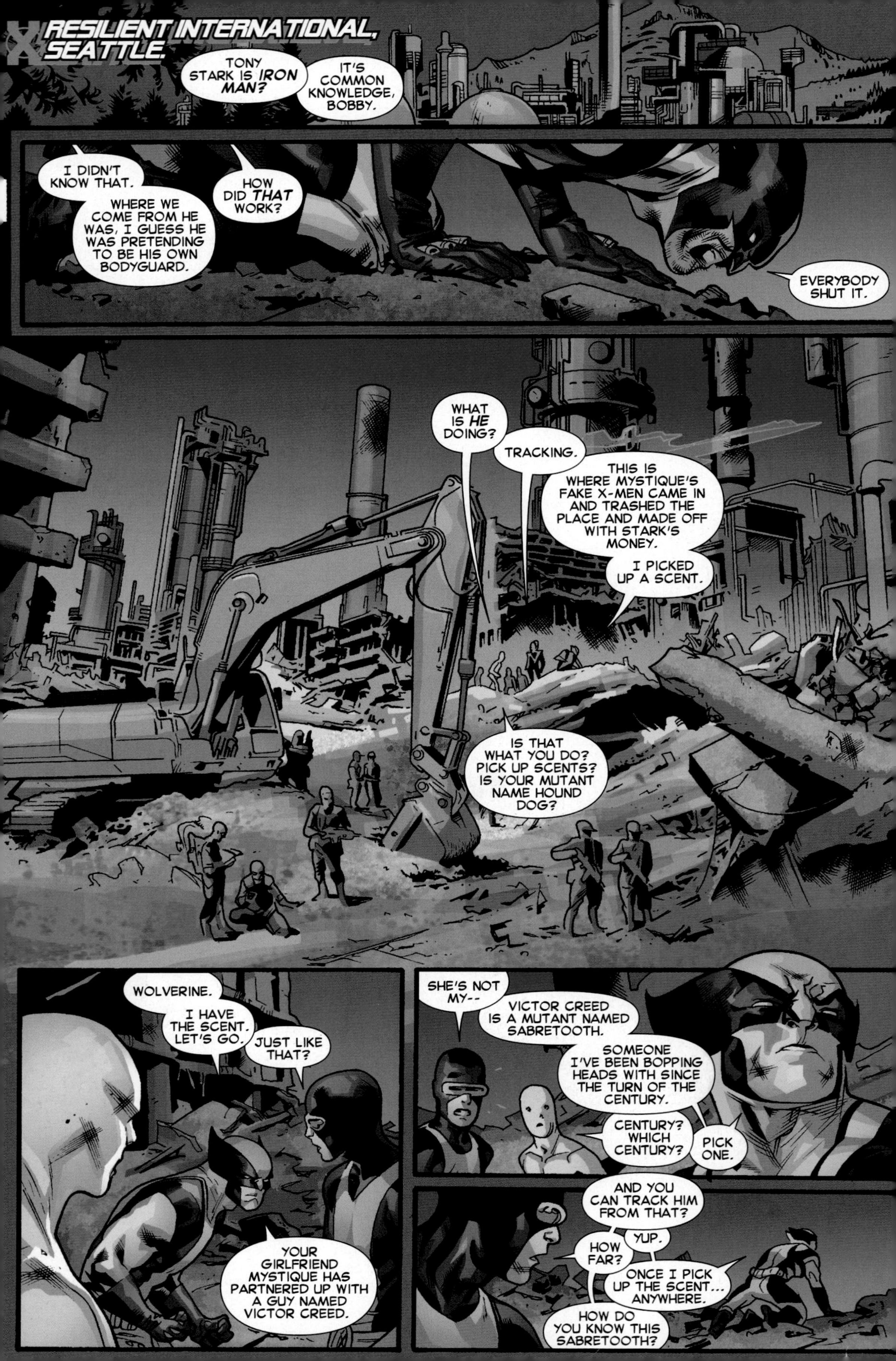
RESILIENT INTERNATIONAL, SEATTLE.
TONY STARK IS IRON MAN?
IT'S COMMON KNOWLEDGE, BOBBY.
I DIDN'T KNOW THAT.
WHERE WE COME FROM HE WAS, I GUESS HE WAS PRETENDING TO BE HIS OWN BODYGUARD.
HOW DID THAT WORK?
EVERYBODY SHUT IT.
WHAT IS HE DOING?
TRACKING.
THIS IS WHERE MYSTIQUE'S FAKE X-MEN CAME IN AND TRASHED THE PLACE AND MADE OFF WITH STARK'S MONEY.
I PICKED UP A SCENT.
IS THAT WHAT YOU DO? PICK UP SCENTS? IS YOUR MUTANT NAME HOUND DOG?
WOLVERINE.
I HAVE THE SCENT. LET'S GO.
JUST LIKE THAT?
YOUR GIRLFRIEND MYSTIQUE HAS PARTNERED UP WITH A GUY NAMED VICTOR CREED.
SHE'S NOT MY--
VICTOR CREED IS A MUTANT NAMED SABRETOOTH.
SOMEONE I'VE BEEN BOPPING HEADS WITH SINCE THE TURN OF THE CENTURY.
CENTURY? WHICH CENTURY?
PICK ONE.
AND YOU CAN TRACK HIM FROM THAT?
YUP.
HOW FAR?
ONCE I PICK UP THE SCENT... ANYWHERE.
HOW DO YOU KNOW THIS SABRETOOTH?

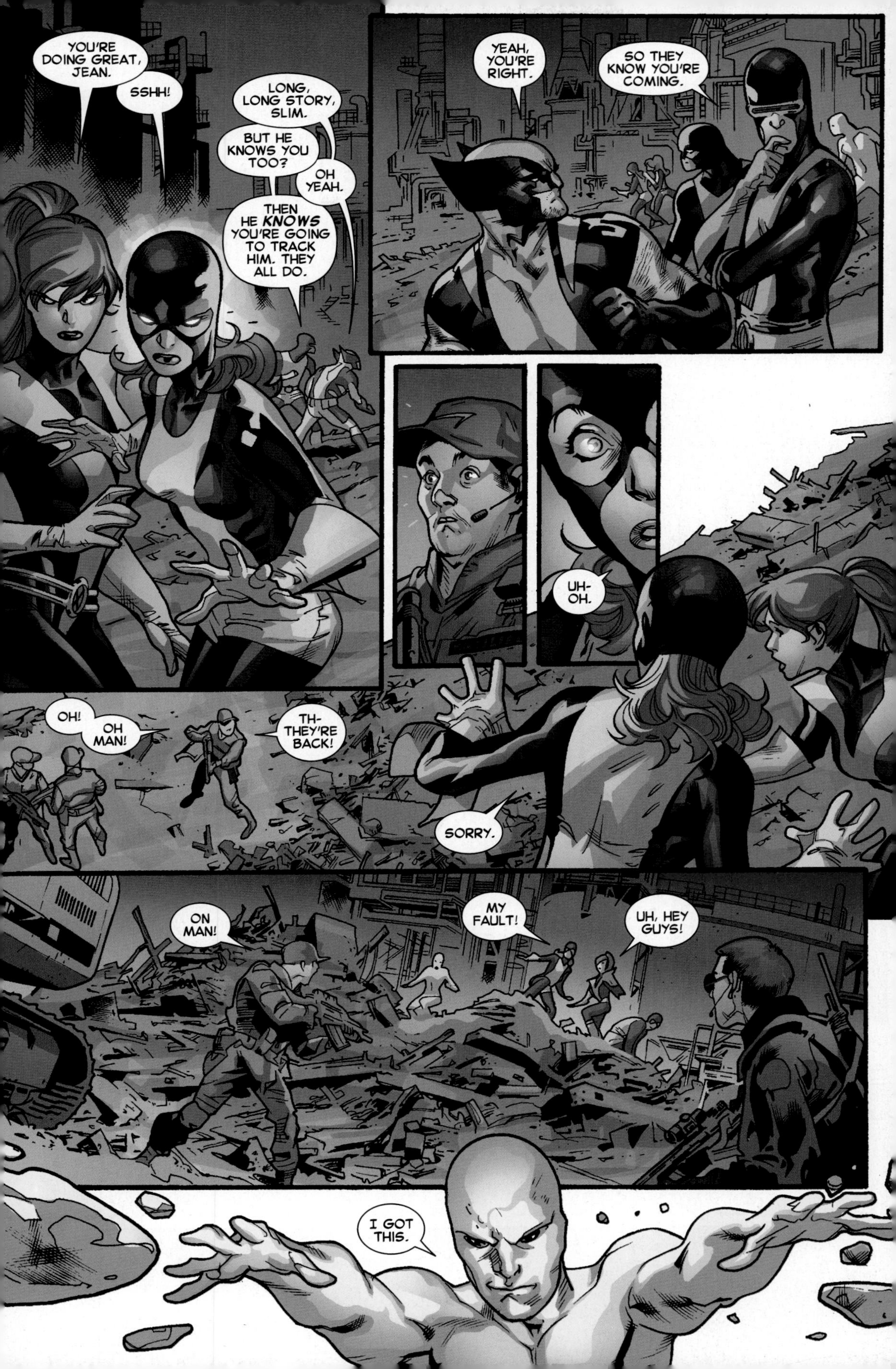
YOU'RE DOING GREAT, JEAN.
SSHH!
LONG, LONG STORY, SLIM.
BUT HE KNOWS YOU TOO?
OH YEAH.
THEN HE KNOWS YOU'RE GOING TO TRACK HIM. THEY ALL DO.
YEAH, YOU'RE RIGHT.
SO THEY KNOW YOU'RE COMING.
UH-OH.
OH!
OH MAN!
TH-THEY'RE BACK!
SORRY.
ON MAN!
MY FAULT!
UH, HEY GUYS!
I GOT THIS.

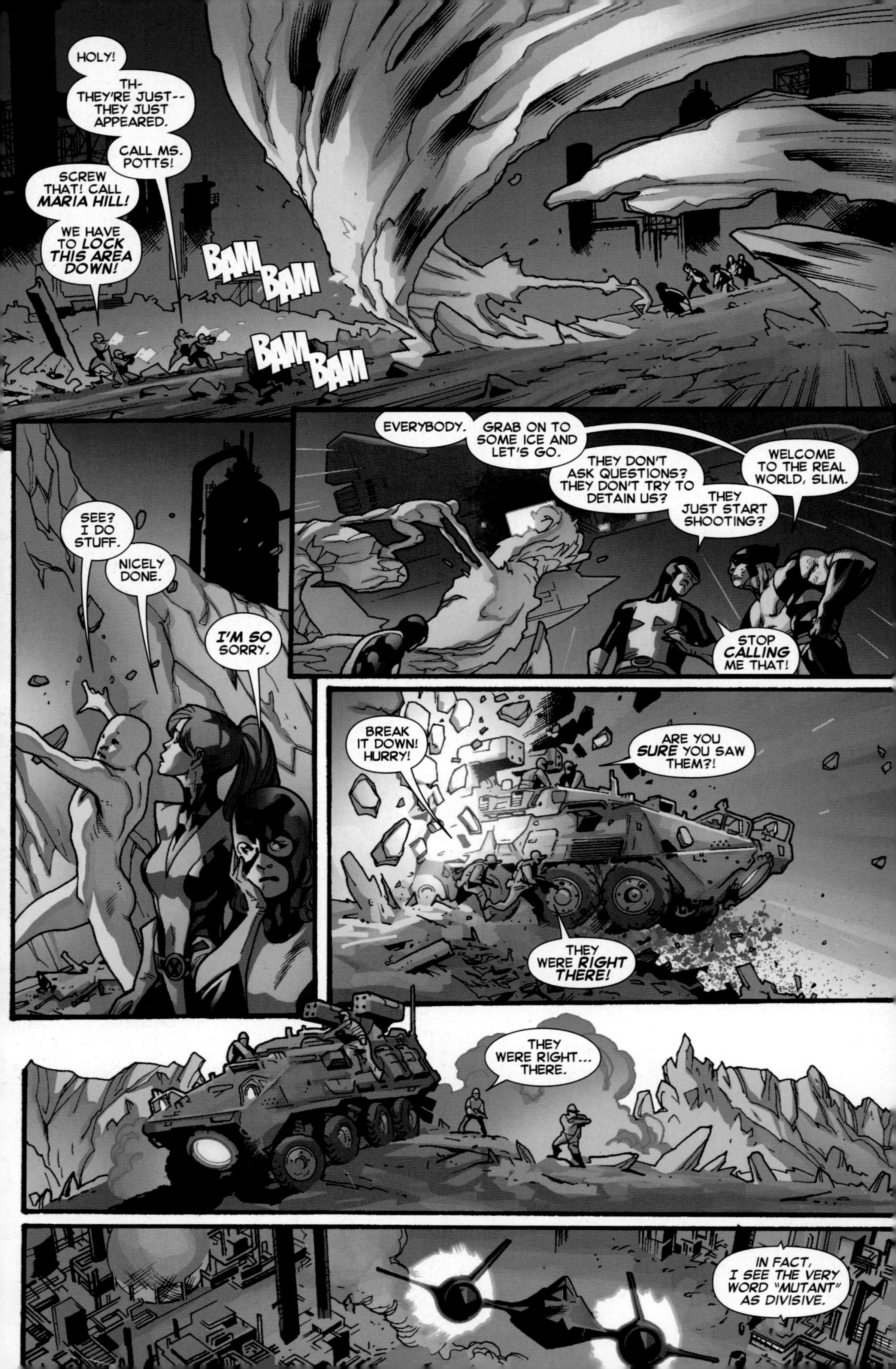
HOLY!
TH- THEY'RE JUST-- THEY JUST APPEARED.
CALL MS. POTTS!
SCREW THAT! CALL MARIA HILL!
WE HAVE TO LOCK THIS AREA DOWN!
BAM BAM
BAM BAM
SEE? I DO STUFF.
NICELY DONE.
I'M SO SORRY.
EVERYBODY.
GRAB ON TO SOME ICE AND LET'S GO.
THEY DON'T ASK QUESTIONS? THEY DON'T TRY TO DETAIN US?
THEY JUST START SHOOTING?
WELCOME TO THE REAL WORLD, SLIM.
STOP CALLING ME THAT!
BREAK IT DOWN! HURRY!
ARE YOU SURE YOU SAW THEM?!
THEY WERE RIGHT THERE!
THEY WERE RIGHT... THERE.
IN FACT, I SEE THE VERY WORD "MUTANT" AS DIVISIVE.

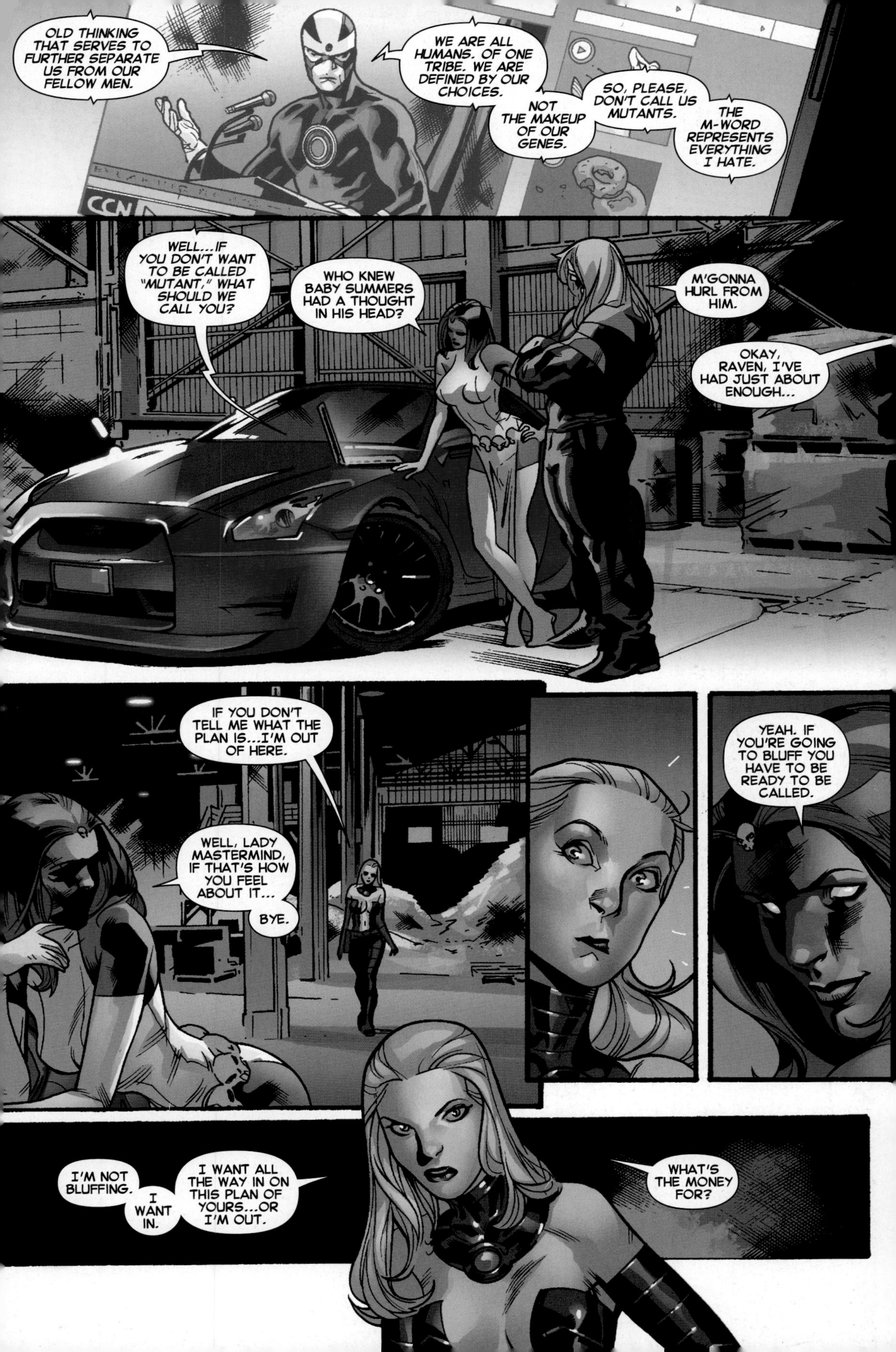
OLD THINKING THAT SERVES TO FURTHER SEPARATE US FROM OUR FELLOW MEN.
WE ARE ALL HUMANS. OF ONE TRIBE. WE ARE DEFINED BY OUR CHOICES.
NOT THE MAKEUP OF OUR GENES.
SO, PLEASE, DON'T CALL US MUTANTS.
THE M-WORD REPRESENTS EVERYTHING I HATE.
CCN
WELL...IF YOU DON'T WANT TO BE CALLED "MUTANT," WHAT SHOULD WE CALL YOU?
WHO KNEW BABY SUMMERS HAD A THOUGHT IN HIS HEAD?
M'GONNA HURL FROM HIM.
OKAY, RAVEN, I'VE HAD JUST ABOUT ENOUGH...
IF YOU DON'T TELL ME WHAT THE PLAN IS...I'M OUT OF HERE.
WELL, LADY MASTERMIND, IF THAT'S HOW YOU FEEL ABOUT IT...
BYE.
YEAH. IF YOU'RE GOING TO BLUFF YOU HAVE TO BE READY TO BE CALLED.
I'M NOT BLUFFING.
I WANT IN.
I WANT ALL THE WAY IN ON THIS PLAN OF YOURS...OR I'M OUT.
WHAT'S THE MONEY FOR?

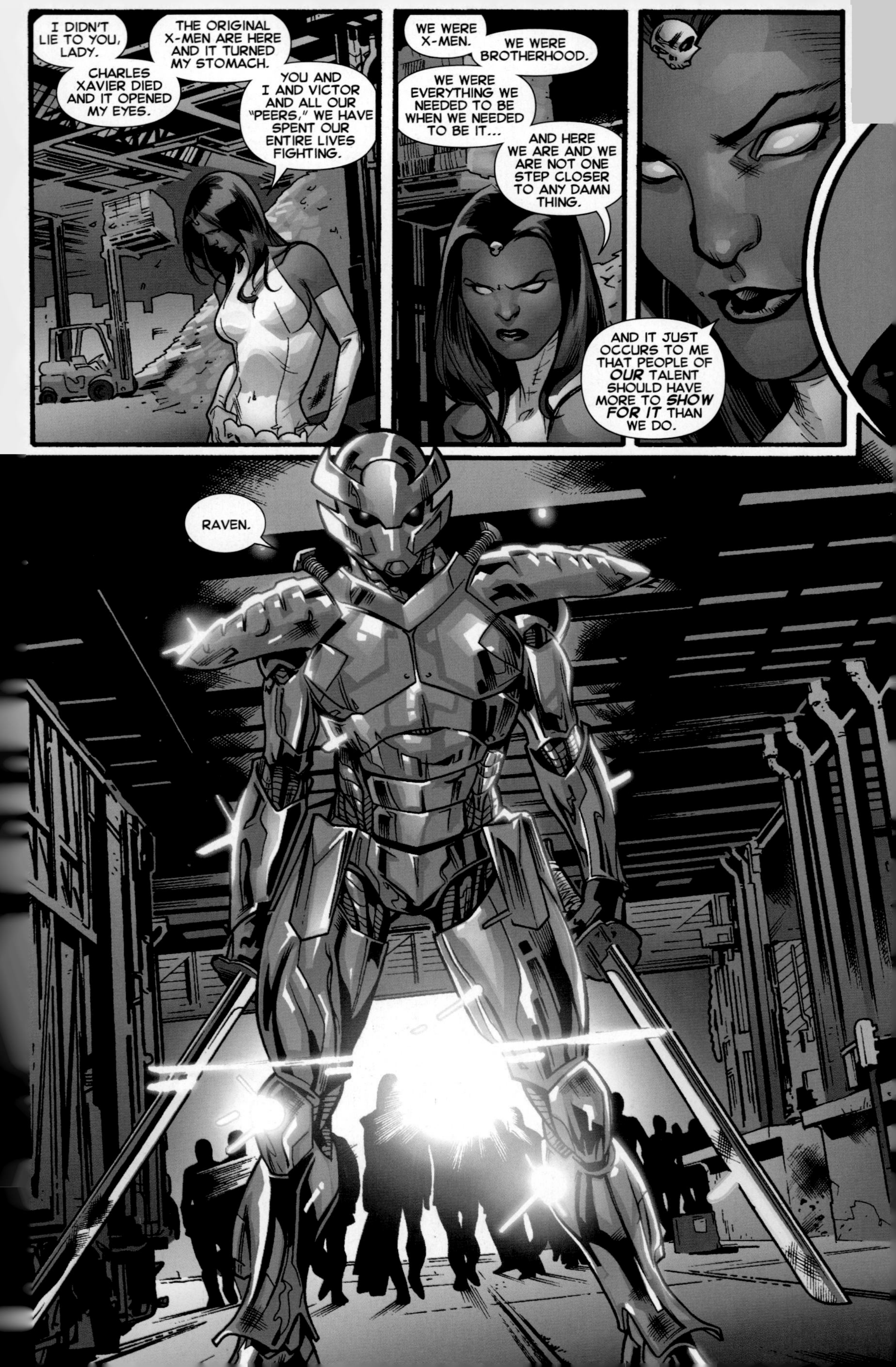
I DIDN'T LIE TO YOU, LADY.
THE ORIGINAL X-MEN ARE HERE AND IT TURNED MY STOMACH.
CHARLES XAVIER DIED AND IT OPENED MY EYES.
YOU AND I AND VICTOR AND ALL OUR "PEERS," WE HAVE SPENT OUR ENTIRE LIVES FIGHTING.
WE WERE X-MEN.
WE WERE BROTHERHOOD.
WE WERE EVERYTHING WE NEEDED TO BE WHEN WE NEEDED TO BE IT...
AND HERE WE ARE AND WE ARE NOT ONE STEP CLOSER TO ANY DAMN THING.
AND IT JUST OCCURS TO ME THAT PEOPLE OF ***OUR*** TALENT SHOULD HAVE MORE TO ***SHOW FOR IT*** THAN WE DO.
RAVEN.

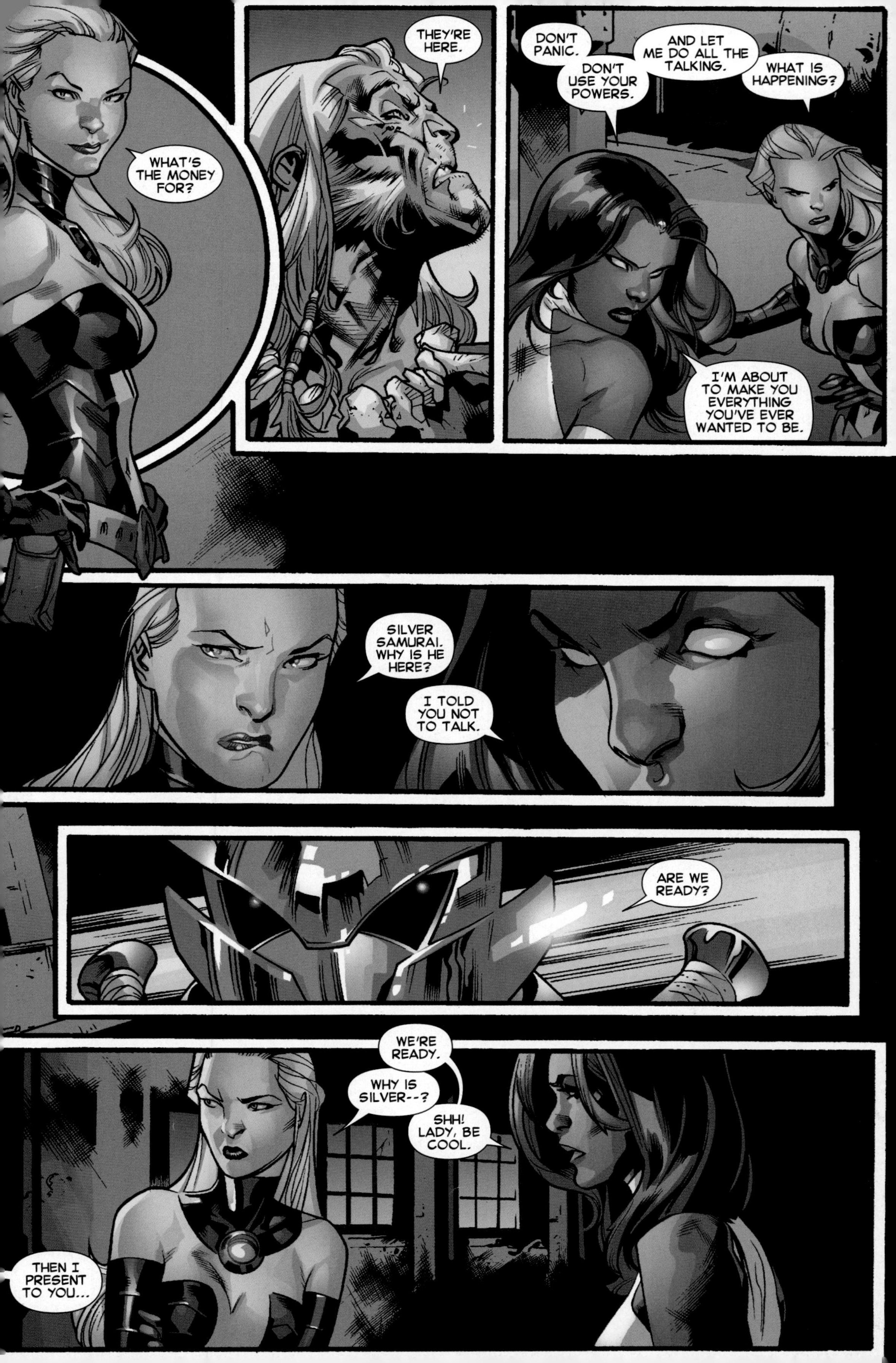
WHAT'S THE MONEY FOR?
THEY'RE HERE.
DON'T PANIC.
DON'T USE YOUR POWERS.
AND LET ME DO ALL THE TALKING.
WHAT IS HAPPENING?
I'M ABOUT TO MAKE YOU EVERYTHING YOU'VE EVER WANTED TO BE.
SILVER SAMURAI. WHY IS HE HERE?
I TOLD YOU NOT TO TALK.
ARE WE READY?
WE'RE READY.
WHY IS SILVER--?
SHH! LADY, BE COOL.
THEN I PRESENT TO YOU...

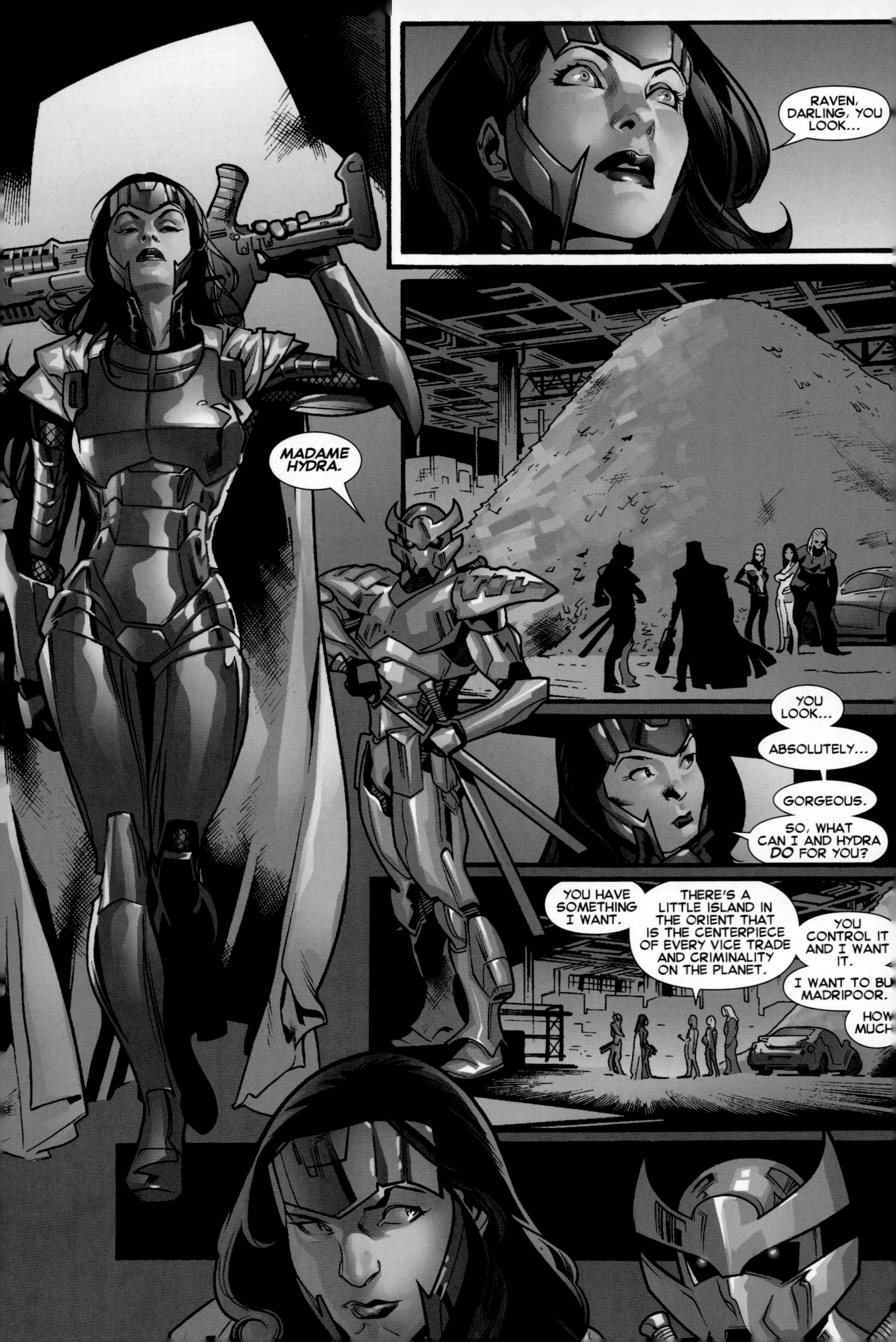
RAVEN, DARLING, YOU LOOK...
MADAME HYDRA.
YOU LOOK...
ABSOLUTELY...
GORGEOUS.
SO, WHAT CAN I AND HYDRA DO FOR YOU?
YOU HAVE SOMETHING I WANT.
THERE'S A LITTLE ISLAND IN THE ORIENT THAT IS THE CENTERPIECE OF EVERY VICE TRADE AND CRIMINALITY ON THE PLANET.
YOU CONTROL IT AND I WANT IT.
MADRIPOOR.

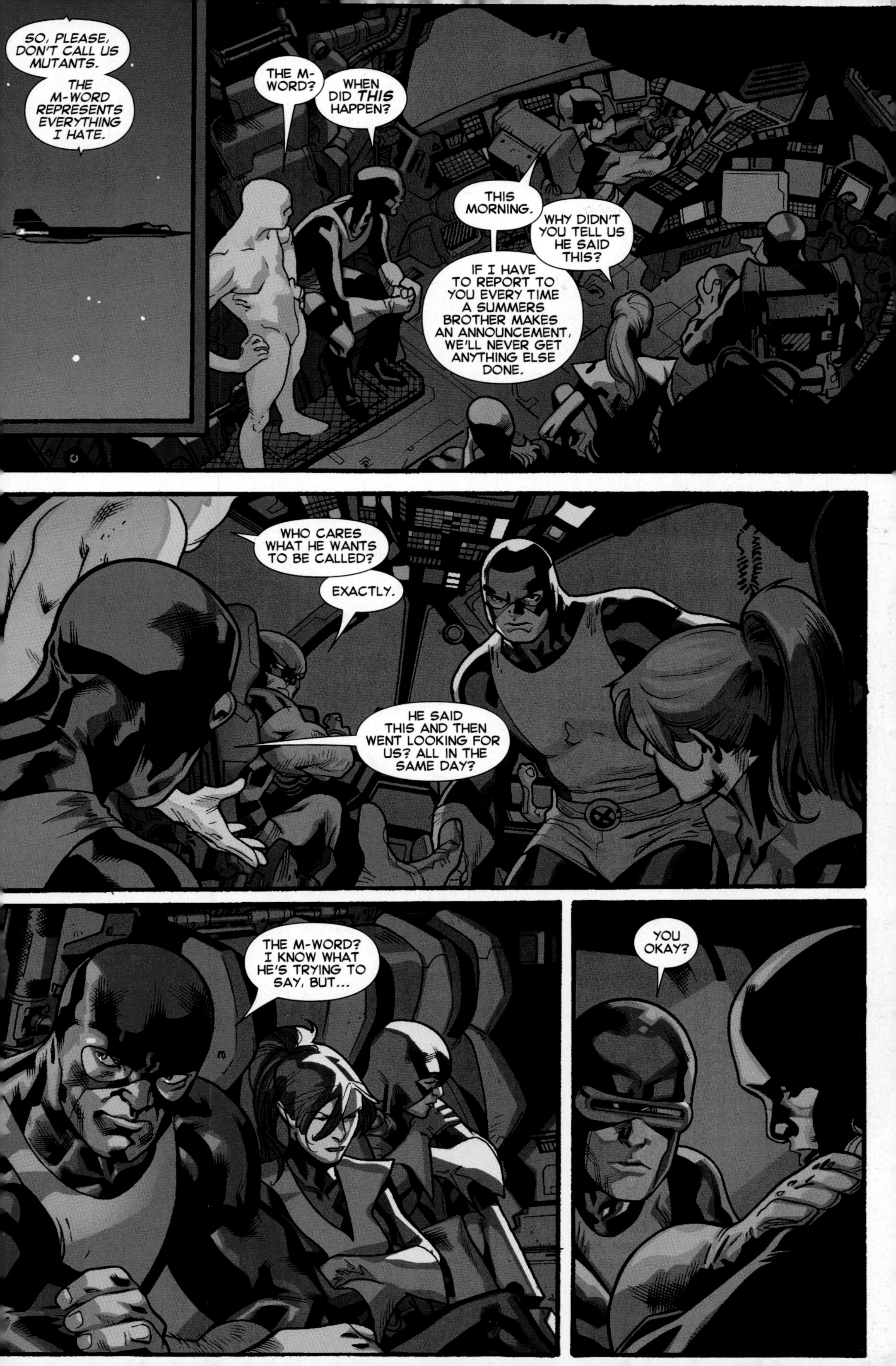
SO, PLEASE, DON'T CALL US MUTANTS.
THE M-WORD REPRESENTS EVERYTHING I HATE.
THE M-WORD?
WHEN DID THIS HAPPEN?
THIS MORNING.
WHY DIDN'T YOU TELL US HE SAID THIS?
IF I HAVE TO REPORT TO YOU EVERY TIME A SUMMERS BROTHER MAKES AN ANNOUNCEMENT, WE'LL NEVER GET ANYTHING ELSE DONE.
WHO CARES WHAT HE WANTS TO BE CALLED?
EXACTLY.
HE SAID THIS AND THEN WENT LOOKING FOR US? ALL IN THE SAME DAY?
THE M-WORD? I KNOW WHAT HE'S TRYING TO SAY, BUT...
YOU OKAY?

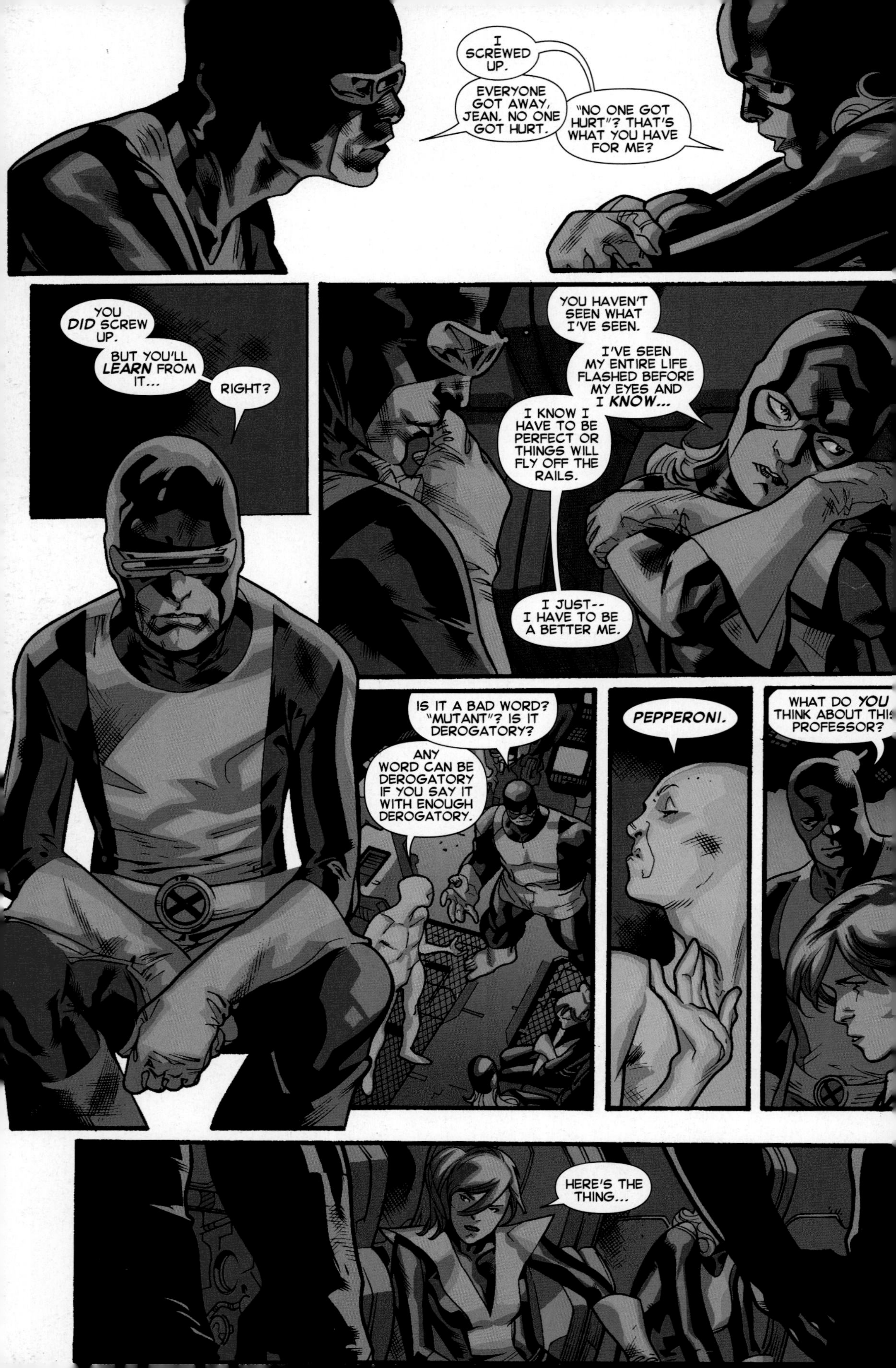
I SCREWED UP.
EVERYONE GOT AWAY, JEAN. NO ONE GOT HURT.
"NO ONE GOT HURT"? THAT'S WHAT YOU HAVE FOR ME?
YOU *DID* SCREW UP.
BUT YOU'LL *LEARN* FROM IT...
RIGHT?
YOU HAVEN'T SEEN WHAT I'VE SEEN.
I'VE SEEN MY ENTIRE LIFE FLASHED BEFORE MY EYES AND I *KNOW...*
I KNOW I HAVE TO BE PERFECT OR THINGS WILL FLY OFF THE RAILS.
I JUST-- I HAVE TO BE A BETTER ME.
IS IT A BAD WORD? "MUTANT"? IS IT DEROGATORY?
ANY WORD CAN BE DEROGATORY IF YOU SAY IT WITH ENOUGH DEROGATORY.
PEPPERONI.
WHAT DO *YOU* THINK ABOUT THIS PROFESSOR?
HERE'S THE THING...

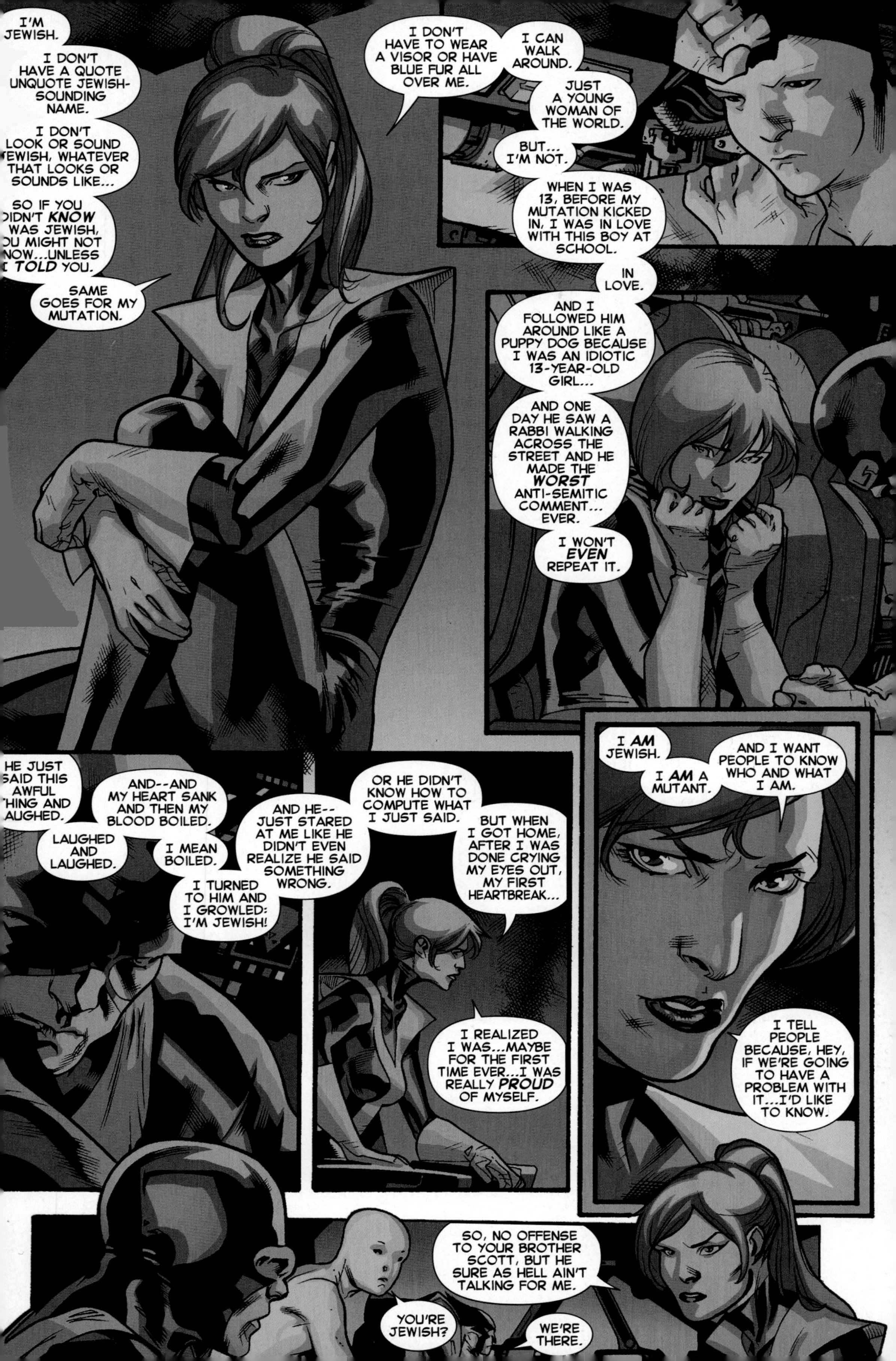

I'M JEWISH.
I DON'T HAVE A QUOTE UNQUOTE JEWISH-SOUNDING NAME.
I DON'T LOOK OR SOUND JEWISH, WHATEVER THAT LOOKS OR SOUNDS LIKE...
SO IF YOU DIDN'T KNOW I WAS JEWISH, YOU MIGHT NOT KNOW...UNLESS I TOLD YOU.
SAME GOES FOR MY MUTATION.
I DON'T HAVE TO WEAR A VISOR OR HAVE BLUE FUR ALL OVER ME.
I CAN WALK AROUND.
JUST A YOUNG WOMAN OF THE WORLD.
BUT... I'M NOT.
WHEN I WAS 13, BEFORE MY MUTATION KICKED IN, I WAS IN LOVE WITH THIS BOY AT SCHOOL.
IN LOVE.
AND I FOLLOWED HIM AROUND LIKE A PUPPY DOG BECAUSE I WAS AN IDIOTIC 13-YEAR-OLD GIRL...
AND ONE DAY HE SAW A RABBI WALKING ACROSS THE STREET AND HE MADE THE WORST ANTI-SEMITIC COMMENT... EVER.
I WON'T EVEN REPEAT IT.
HE JUST SAID THIS AWFUL THING AND LAUGHED.
LAUGHED AND LAUGHED.
AND--AND MY HEART SANK AND THEN MY BLOOD BOILED.
I MEAN BOILED.
I TURNED TO HIM AND I GROWLED: I'M JEWISH!
AND HE--JUST STARED AT ME LIKE HE DIDN'T EVEN REALIZE HE SAID SOMETHING WRONG.
OR HE DIDN'T KNOW HOW TO COMPUTE WHAT I JUST SAID.
BUT WHEN I GOT HOME, AFTER I WAS DONE CRYING MY EYES OUT, MY FIRST HEARTBREAK...
I REALIZED I WAS...MAYBE FOR THE FIRST TIME EVER...I WAS REALLY PROUD OF MYSELF.
I AM JEWISH.
I AM A MUTANT.
AND I WANT PEOPLE TO KNOW WHO AND WHAT I AM.
I TELL PEOPLE BECAUSE, HEY, IF WE'RE GOING TO HAVE A PROBLEM WITH IT...I'D LIKE TO KNOW.
SO, NO OFFENSE TO YOUR BROTHER SCOTT, BUT HE SURE AS HELL AIN'T TALKING FOR ME.
YOU'RE JEWISH?
WE'RE THERE.

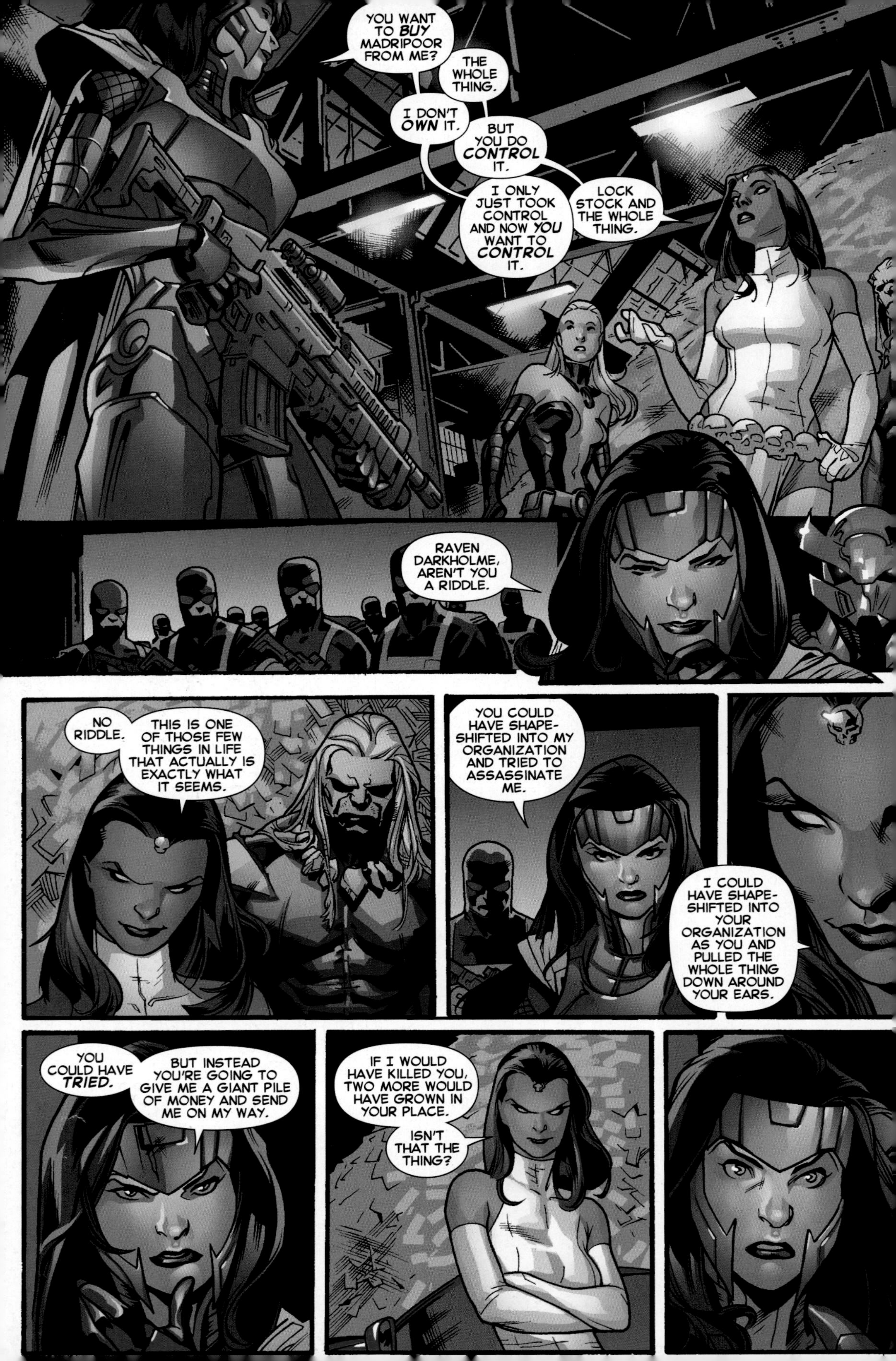
YOU WANT TO BUY MADRIPOOR FROM ME?
THE WHOLE THING.
I DON'T OWN IT.
BUT YOU DO CONTROL IT.
I ONLY JUST TOOK CONTROL AND NOW YOU WANT TO CONTROL IT.
LOCK STOCK AND THE WHOLE THING.
RAVEN DARKHOLME, AREN'T YOU A RIDDLE.
NO RIDDLE.
THIS IS ONE OF THOSE FEW THINGS IN LIFE THAT ACTUALLY IS EXACTLY WHAT IT SEEMS.
YOU COULD HAVE SHAPE-SHIFTED INTO MY ORGANIZATION AND TRIED TO ASSASSINATE ME.
I COULD HAVE SHAPE-SHIFTED INTO YOUR ORGANIZATION AS YOU AND PULLED THE WHOLE THING DOWN AROUND YOUR EARS.
YOU COULD HAVE TRIED.
BUT INSTEAD YOU'RE GOING TO GIVE ME A GIANT PILE OF MONEY AND SEND ME ON MY WAY.
IF I WOULD HAVE KILLED YOU, TWO MORE WOULD HAVE GROWN IN YOUR PLACE.
ISN'T THAT THE THING?

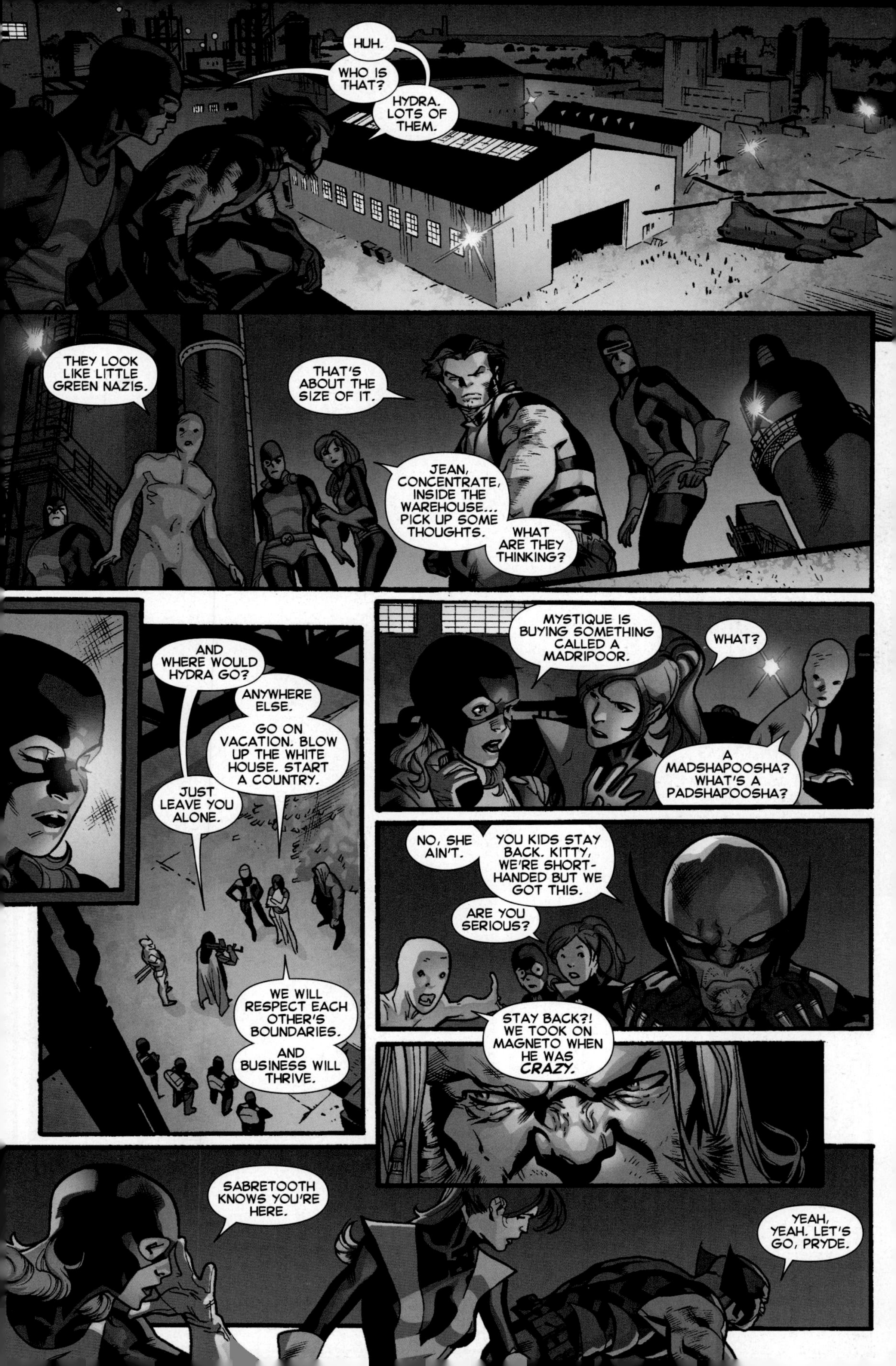
HUH.
WHO IS THAT?
HYDRA. LOTS OF THEM.
THEY LOOK LIKE LITTLE GREEN NAZIS.
THAT'S ABOUT THE SIZE OF IT.
JEAN, CONCENTRATE, INSIDE THE WAREHOUSE... PICK UP SOME THOUGHTS.
WHAT ARE THEY THINKING?
AND WHERE WOULD HYDRA GO?
ANYWHERE ELSE.
GO ON VACATION. BLOW UP THE WHITE HOUSE. START A COUNTRY.
JUST LEAVE YOU ALONE.
WE WILL RESPECT EACH OTHER'S BOUNDARIES.
AND BUSINESS WILL THRIVE.
MYSTIQUE IS BUYING SOMETHING CALLED A MADRIPOOR.
WHAT?
A MADSHAPOOSHA? WHAT'S A PADSHAPOOSHA?
NO, SHE AIN'T.
YOU KIDS STAY BACK. KITTY, WE'RE SHORT-HANDED BUT WE GOT THIS.
ARE YOU SERIOUS?
STAY BACK?! WE TOOK ON MAGNETO WHEN HE WAS CRAZY.
SABRETOOTH KNOWS YOU'RE HERE.
YEAH, YEAH. LET'S GO, PRYDE.

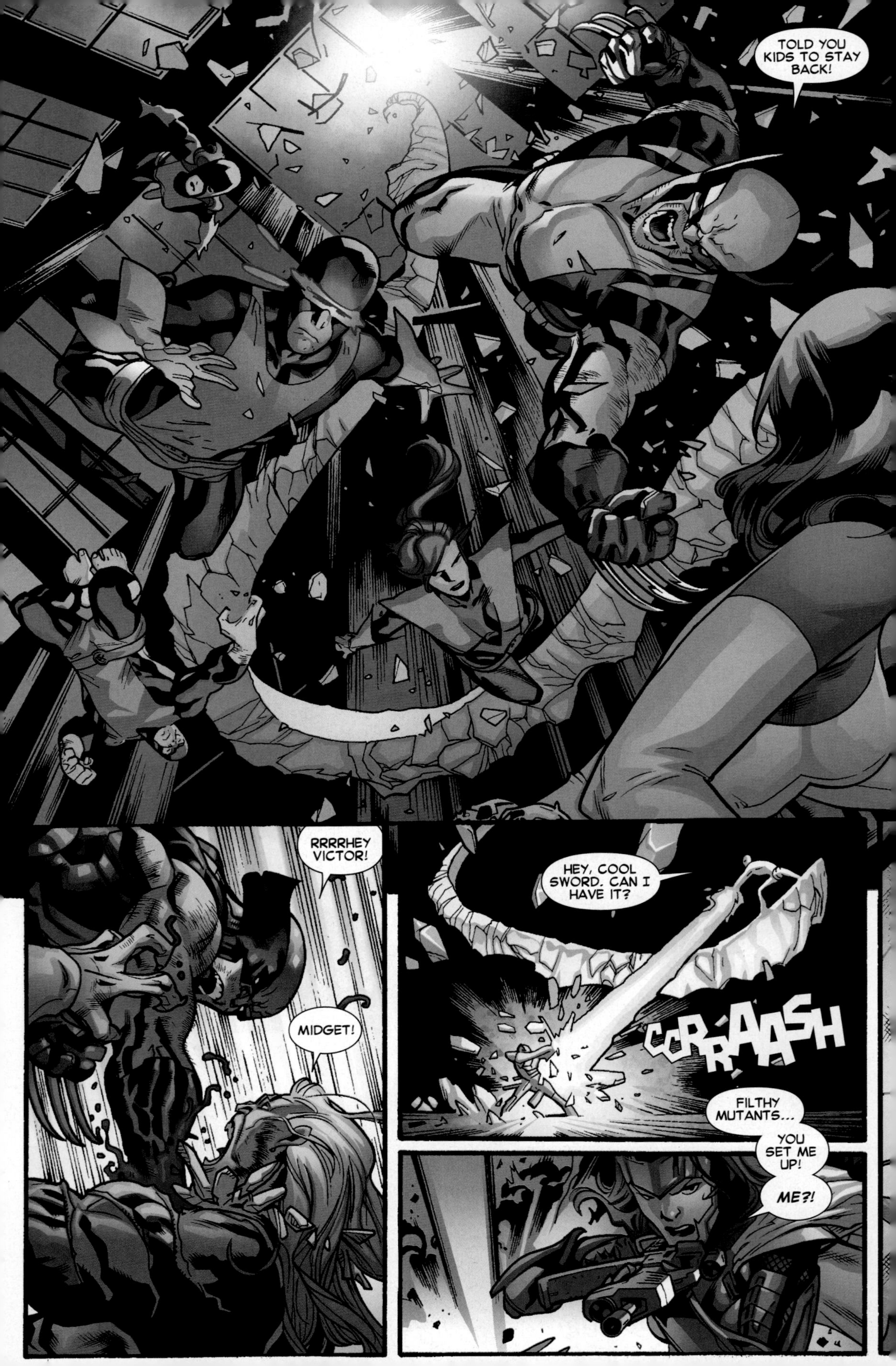
TOLD YOU KIDS TO STAY BACK!
RRRRHEY VICTOR!
MIDGET!
HEY, COOL SWORD. CAN I HAVE IT?
CCRRAASH
FILTHY MUTANTS...
YOU SET ME UP!
ME?!

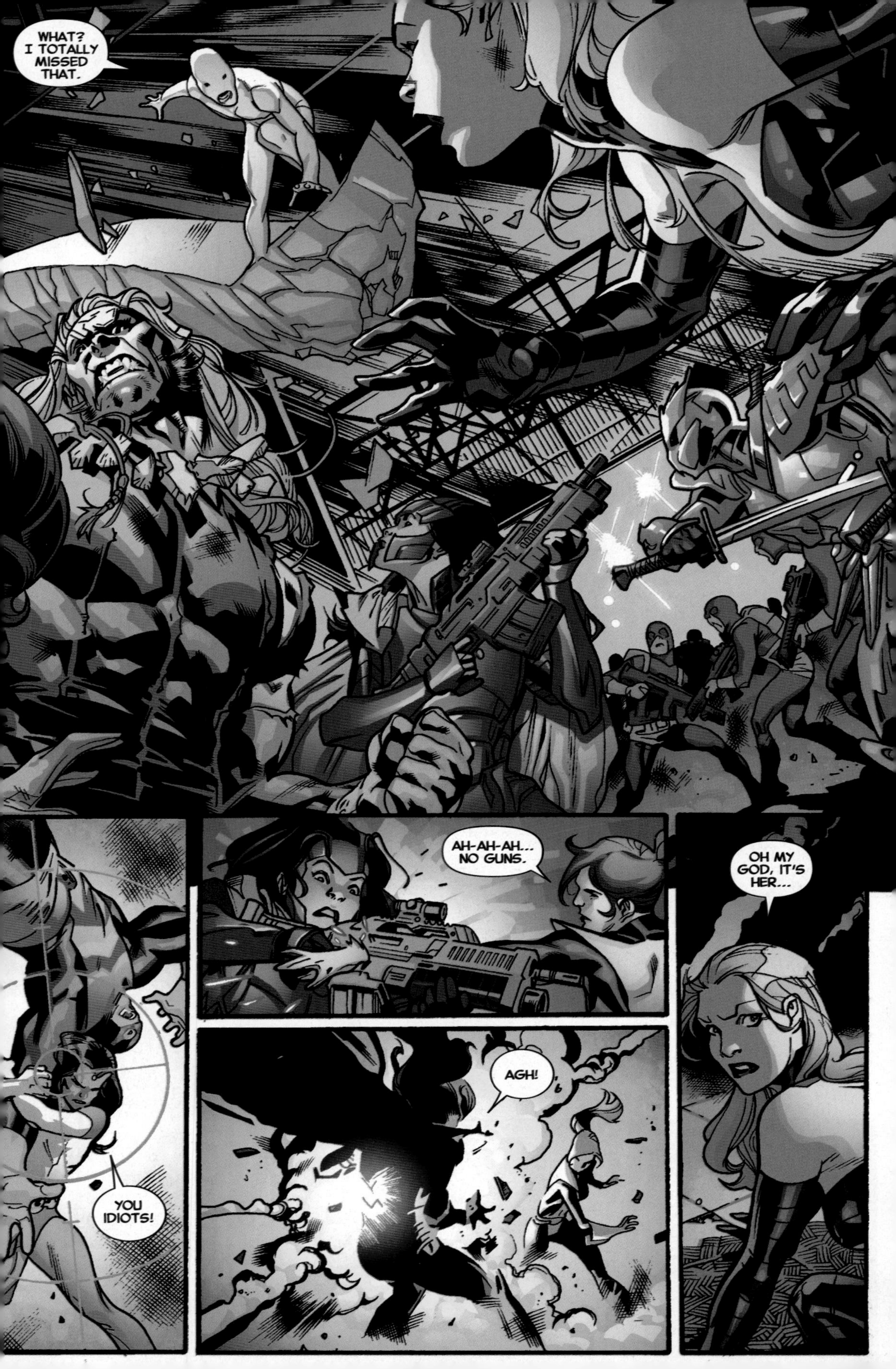

WHAT? I TOTALLY MISSED THAT.
AH-AH-AH... NO GUNS.
OH MY GOD, IT'S HER...
AGH!
YOU IDIOTS!

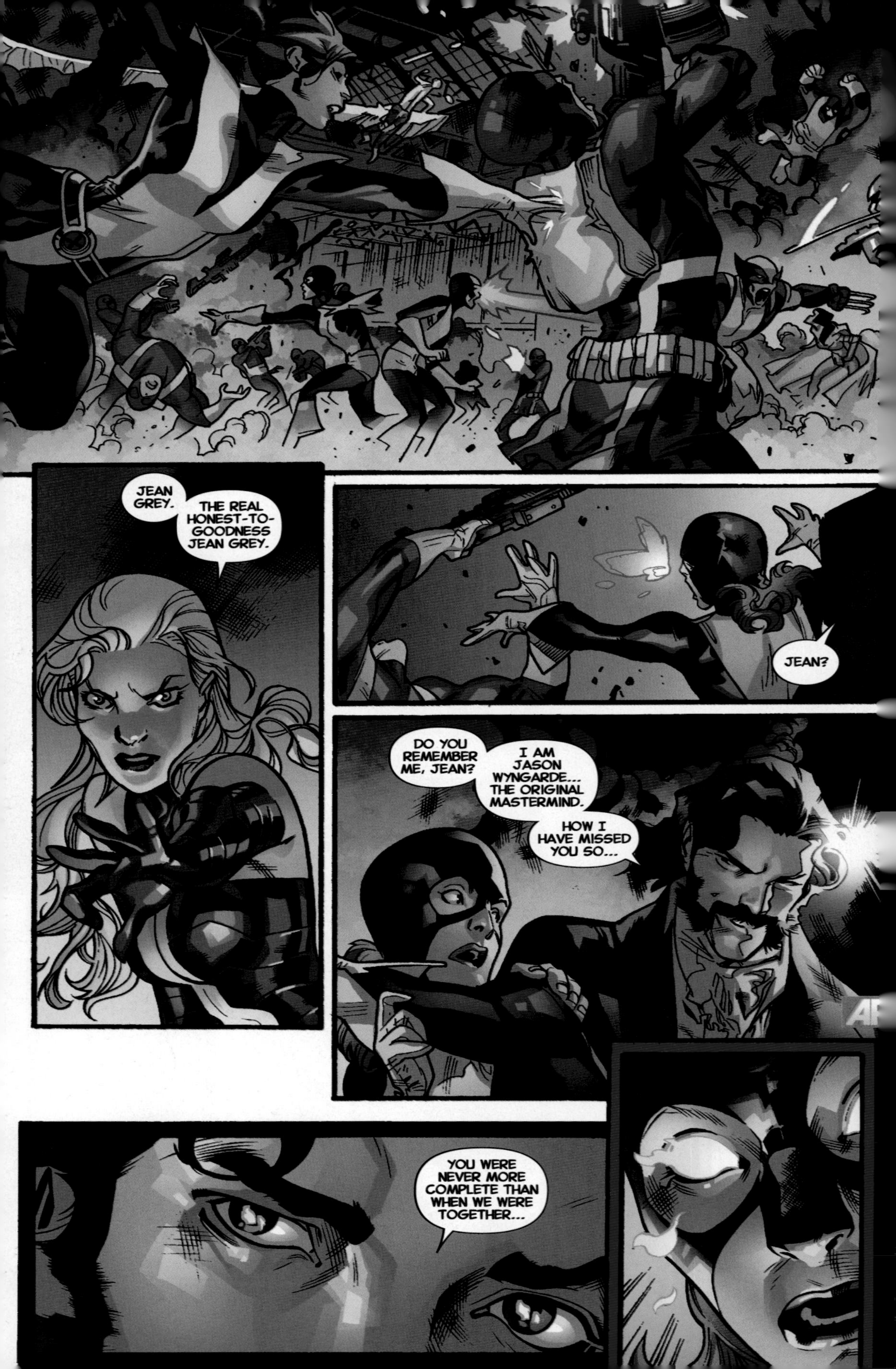
JEAN GREY.
THE REAL HONEST-TO-GOODNESS JEAN GREY.
JEAN?
DO YOU REMEMBER ME, JEAN?
I AM JASON WYNGARDE... THE ORIGINAL MASTERMIND.
HOW I HAVE MISSED YOU SO...
YOU WERE NEVER MORE COMPLETE THAN WHEN WE WERE TOGETHER...

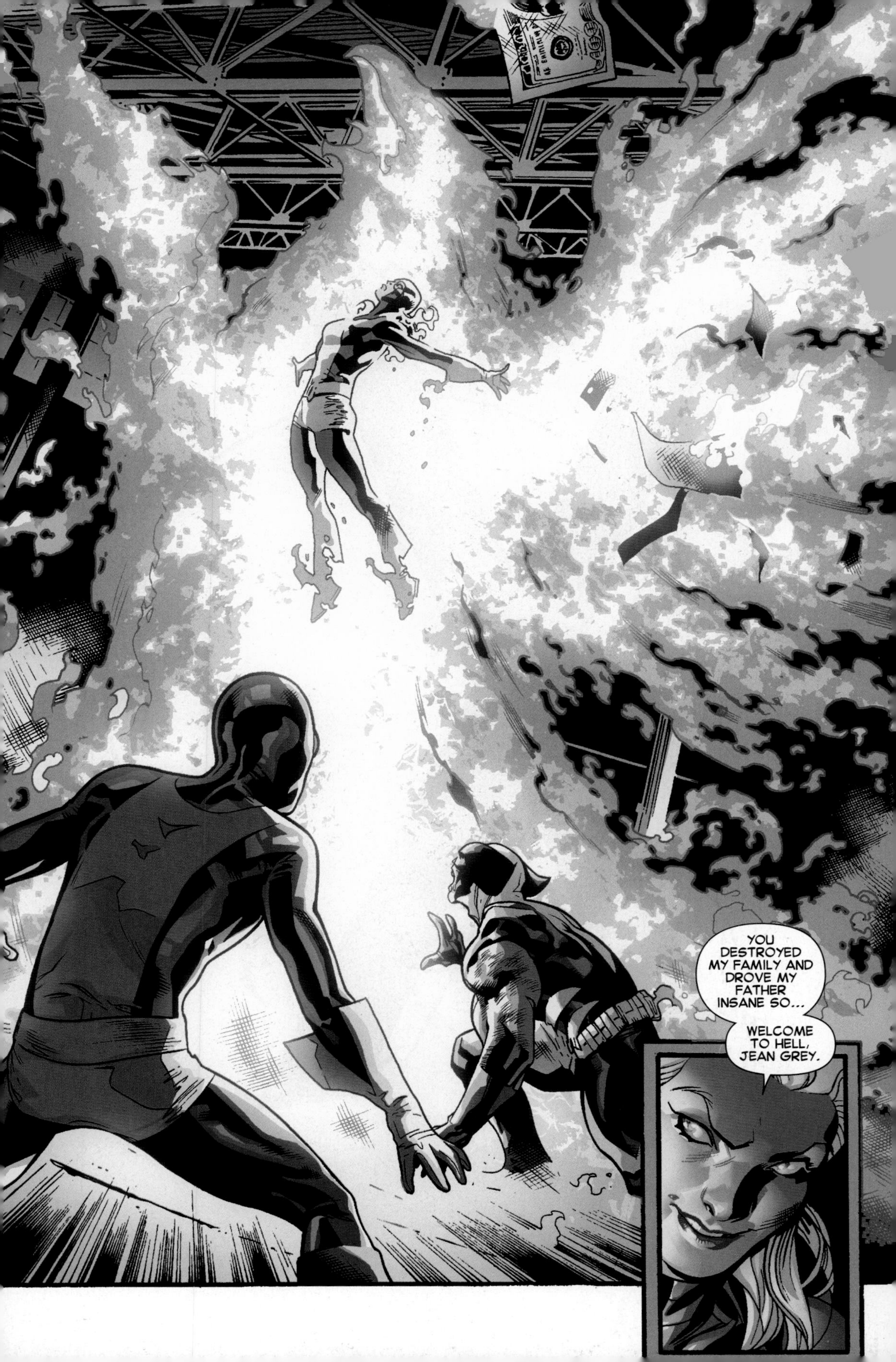
YOU DESTROYED MY FAMILY AND DROVE MY FATHER INSANE SO...
WELCOME TO HELL, JEAN GREY.

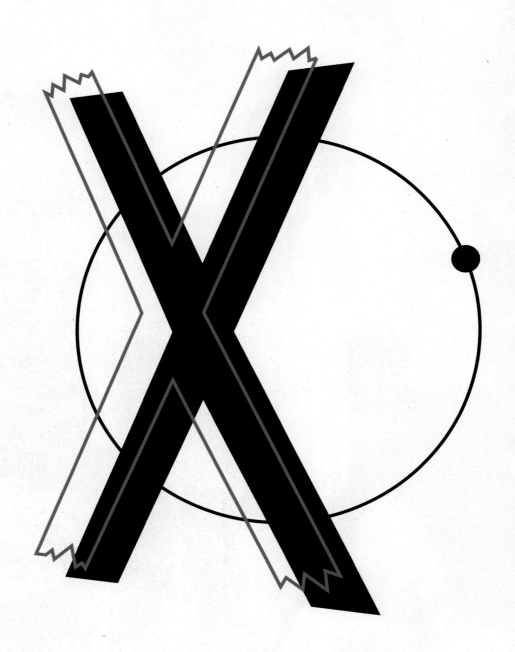

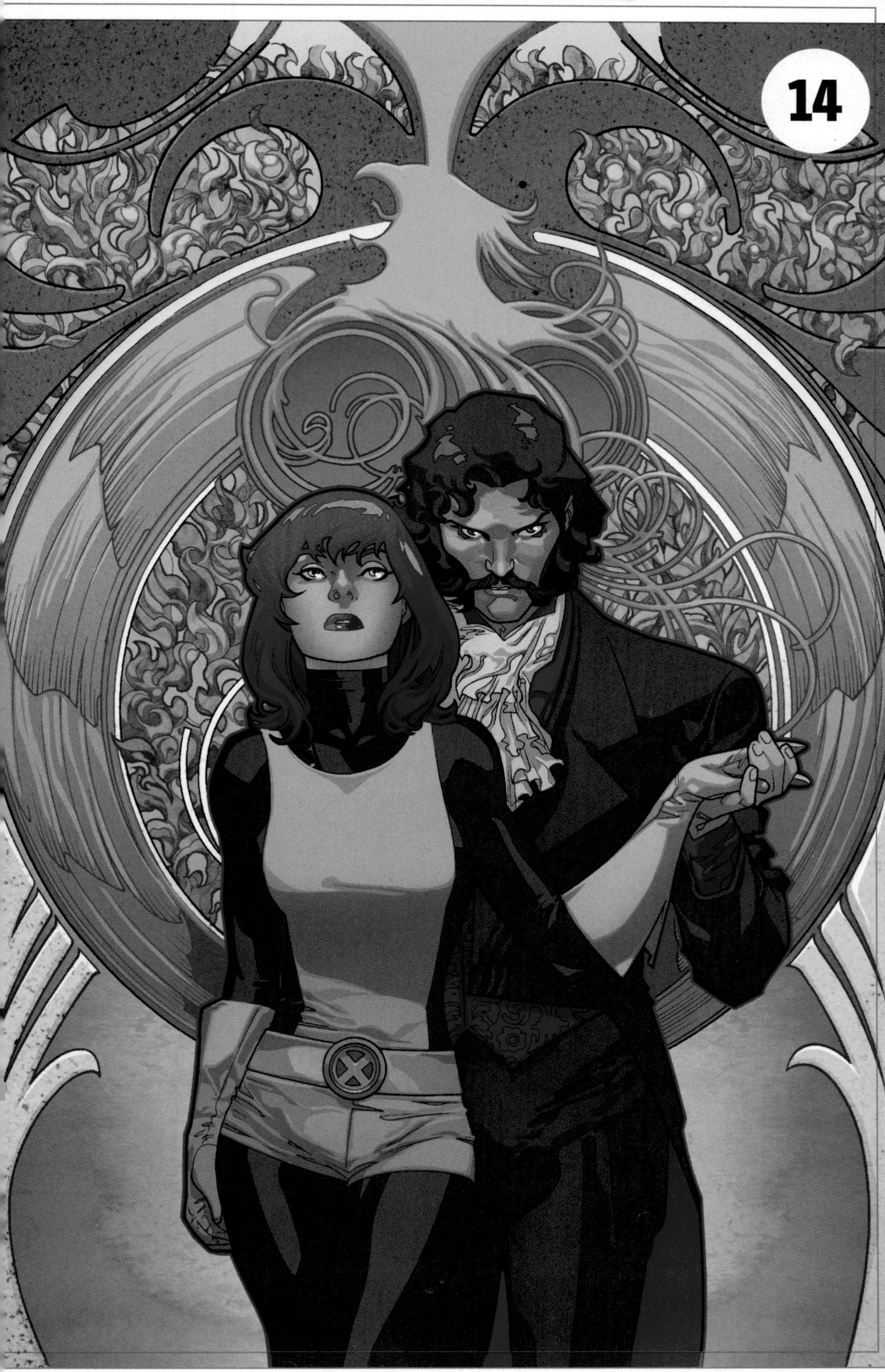
14

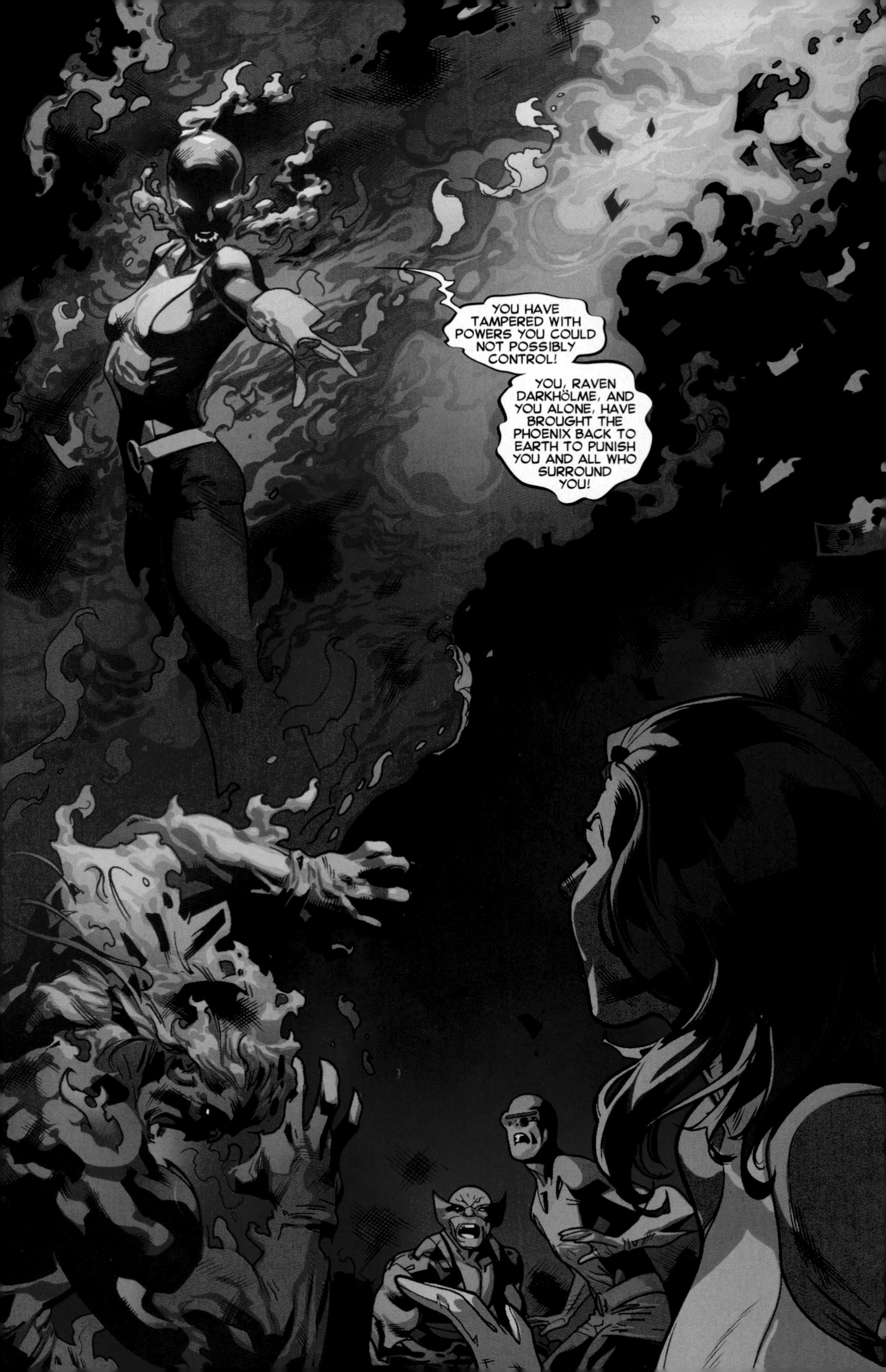
YOU HAVE TAMPERED WITH POWERS YOU COULD NOT POSSIBLY CONTROL!
YOU, RAVEN DARKHÖLME, AND YOU ALONE, HAVE BROUGHT THE PHOENIX BACK TO EARTH TO PUNISH YOU AND ALL WHO SURROUND YOU!

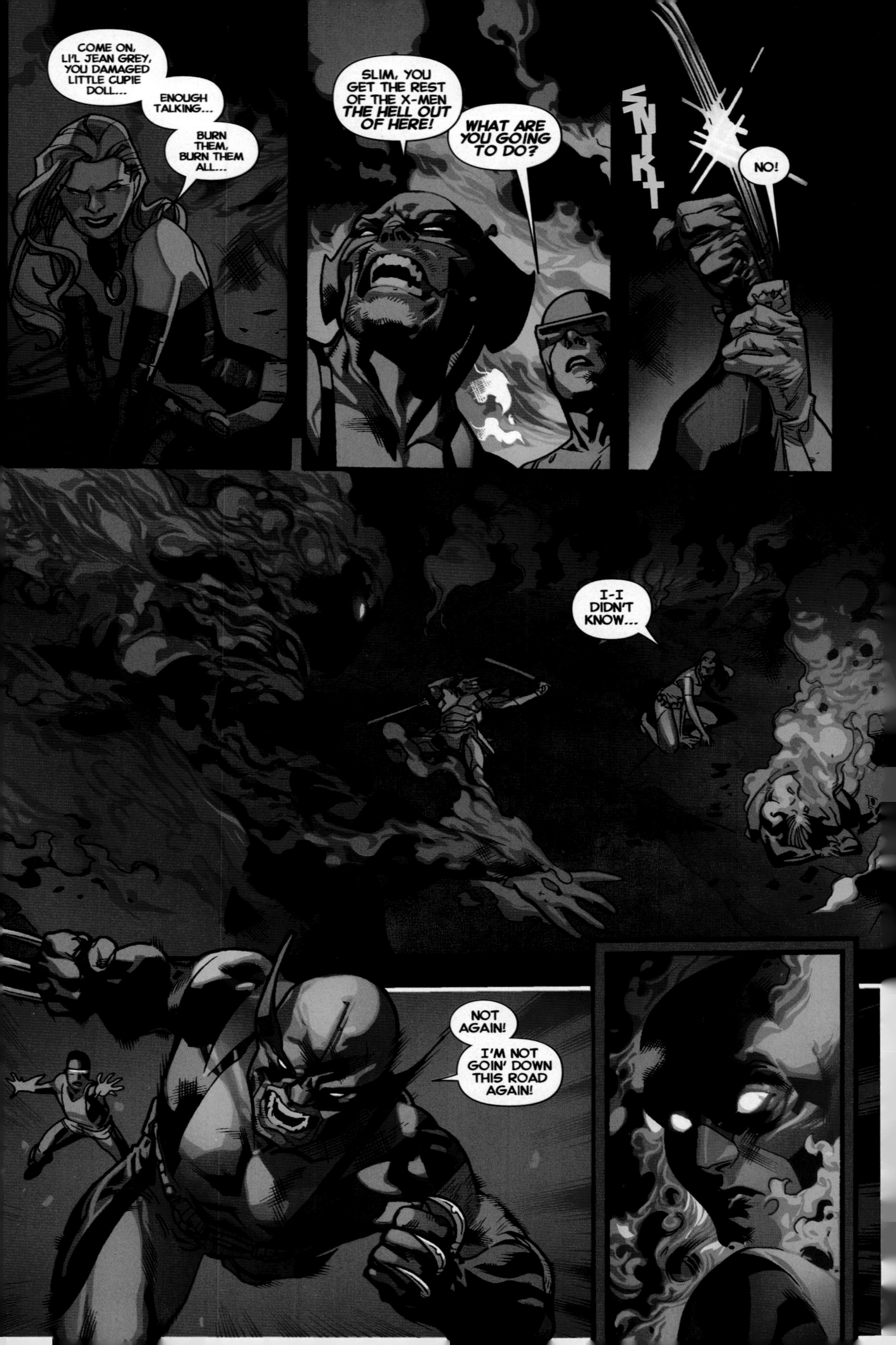
COME ON, LI'L JEAN GREY, YOU DAMAGED LITTLE CUPIE DOLL...
ENOUGH TALKING...
BURN THEM, BURN THEM ALL...
SLIM, YOU GET THE REST OF THE X-MEN THE HELL OUT OF HERE!
WHAT ARE YOU GOING TO DO?
SNIKT
NO!
I-I DIDN'T KNOW...
NOT AGAIN!
I'M NOT GOIN' DOWN THIS ROAD AGAIN!

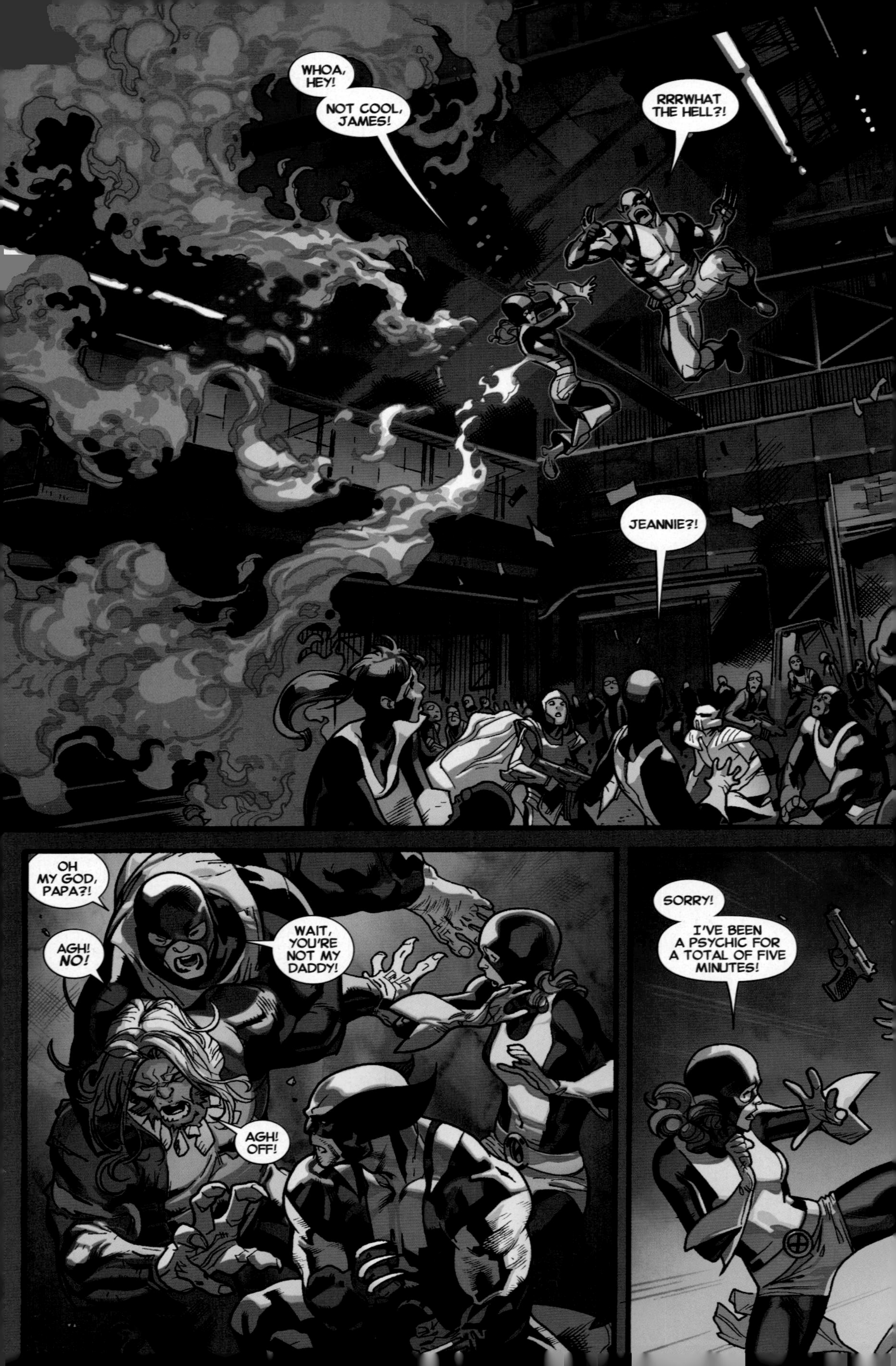

WHOA, HEY!
NOT COOL, JAMES!
RRRWHAT THE HELL?!
JEANNIE?!
OH MY GOD, PAPA?!
AGH! NO!
WAIT, YOU'RE NOT MY DADDY!
AGH! OFF!
SORRY!
I'VE BEEN A PSYCHIC FOR A TOTAL OF FIVE MINUTES!

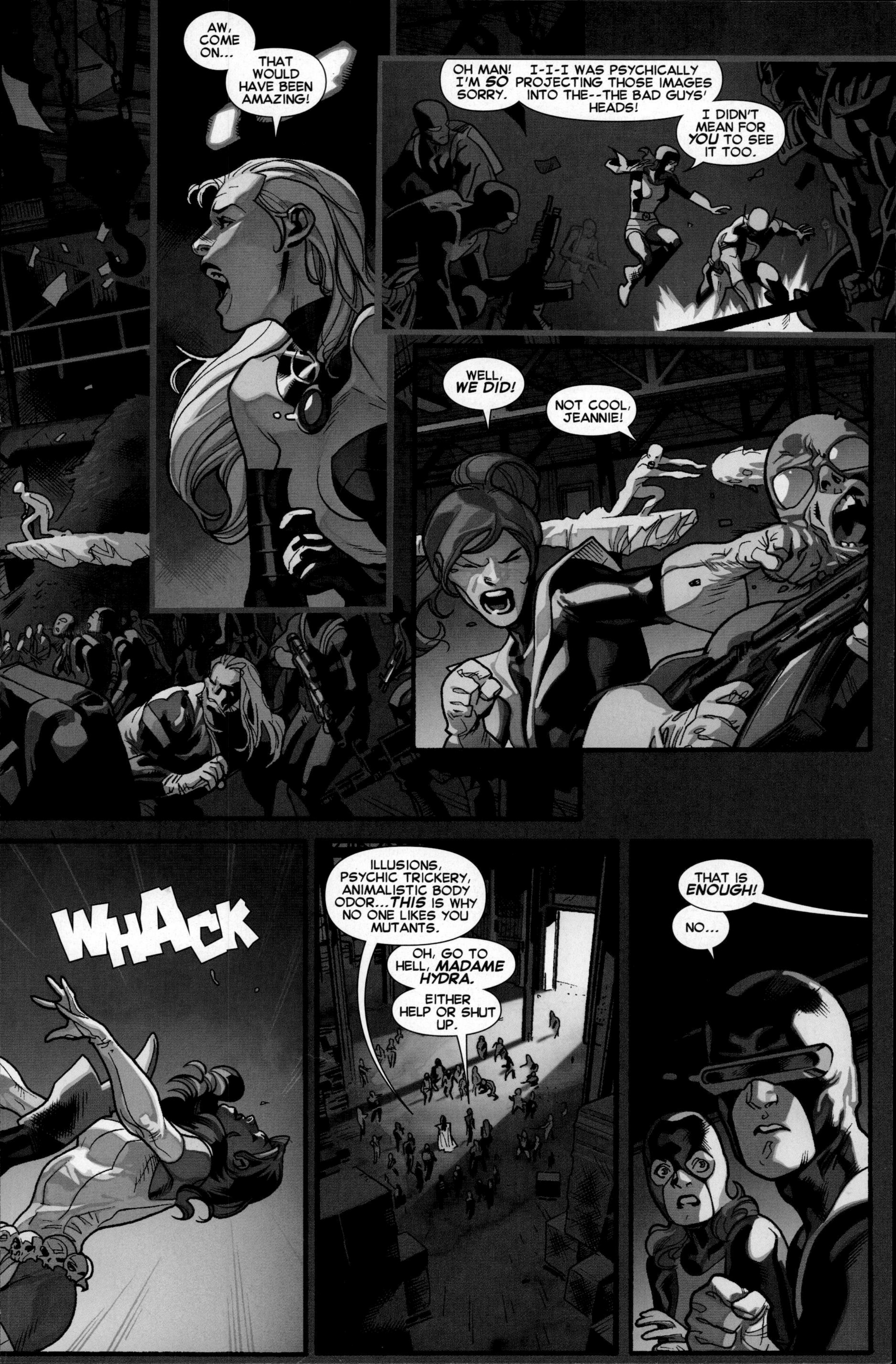
AW, COME ON...
THAT WOULD HAVE BEEN AMAZING!
OH MAN! I'M SO SORRY.
I-I-I WAS PSYCHICALLY PROJECTING THOSE IMAGES INTO THE--THE BAD GUYS' HEADS!
I DIDN'T MEAN FOR YOU TO SEE IT TOO.
WELL, WE DID!
NOT COOL, JEANNIE!
WHACK
ILLUSIONS, PSYCHIC TRICKERY, ANIMALISTIC BODY ODOR...THIS IS WHY NO ONE LIKES YOU MUTANTS.
OH, GO TO HELL, MADAME HYDRA.
EITHER HELP OR SHUT UP.
THAT IS ENOUGH!
NO...

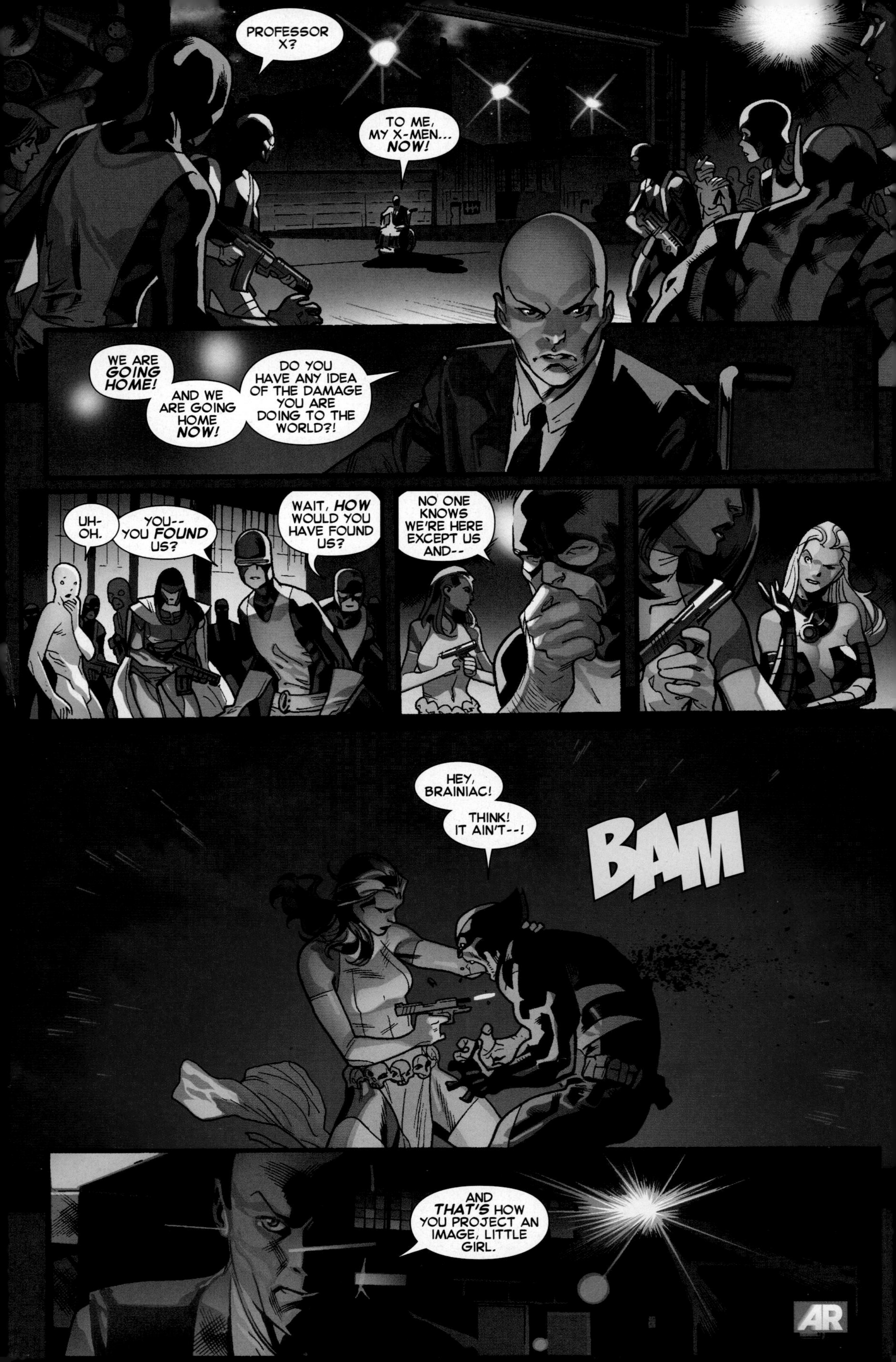
PROFESSOR X?
TO ME, MY X-MEN... NOW!
WE ARE GOING HOME!
AND WE ARE GOING HOME NOW!
DO YOU HAVE ANY IDEA OF THE DAMAGE YOU ARE DOING TO THE WORLD?!
UH-OH.
YOU-- YOU FOUND US?
WAIT, HOW WOULD YOU HAVE FOUND US?
NO ONE KNOWS WE'RE HERE EXCEPT US AND--
HEY, BRAINIAC!
THINK! IT AIN'T--!
BAM
AND THAT'S HOW YOU PROJECT AN IMAGE, LITTLE GIRL.
AR

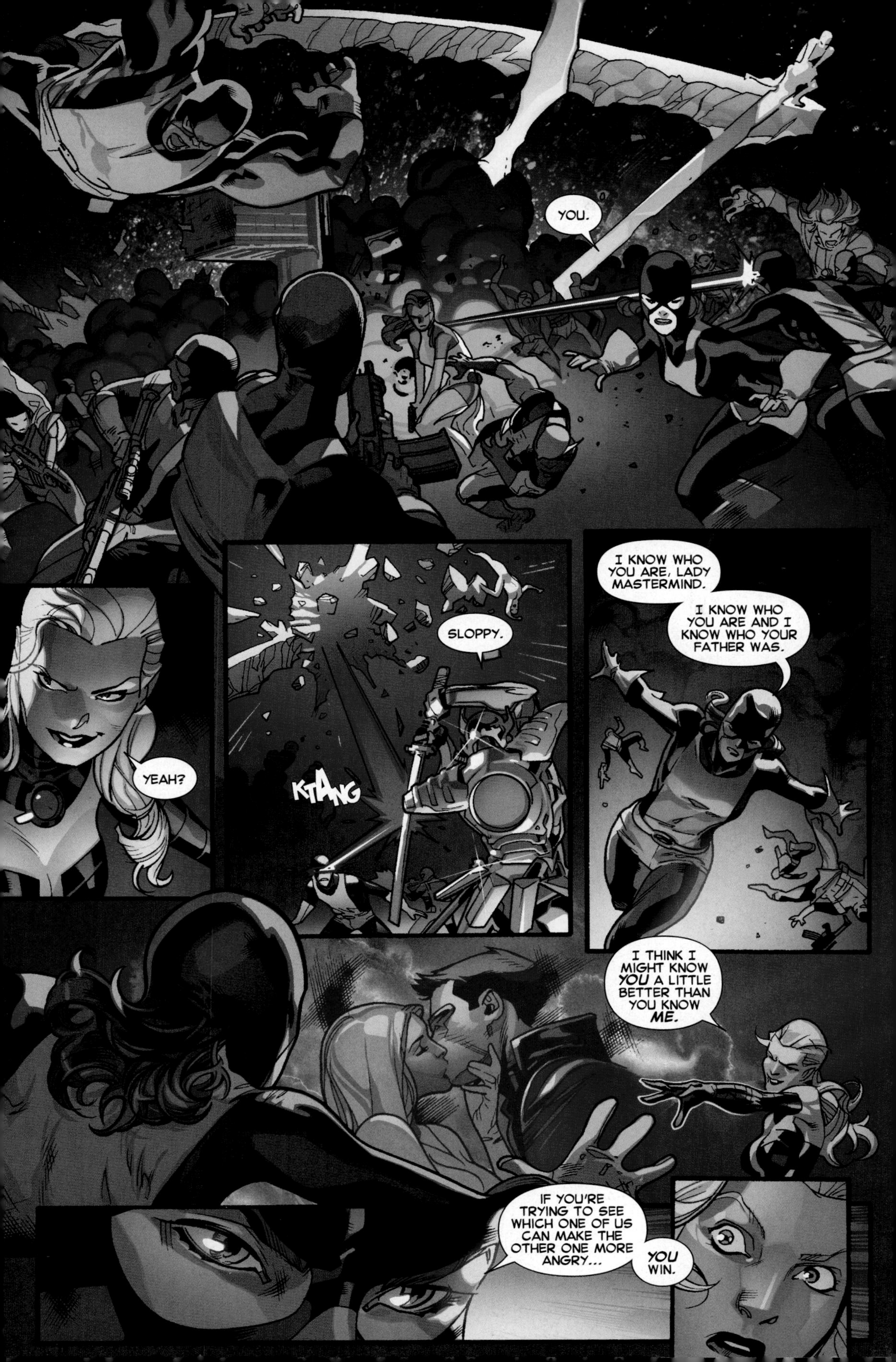
YOU.
YEAH?
SLOPPY.
KTANG
I KNOW WHO YOU ARE, LADY MASTERMIND.
I KNOW WHO YOU ARE AND I KNOW WHO YOUR FATHER WAS.
I THINK I MIGHT KNOW *YOU* A LITTLE BETTER THAN YOU KNOW *ME.*
IF YOU'RE TRYING TO SEE WHICH ONE OF US CAN MAKE THE OTHER ONE MORE ANGRY...
YOU WIN.

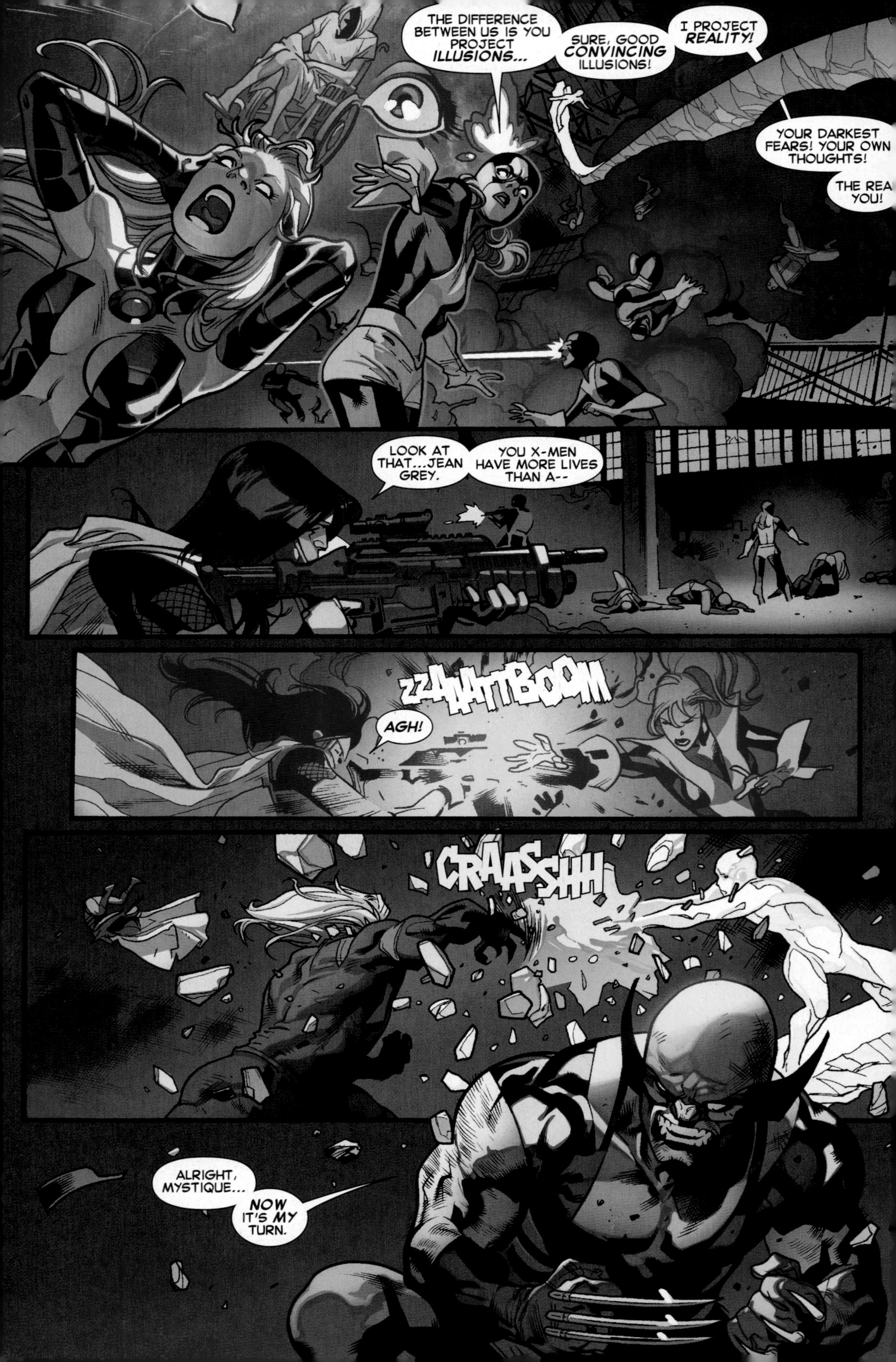

THE DIFFERENCE BETWEEN US IS YOU PROJECT ILLUSIONS...
SURE, GOOD CONVINCING ILLUSIONS!
I PROJECT REALITY!
YOUR DARKEST FEARS! YOUR OWN THOUGHTS!
THE REA YOU!
LOOK AT THAT...JEAN GREY.
YOU X-MEN HAVE MORE LIVES THAN A--
ZZAAATTBOOM
AGH!
CRAASSHHH
ALRIGHT, MYSTIQUE...
NOW IT'S MY TURN.

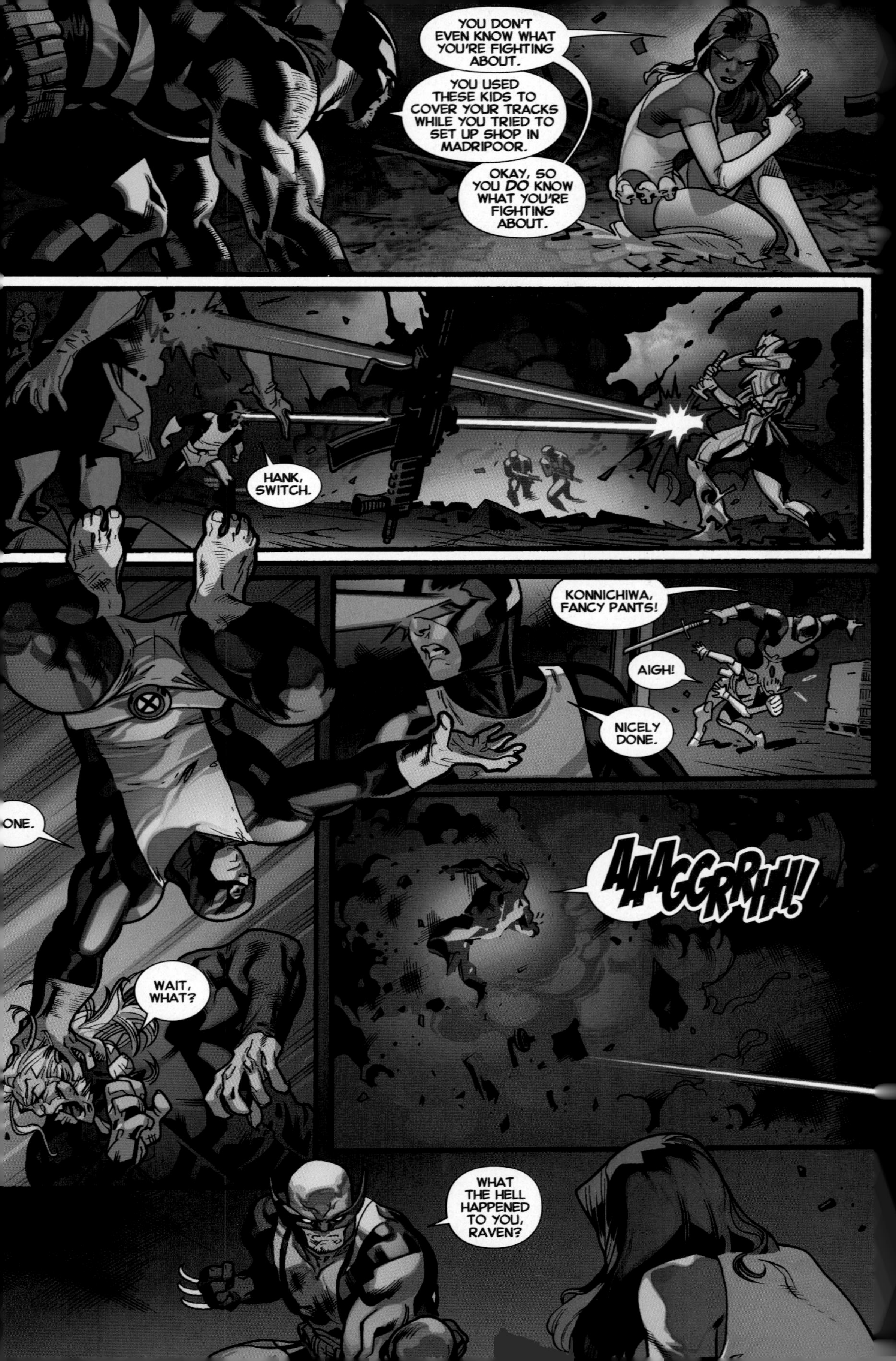
YOU DON'T EVEN KNOW WHAT YOU'RE FIGHTING ABOUT.
YOU USED THESE KIDS TO COVER YOUR TRACKS WHILE YOU TRIED TO SET UP SHOP IN MADRIPOOR.
OKAY, SO YOU DO KNOW WHAT YOU'RE FIGHTING ABOUT.
HANK, SWITCH.
KONNICHIWA, FANCY PANTS!
AIGH!
NICELY DONE.
ONE.
WAIT, WHAT?
AAAGGRRHH!
WHAT THE HELL HAPPENED TO YOU, RAVEN?

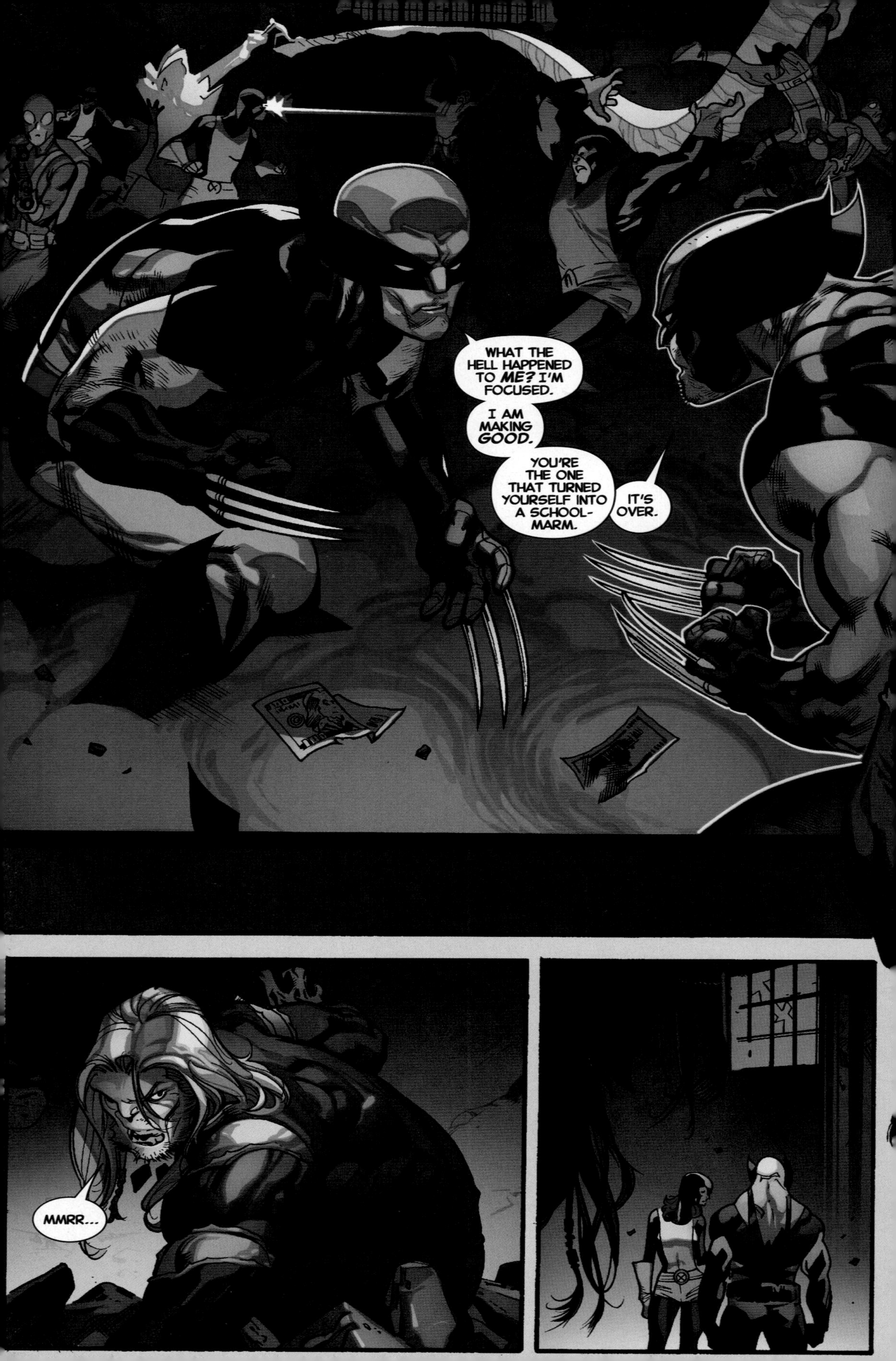
WHAT THE HELL HAPPENED TO *ME?* I'M FOCUSED.
I AM MAKING *GOOD.*
YOU'RE THE ONE THAT TURNED YOURSELF INTO A SCHOOL-MARM.
IT'S OVER.
MMRR...

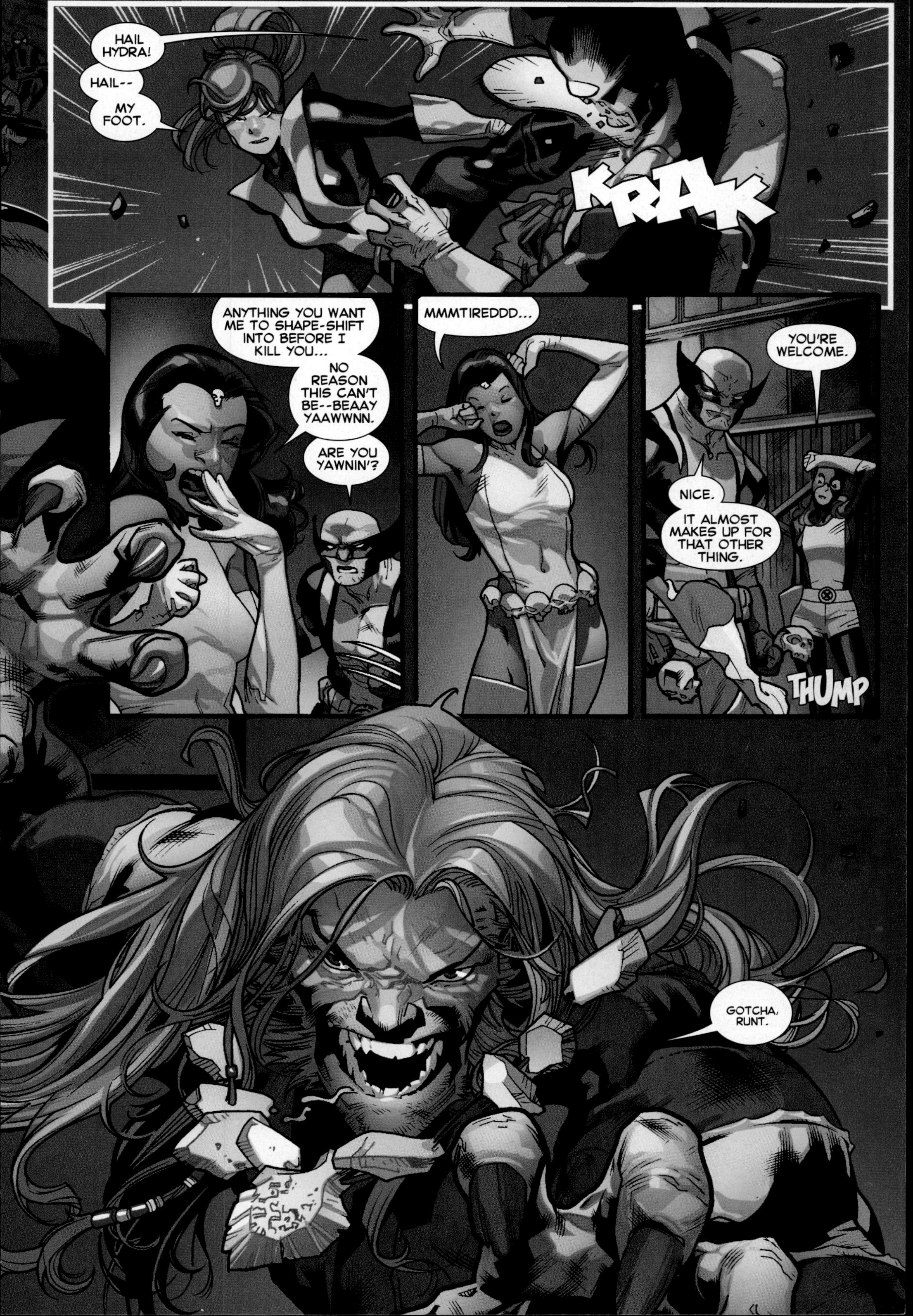
HAIL HYDRA!
HAIL--
MY FOOT.
KRAK
ANYTHING YOU WANT ME TO SHAPE-SHIFT INTO BEFORE I KILL YOU...
NO REASON THIS CAN'T BE--BEAAY YAAWWNN.
ARE YOU YAWNIN'?
MMMTIREDDD...
YOU'RE WELCOME.
NICE.
IT ALMOST MAKES UP FOR THAT OTHER THING.
THUMP
GOTCHA, RUNT.

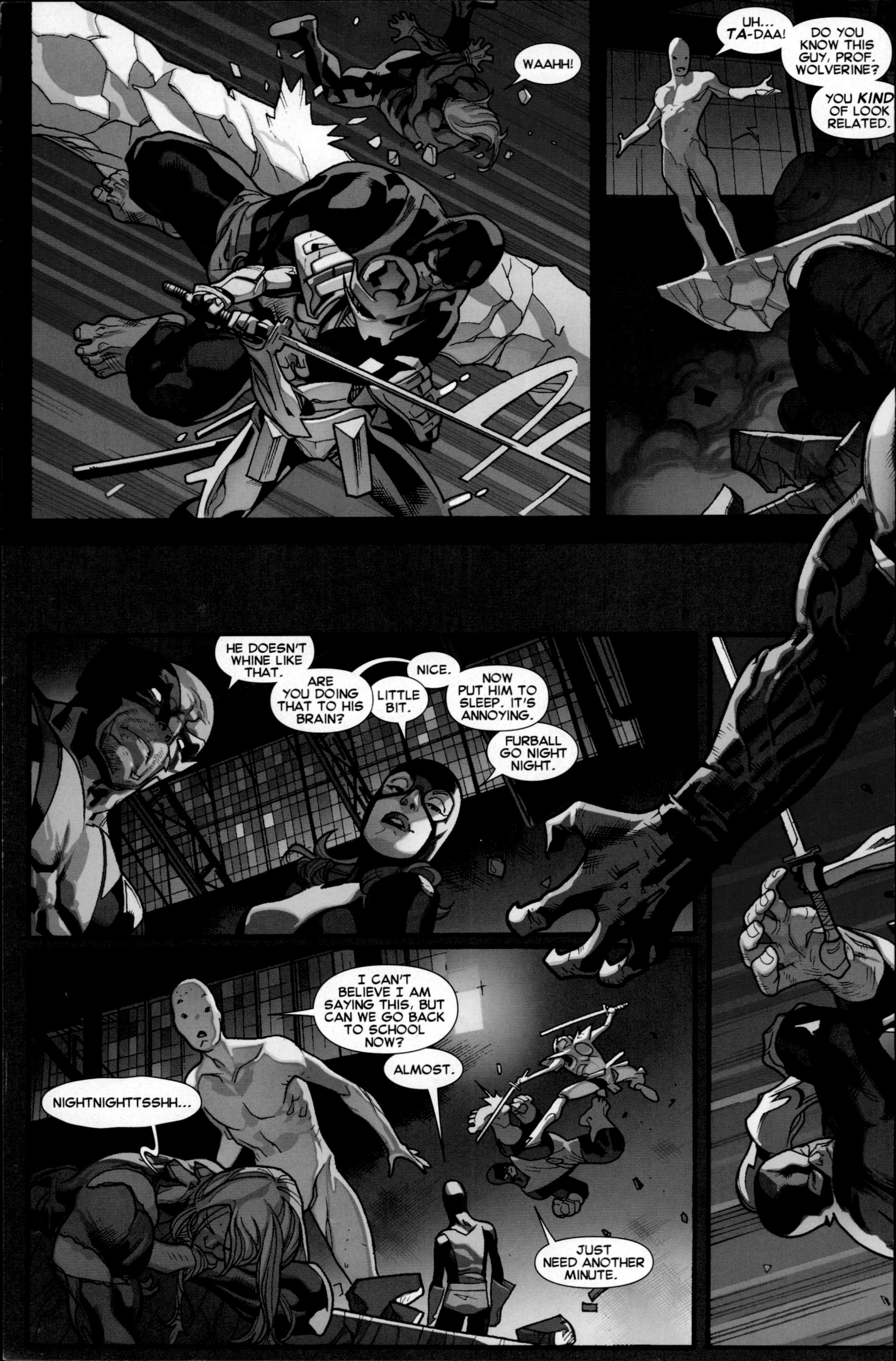
WAAHH!
UH... TA-DAA!
DO YOU KNOW THIS GUY, PROF. WOLVERINE?
YOU KIND OF LOOK RELATED.
HE DOESN'T WHINE LIKE THAT.
ARE YOU DOING THAT TO HIS BRAIN?
LITTLE BIT.
NICE.
NOW PUT HIM TO SLEEP. IT'S ANNOYING.
FURBALL GO NIGHT NIGHT.
I CAN'T BELIEVE I AM SAYING THIS, BUT CAN WE GO BACK TO SCHOOL NOW?
ALMOST.
NIGHTNIGHTTSSHH...
JUST NEED ANOTHER MINUTE.

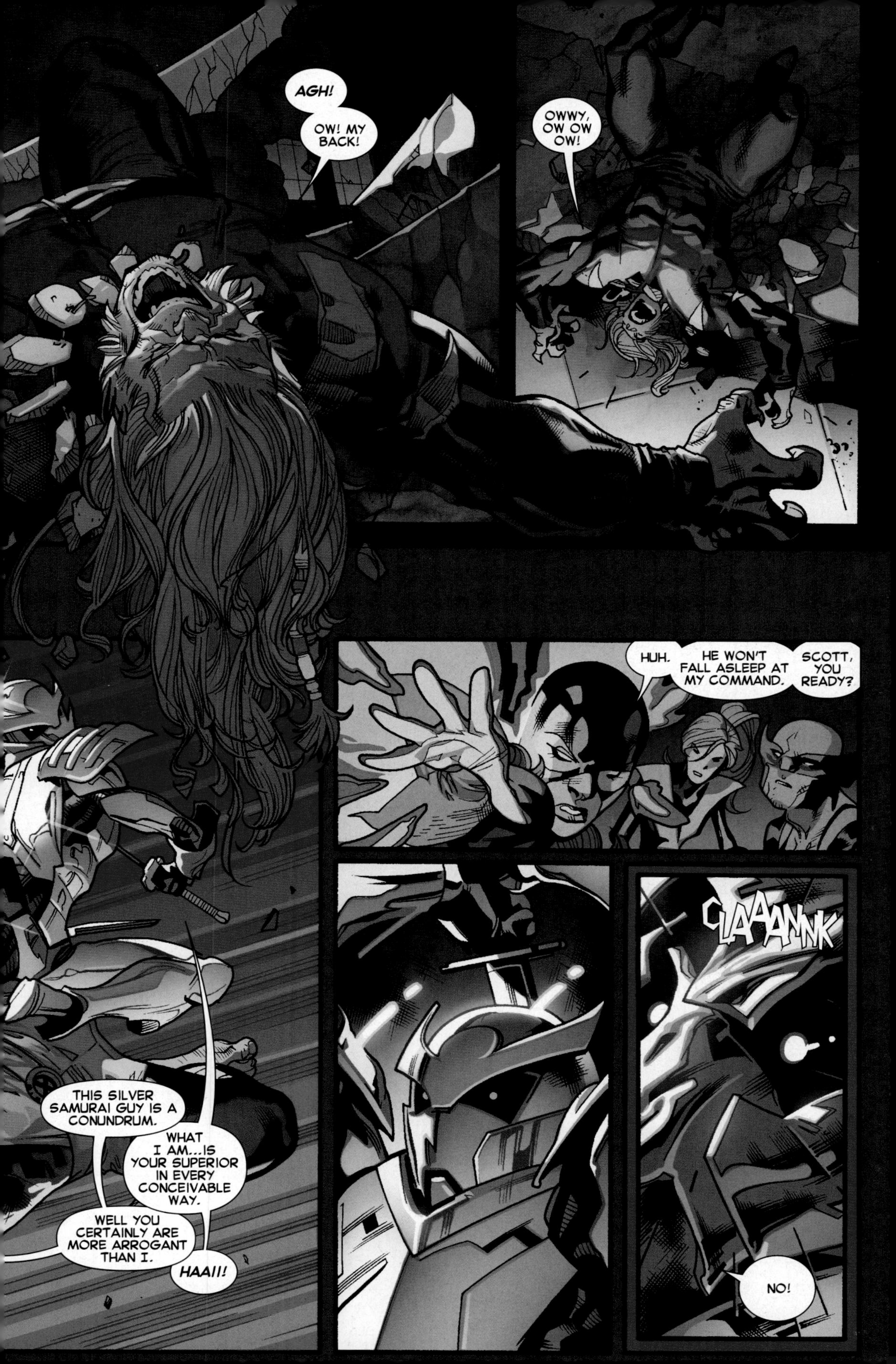
AGH!
OW! MY BACK!
OWWY, OW OW OW!
HUH.
HE WON'T FALL ASLEEP AT MY COMMAND.
SCOTT, YOU READY?
THIS SILVER SAMURAI GUY IS A CONUNDRUM.
WHAT I AM...IS YOUR SUPERIOR IN EVERY CONCEIVABLE WAY.
WELL YOU CERTAINLY ARE MORE ARROGANT THAN I.
HAAI!!
CLAAAANNK
NO!

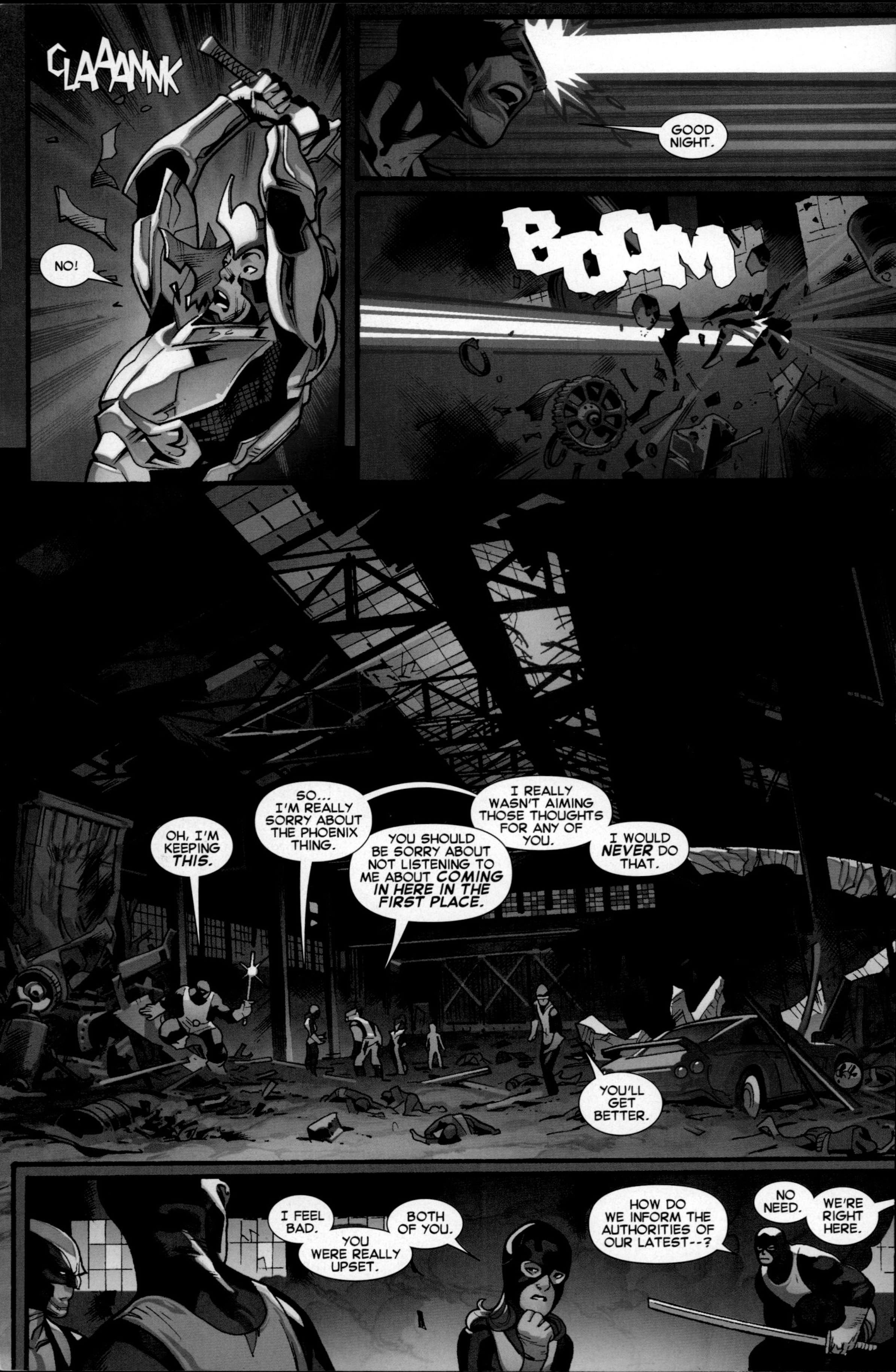
CLAAANNK
NO!
GOOD NIGHT.
BOOM
OH, I'M KEEPING *THIS.*
SO... I'M REALLY SORRY ABOUT THE PHOENIX THING.
I REALLY WASN'T AIMING THOSE THOUGHTS FOR ANY OF YOU.
I WOULD *NEVER* DO THAT.
YOU SHOULD BE SORRY ABOUT NOT LISTENING TO ME ABOUT *COMING IN HERE IN THE FIRST PLACE.*
YOU'LL GET BETTER.
I FEEL BAD.
YOU WERE REALLY UPSET.
BOTH OF YOU.
HOW DO WE INFORM THE AUTHORITIES OF OUR LATEST--?
NO NEED.
WE'RE RIGHT HERE.

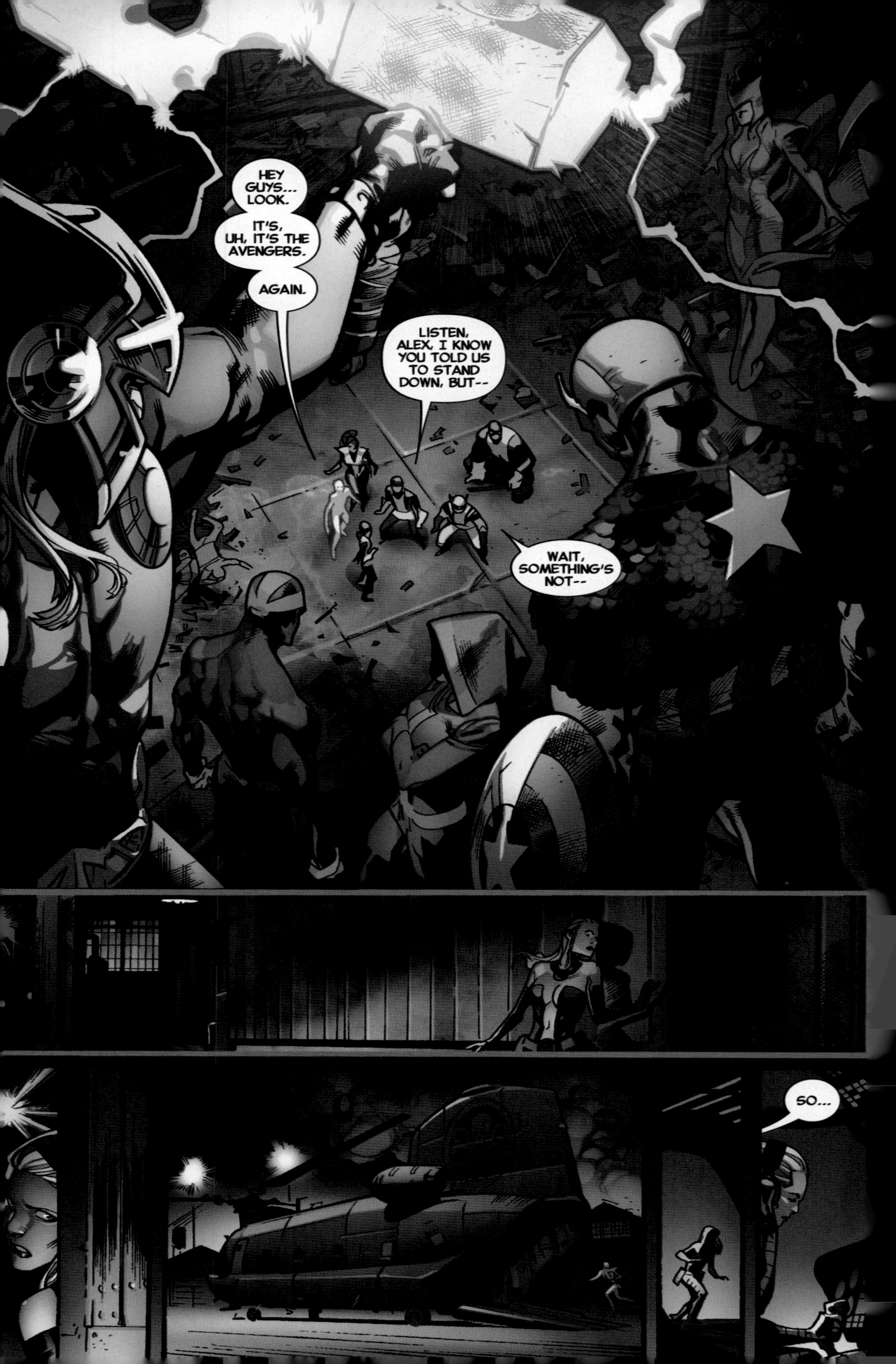
HEY GUYS... LOOK.
IT'S, UH, IT'S THE AVENGERS.
AGAIN.
LISTEN, ALEX, I KNOW YOU TOLD US TO STAND DOWN, BUT--
WAIT, SOMETHING'S NOT--
SO...

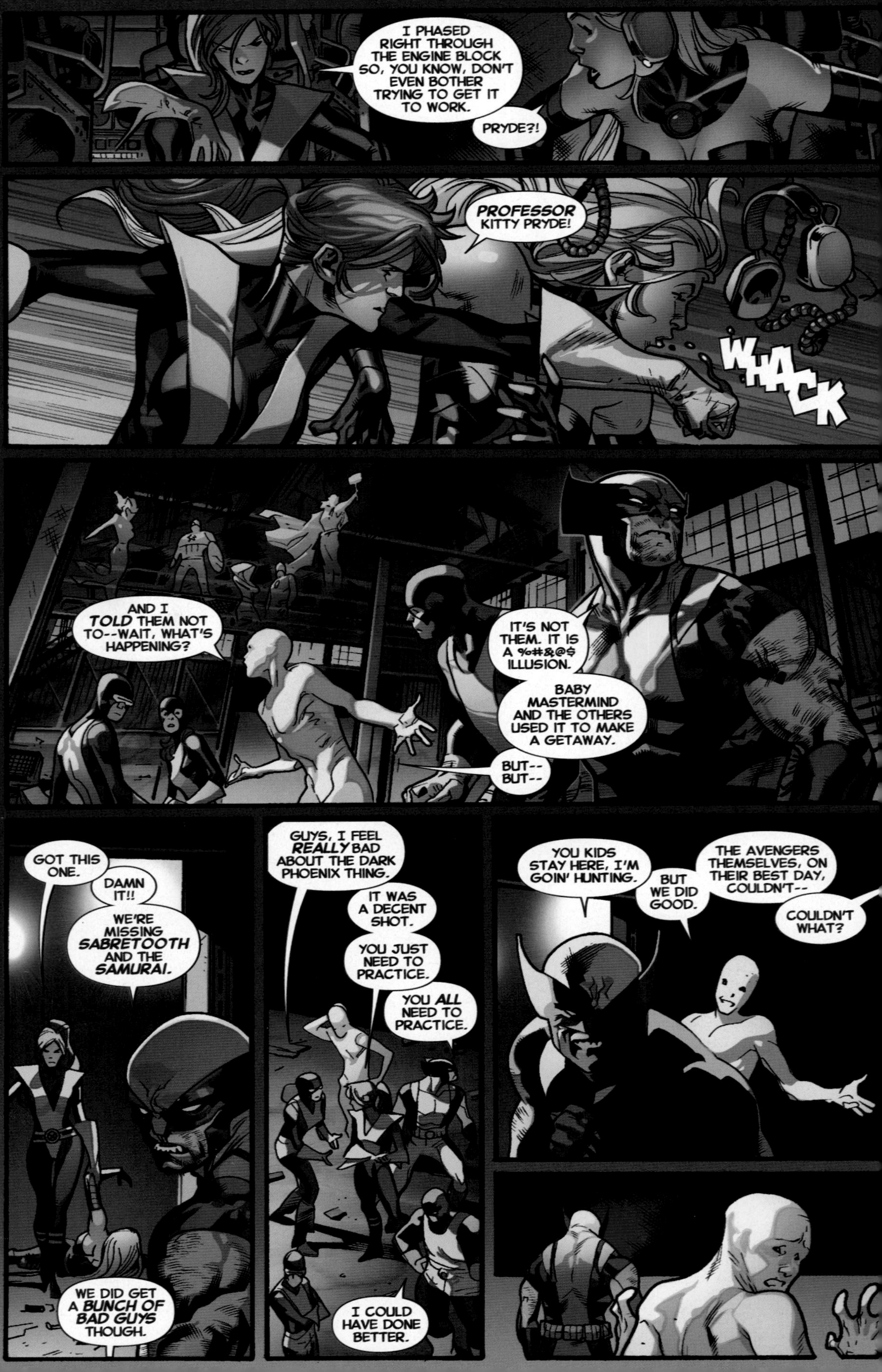
I PHASED RIGHT THROUGH THE ENGINE BLOCK SO, YOU KNOW, DON'T EVEN BOTHER TRYING TO GET IT TO WORK.
PRYDE?!
PROFESSOR KITTY PRYDE!
WHACK
AND I TOLD THEM NOT TO--WAIT, WHAT'S HAPPENING?
IT'S NOT THEM. IT IS A %#&@$ ILLUSION.
BABY MASTERMIND AND THE OTHERS USED IT TO MAKE A GETAWAY.
BUT-- BUT--
GOT THIS ONE.
DAMN IT!!
WE'RE MISSING SABRETOOTH AND THE SAMURAI.
WE DID GET A BUNCH OF BAD GUYS THOUGH.
GUYS, I FEEL REALLY BAD ABOUT THE DARK PHOENIX THING.
IT WAS A DECENT SHOT.
YOU JUST NEED TO PRACTICE.
YOU ALL NEED TO PRACTICE.
I COULD HAVE DONE BETTER.
YOU KIDS STAY HERE, I'M GOIN' HUNTING.
BUT WE DID GOOD.
THE AVENGERS THEMSELVES, ON THEIR BEST DAY, COULDN'T--
COULDN'T WHAT?

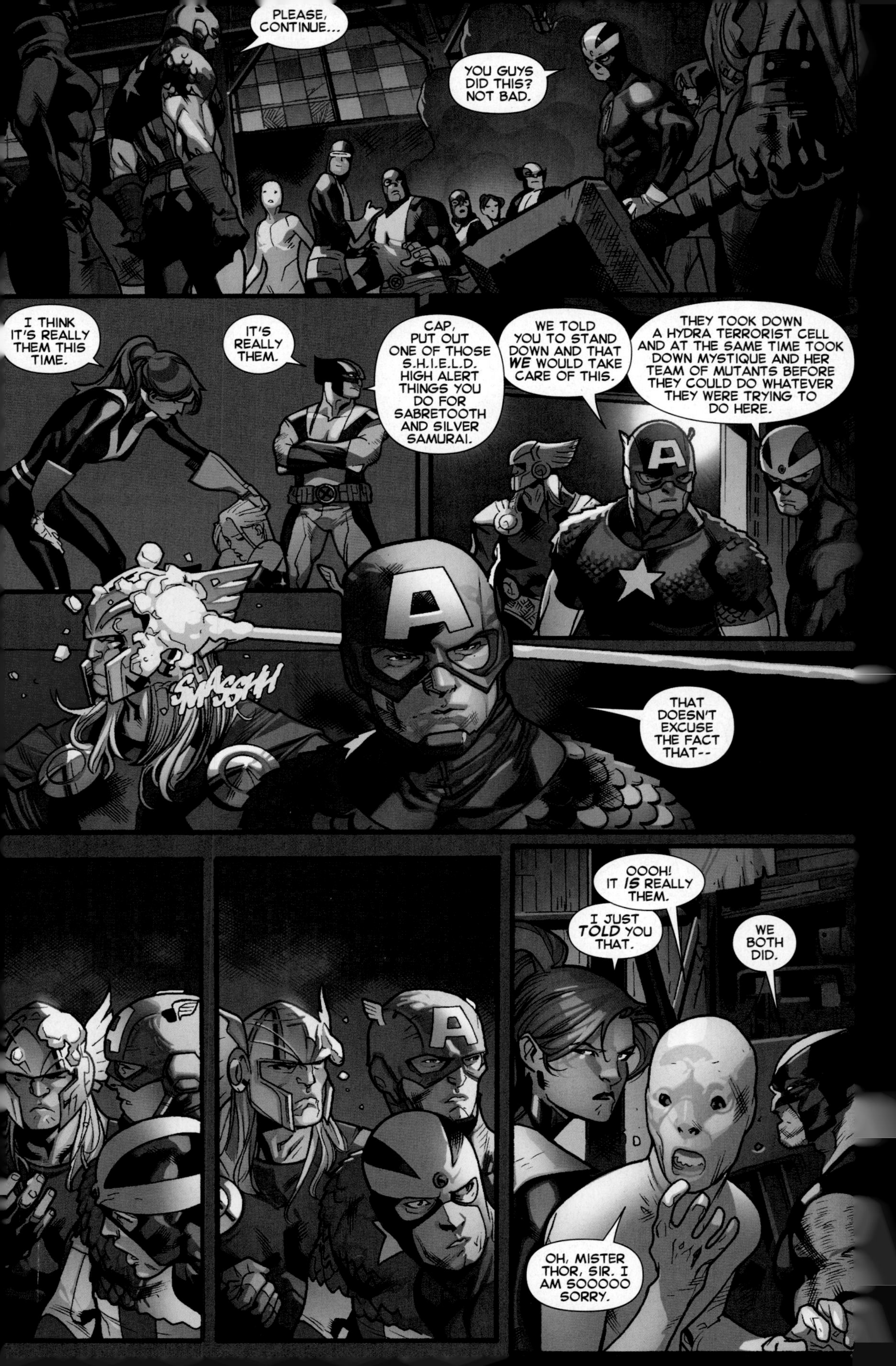
PLEASE, CONTINUE...
YOU GUYS DID THIS? NOT BAD.
I THINK IT'S REALLY THEM THIS TIME.
IT'S REALLY THEM.
CAP, PUT OUT ONE OF THOSE S.H.I.E.L.D. HIGH ALERT THINGS YOU DO FOR SABRETOOTH AND SILVER SAMURAI.
WE TOLD YOU TO STAND DOWN AND THAT WE WOULD TAKE CARE OF THIS.
THEY TOOK DOWN A HYDRA TERRORIST CELL AND AT THE SAME TIME TOOK DOWN MYSTIQUE AND HER TEAM OF MUTANTS BEFORE THEY COULD DO WHATEVER THEY WERE TRYING TO DO HERE.
SMASSHH
THAT DOESN'T EXCUSE THE FACT THAT--
OOOH! IT IS REALLY THEM.
I JUST TOLD YOU THAT.
WE BOTH DID.
OH, MISTER THOR, SIR. I AM SOOOOO SORRY.

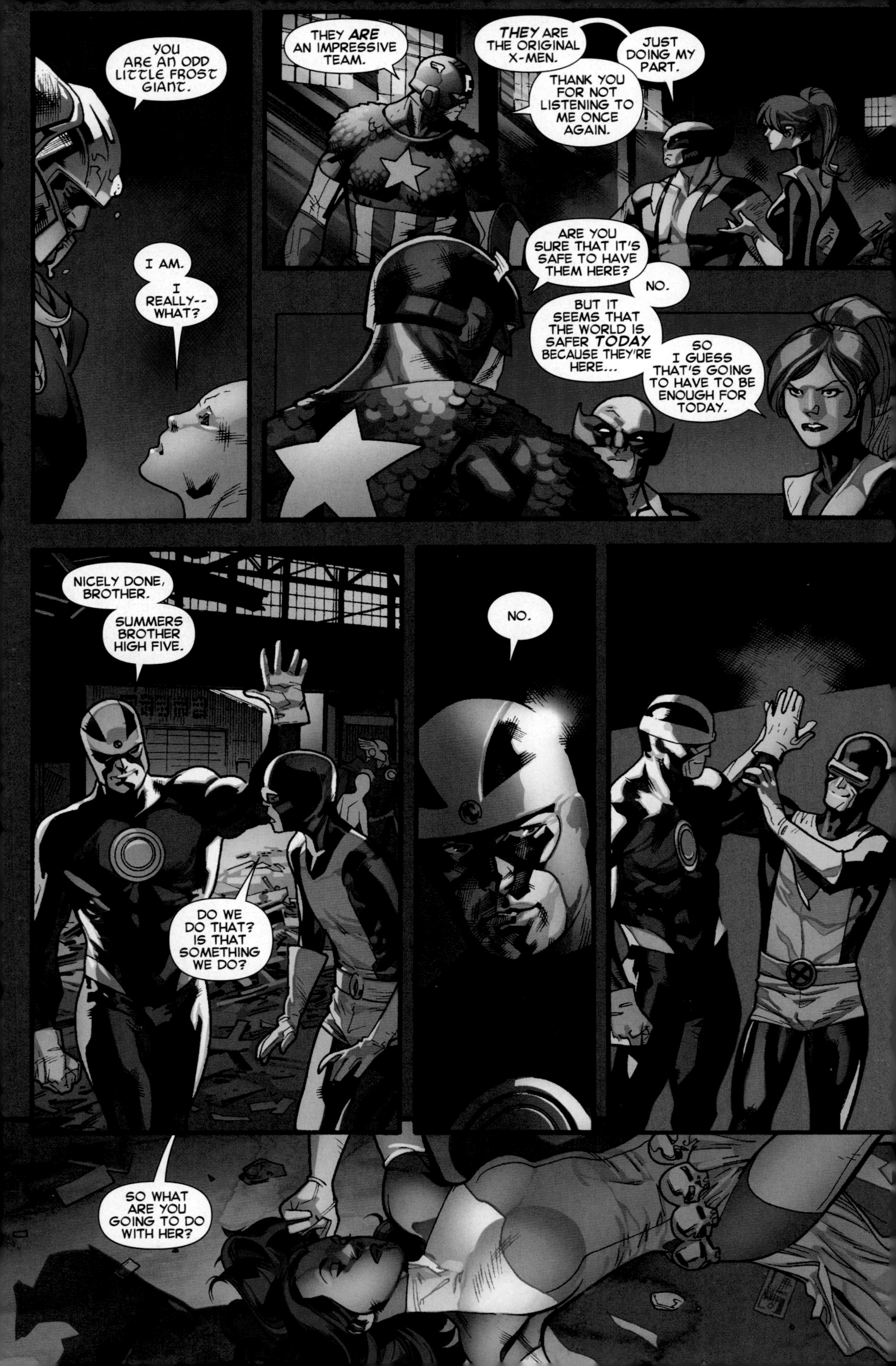
YOU ARE AN ODD LITTLE FROST GIANT.
I AM.
I REALLY-- WHAT?
THEY ARE AN IMPRESSIVE TEAM.
THEY ARE THE ORIGINAL X-MEN.
JUST DOING MY PART.
THANK YOU FOR NOT LISTENING TO ME ONCE AGAIN.
ARE YOU SURE THAT IT'S SAFE TO HAVE THEM HERE?
NO.
BUT IT SEEMS THAT THE WORLD IS SAFER TODAY BECAUSE THEY'RE HERE...
SO I GUESS THAT'S GOING TO HAVE TO BE ENOUGH FOR TODAY.
NICELY DONE, BROTHER.
SUMMERS BROTHER HIGH FIVE.
DO WE DO THAT? IS THAT SOMETHING WE DO?
NO.
SO WHAT ARE YOU GOING TO DO WITH HER?

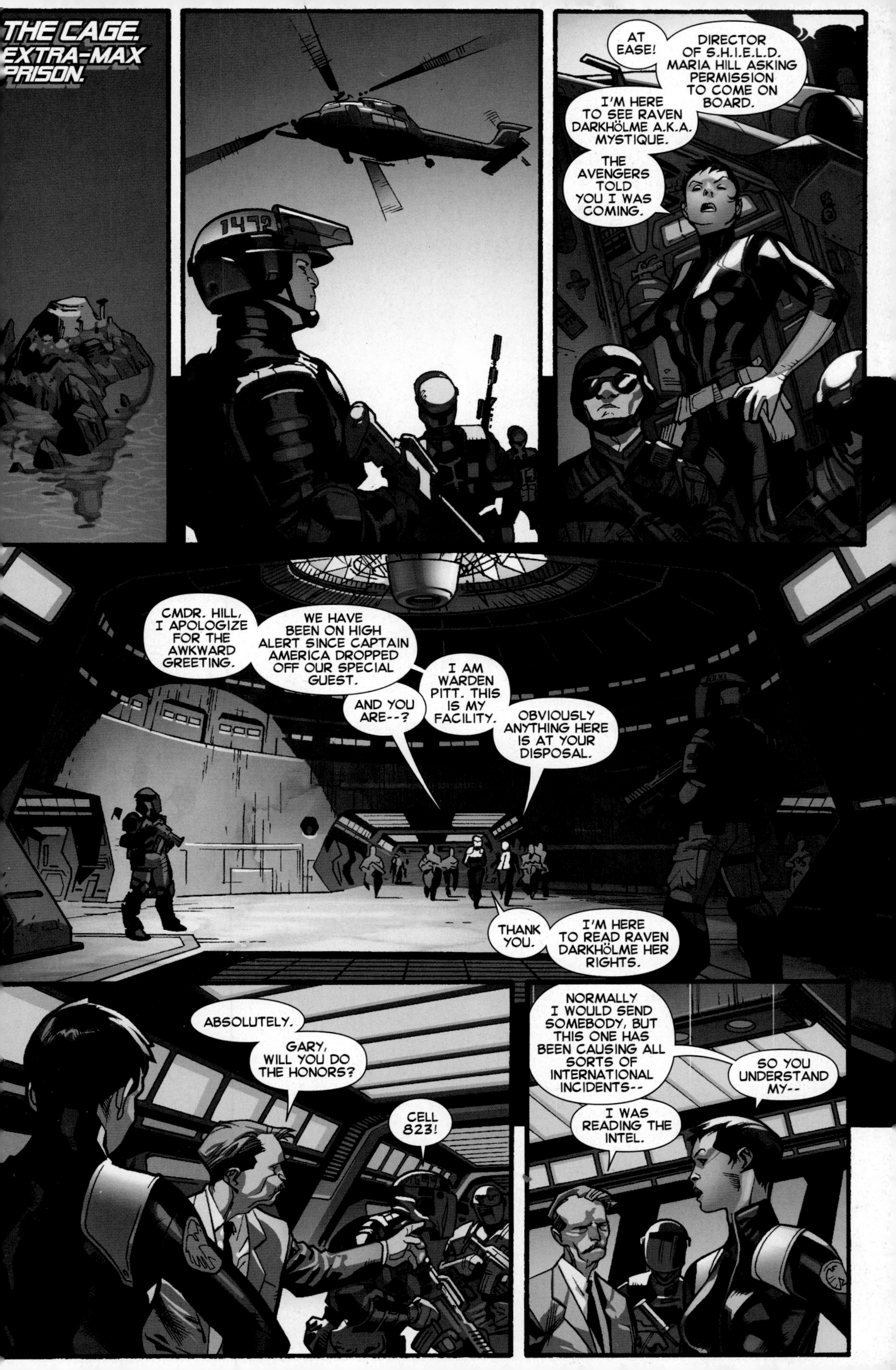
THE CAGE. EXTRA-MAX PRISON.
DIRECTOR OF S.H.I.E.L.D. MARIA HILL ASKING PERMISSION TO COME ON BOARD.
AT EASE!
I'M HERE TO SEE RAVEN DARKHÖLME A.K.A. MYSTIQUE.
THE AVENGERS TOLD YOU I WAS COMING.
CMDR. HILL, I APOLOGIZE FOR THE AWKWARD GREETING.
WE HAVE BEEN ON HIGH ALERT SINCE CAPTAIN AMERICA DROPPED OFF OUR SPECIAL GUEST.
AND YOU ARE--?
I AM WARDEN PITT. THIS IS MY FACILITY.
OBVIOUSLY ANYTHING HERE IS AT YOUR DISPOSAL.
THANK YOU.
I'M HERE TO READ RAVEN DARKHÖLME HER RIGHTS.
ABSOLUTELY.
GARY, WILL YOU DO THE HONORS?
CELL 823!
NORMALLY I WOULD SEND SOMEBODY, BUT THIS ONE HAS BEEN CAUSING ALL SORTS OF INTERNATIONAL INCIDENTS--
SO YOU UNDERSTAND MY--
I WAS READING THE INTEL.

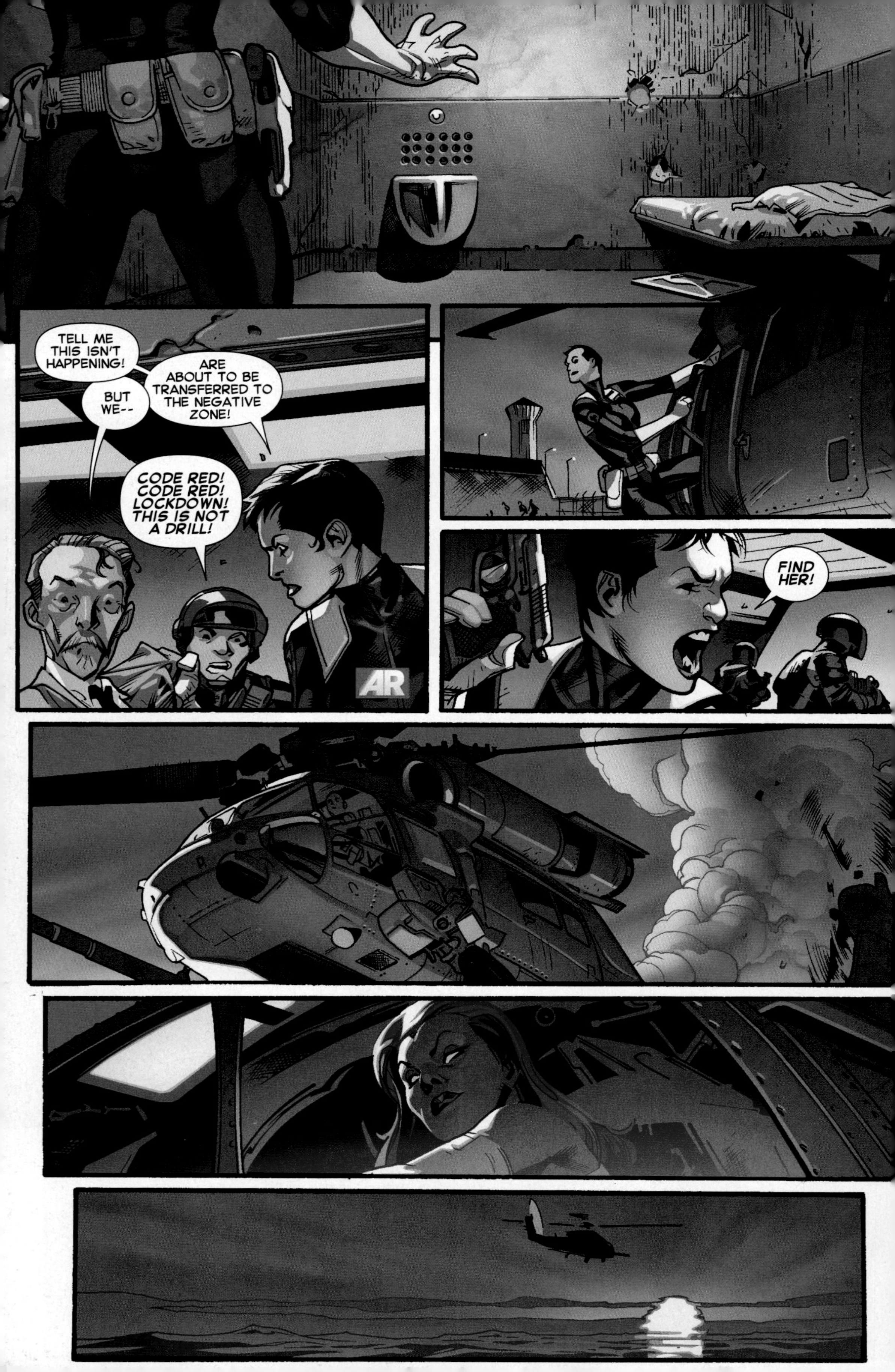

TELL ME THIS ISN'T HAPPENING!
BUT WE--
ARE ABOUT TO BE TRANSFERRED TO THE NEGATIVE ZONE!
CODE RED! CODE RED! LOCKDOWN! THIS IS NOT A DRILL!
FIND HER!

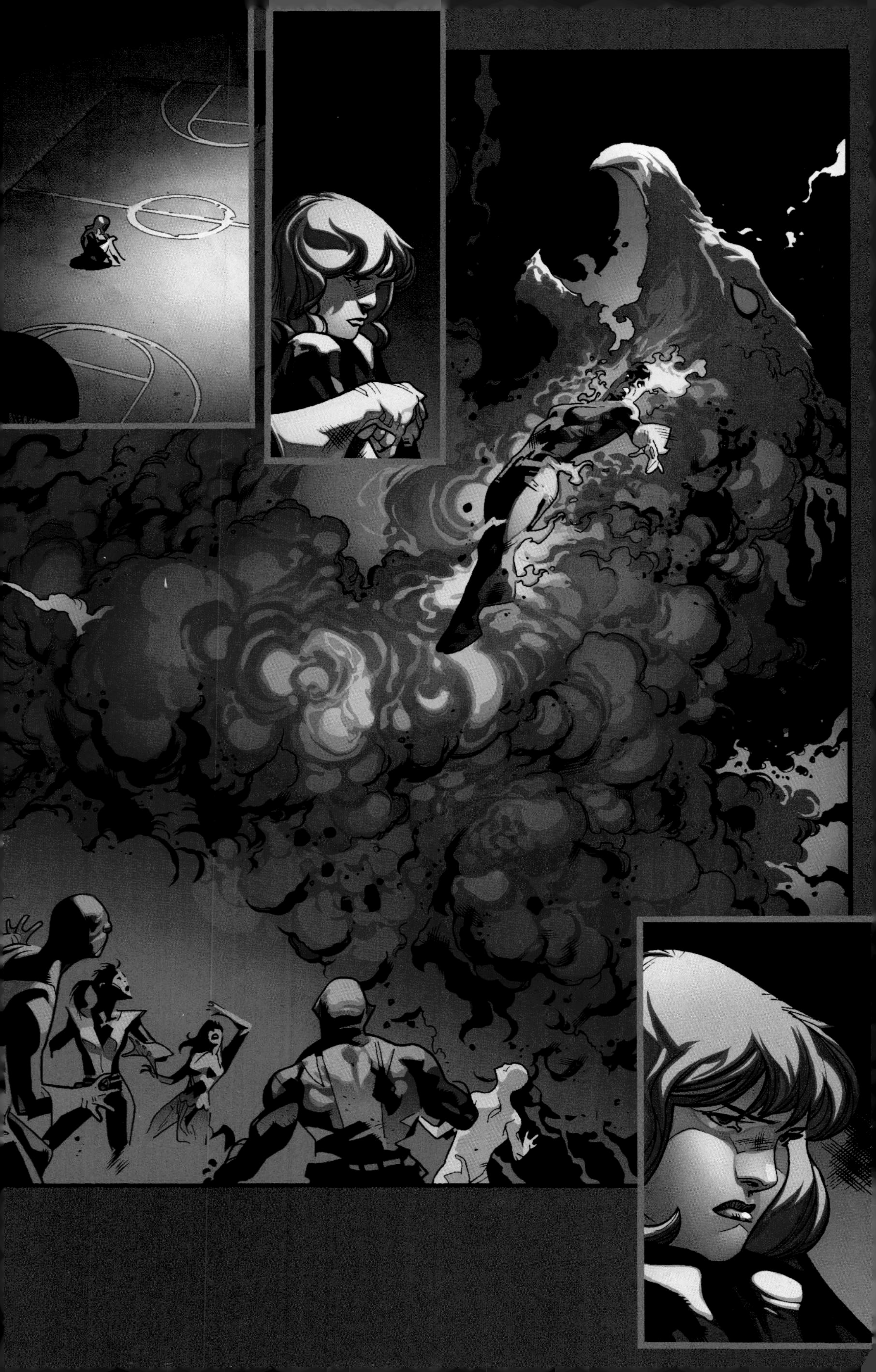

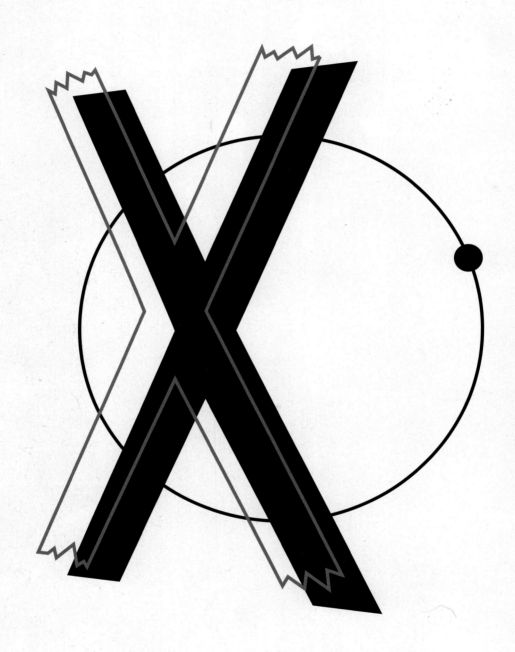

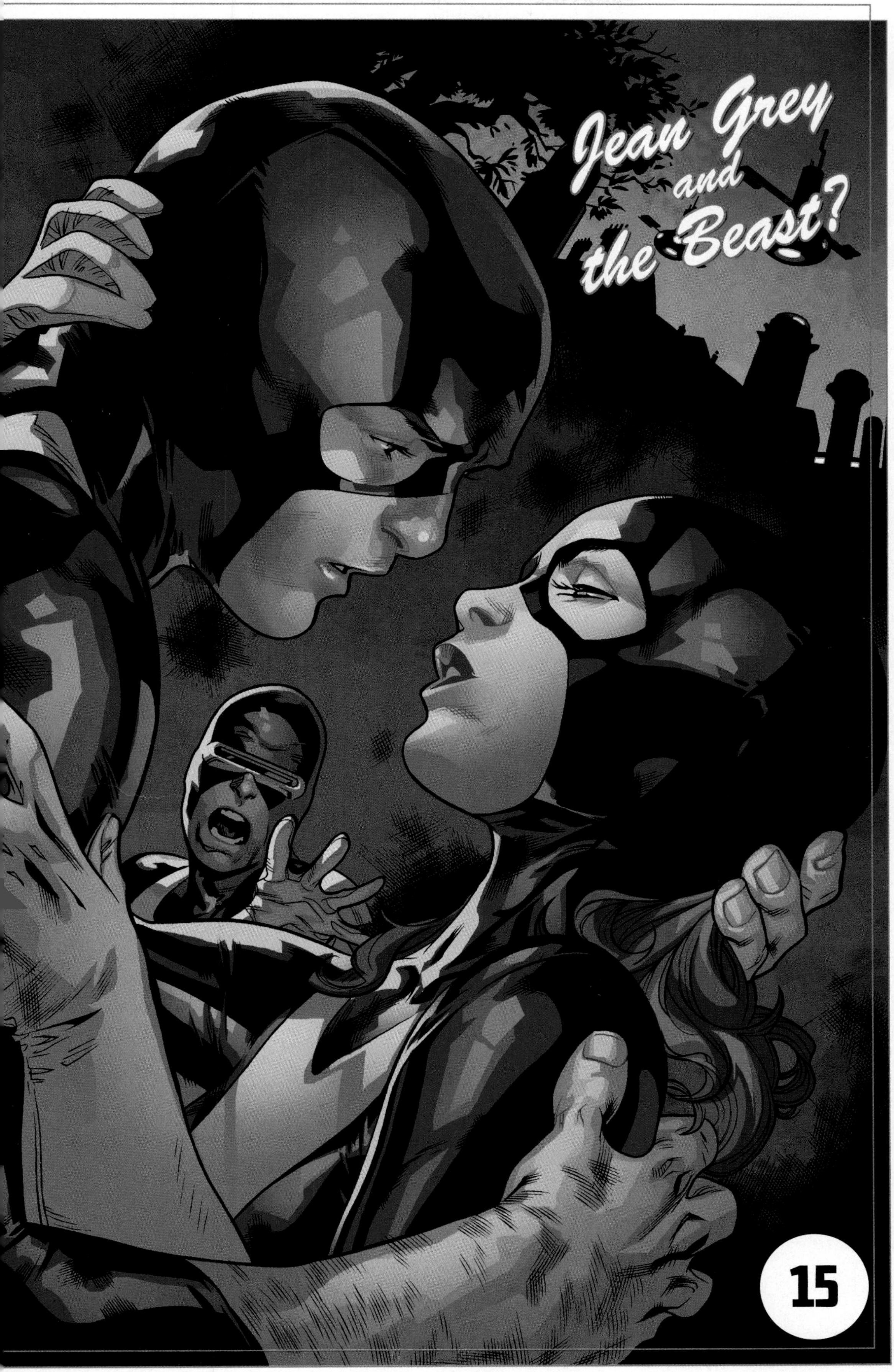
Jean Grey
and
the Beast?
15

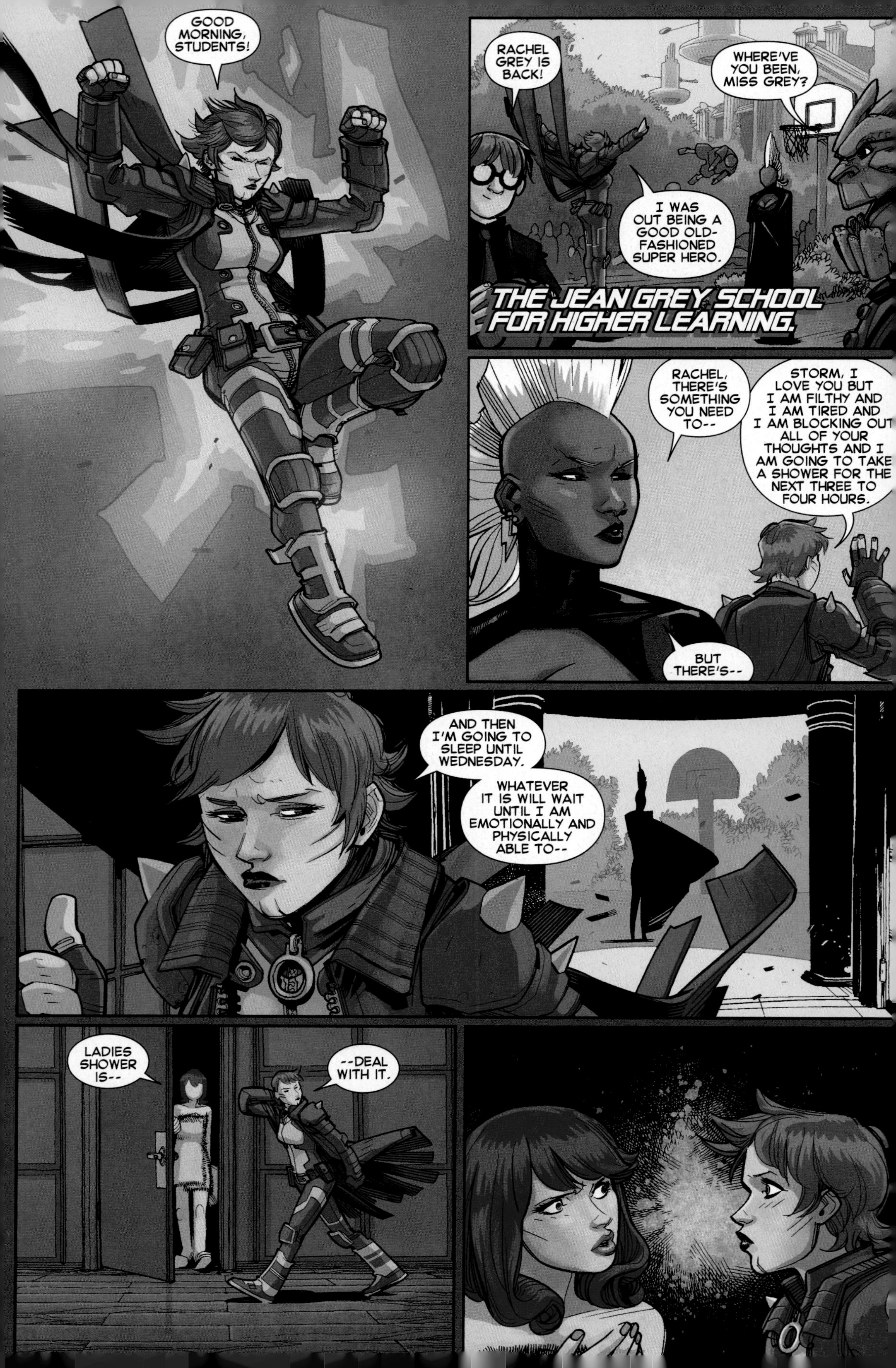
GOOD MORNING, STUDENTS!
RACHEL GREY IS BACK!
WHERE'VE YOU BEEN, MISS GREY?
I WAS OUT BEING A GOOD OLD-FASHIONED SUPER HERO.
THE JEAN GREY SCHOOL FOR HIGHER LEARNING.
RACHEL, THERE'S SOMETHING YOU NEED TO--
STORM, I LOVE YOU BUT I AM FILTHY AND I AM TIRED AND I AM BLOCKING OUT ALL OF YOUR THOUGHTS AND I AM GOING TO TAKE A SHOWER FOR THE NEXT THREE TO FOUR HOURS.
BUT THERE'S--
AND THEN I'M GOING TO SLEEP UNTIL WEDNESDAY.
WHATEVER IT IS WILL WAIT UNTIL I AM EMOTIONALLY AND PHYSICALLY ABLE TO--
LADIES SHOWER IS--
--DEAL WITH IT.

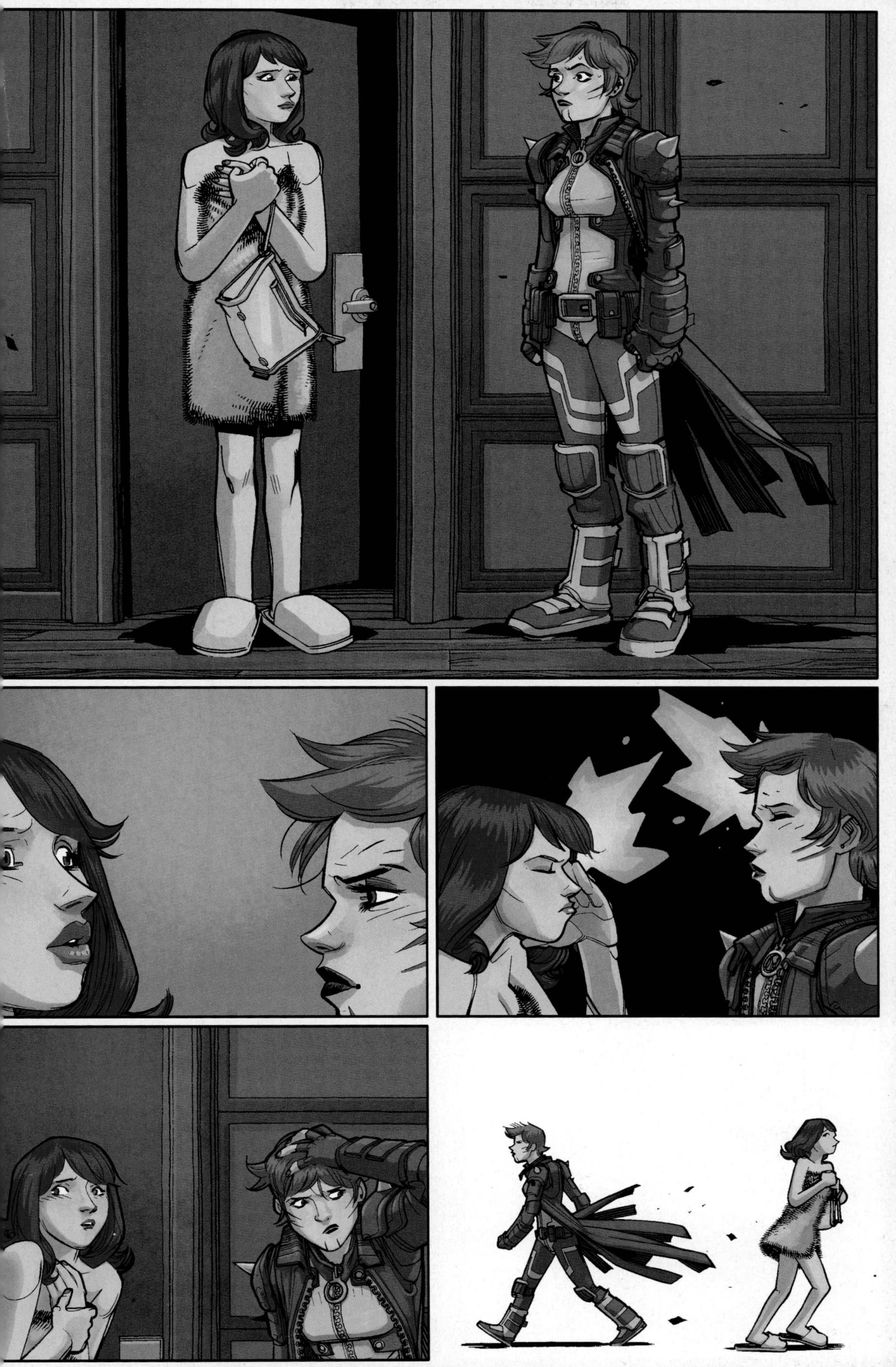

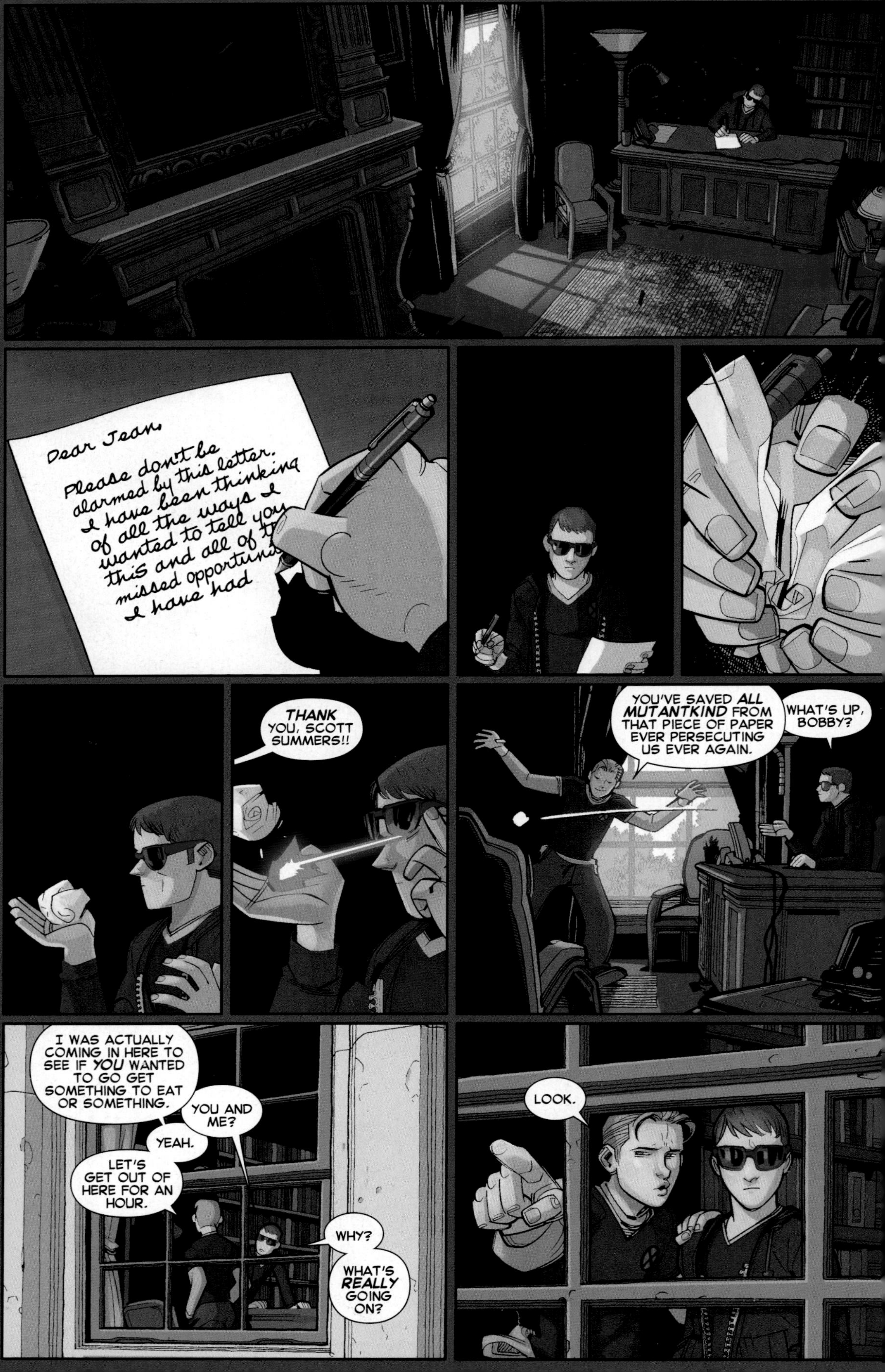

Dear Jean,
Please don't be alarmed by this letter. I have been thinking of all the ways I wanted to tell you this and all of th
missed opportuni
I have had
THANK YOU, SCOTT SUMMERS!!
YOU'VE SAVED ALL MUTANTKIND FROM THAT PIECE OF PAPER EVER PERSECUTING US EVER AGAIN.
WHAT'S UP, BOBBY?
I WAS ACTUALLY COMING IN HERE TO SEE IF YOU WANTED TO GO GET SOMETHING TO EAT OR SOMETHING.
YOU AND ME?
YEAH.
LET'S GET OUT OF HERE FOR AN HOUR.
WHY?
WHAT'S REALLY GOING ON?
LOOK.

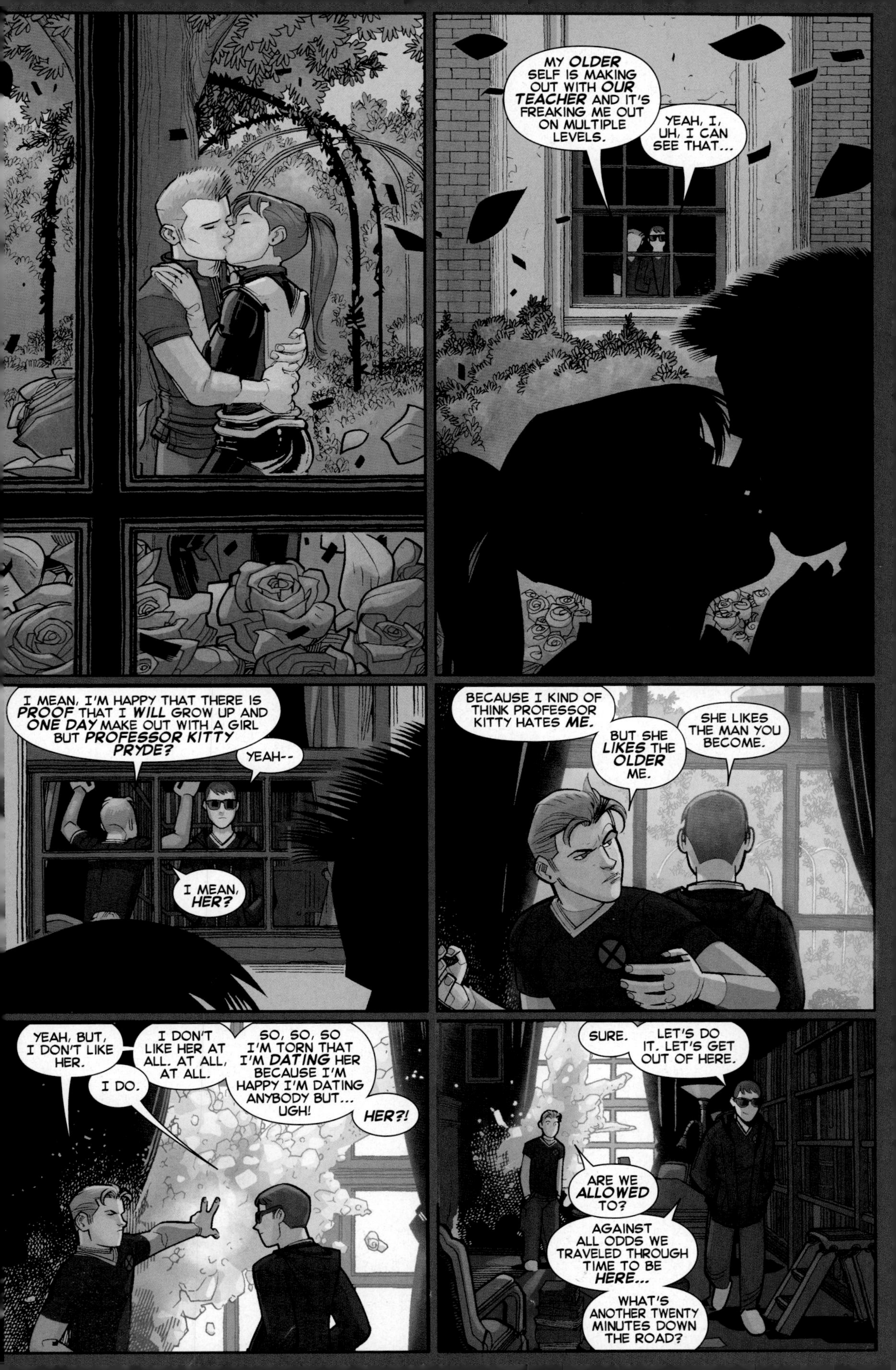
MY OLDER SELF IS MAKING OUT WITH OUR TEACHER AND IT'S FREAKING ME OUT ON MULTIPLE LEVELS.
YEAH, I, UH, I CAN SEE THAT...
I MEAN, I'M HAPPY THAT THERE IS PROOF THAT I WILL GROW UP AND ONE DAY MAKE OUT WITH A GIRL BUT PROFESSOR KITTY PRYDE?
YEAH--
I MEAN, HER?
BECAUSE I KIND OF THINK PROFESSOR KITTY HATES ME.
BUT SHE LIKES THE OLDER ME.
SHE LIKES THE MAN YOU BECOME.
YEAH, BUT, I DON'T LIKE HER.
I DON'T LIKE HER AT ALL. AT ALL, AT ALL.
I DO.
SO, SO, SO I'M TORN THAT I'M DATING HER BECAUSE I'M HAPPY I'M DATING ANYBODY BUT... UGH!
HER?!
SURE.
LET'S DO IT. LET'S GET OUT OF HERE.
ARE WE ALLOWED TO?
AGAINST ALL ODDS WE TRAVELED THROUGH TIME TO BE HERE...
WHAT'S ANOTHER TWENTY MINUTES DOWN THE ROAD?

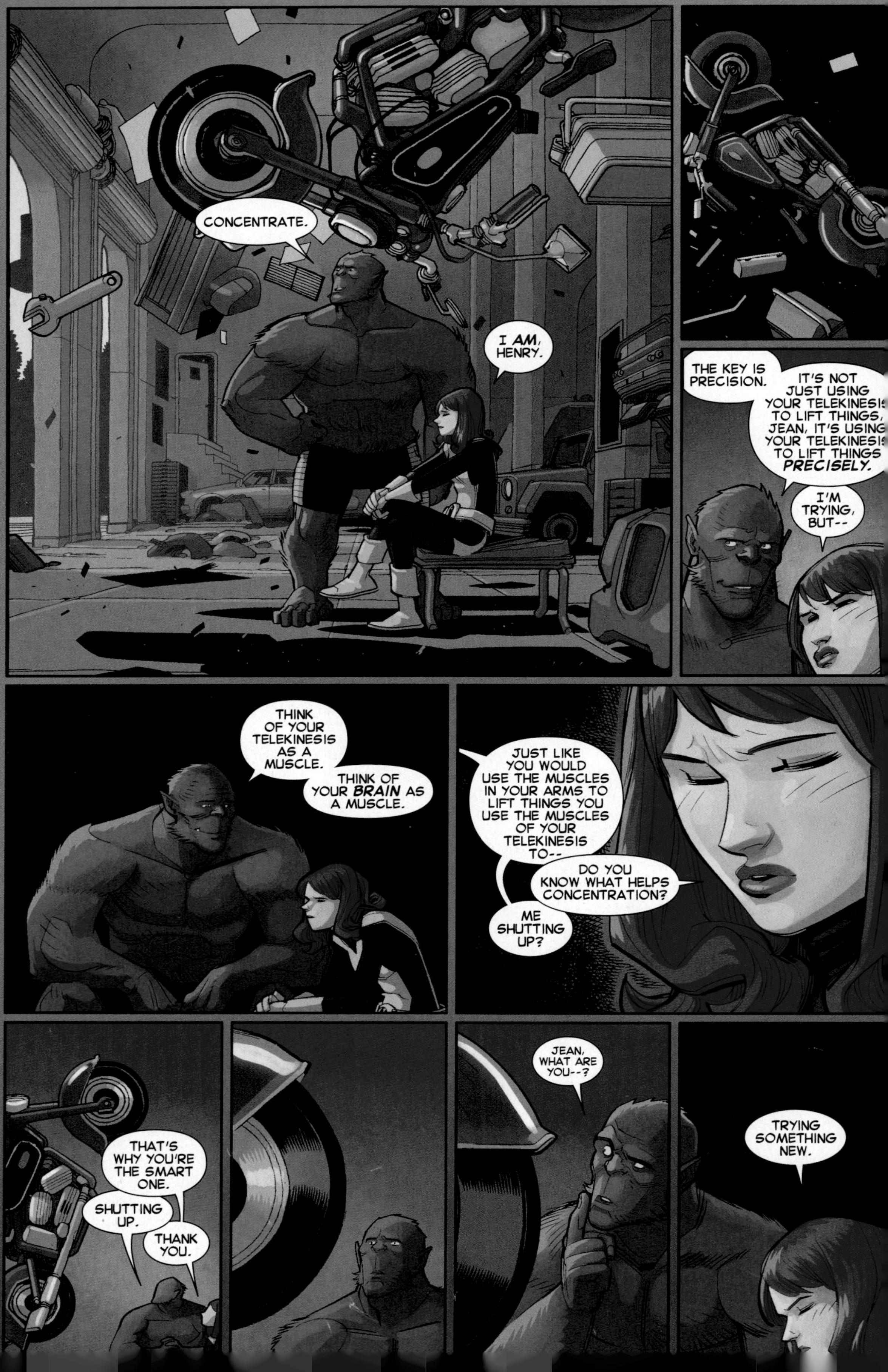
CONCENTRATE.
I AM, HENRY.
THE KEY IS PRECISION.
IT'S NOT JUST USING YOUR TELEKINESIS TO LIFT THINGS, JEAN, IT'S USING YOUR TELEKINESIS TO LIFT THINGS PRECISELY.
I'M TRYING, BUT--
THINK OF YOUR TELEKINESIS AS A MUSCLE.
THINK OF YOUR BRAIN AS A MUSCLE.
JUST LIKE YOU WOULD USE THE MUSCLES IN YOUR ARMS TO LIFT THINGS YOU USE THE MUSCLES OF YOUR TELEKINESIS TO--
DO YOU KNOW WHAT HELPS CONCENTRATION?
ME SHUTTING UP?
THAT'S WHY YOU'RE THE SMART ONE.
SHUTTING UP.
THANK YOU.
JEAN, WHAT ARE YOU--?
TRYING SOMETHING NEW.

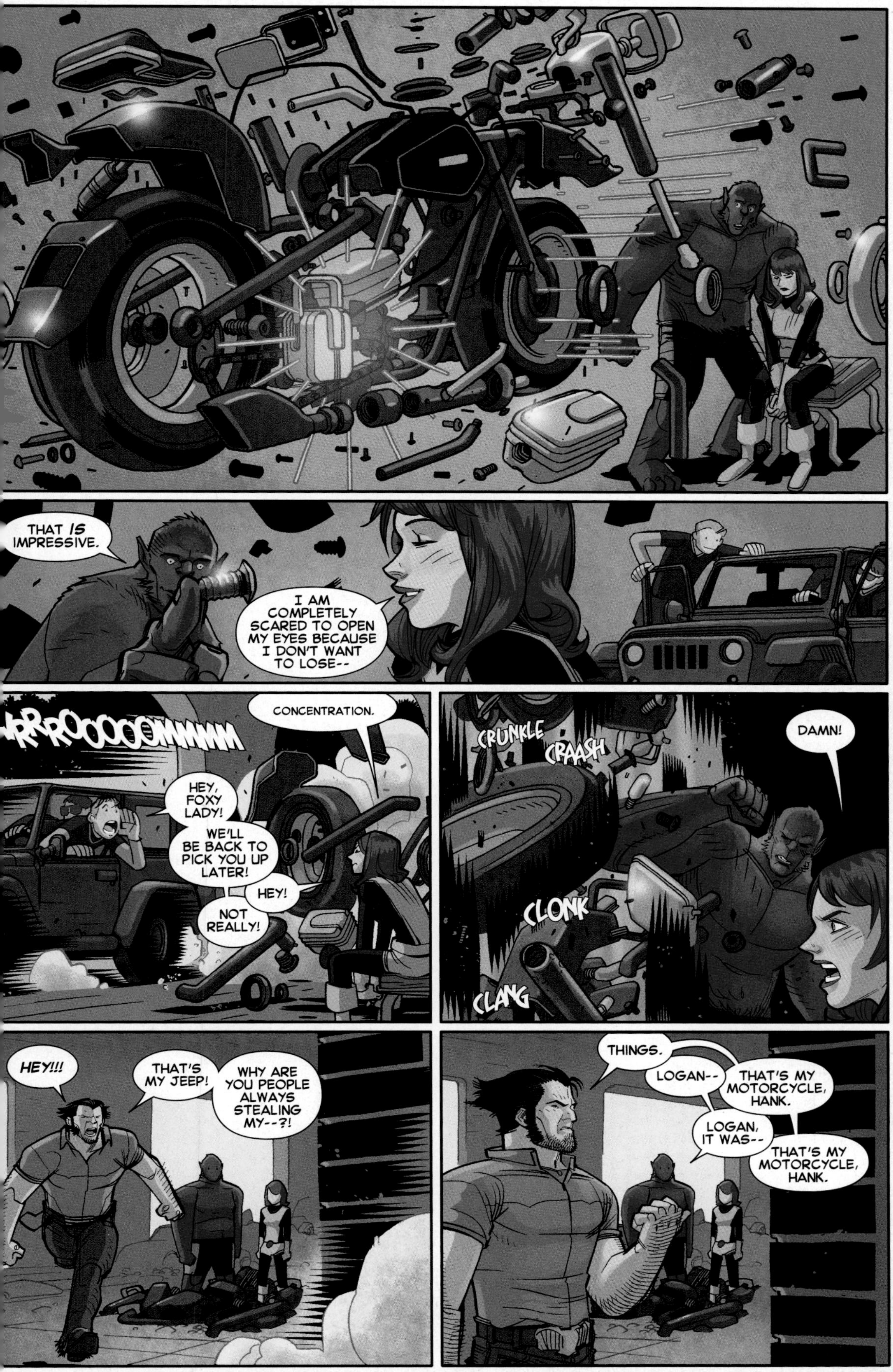
THAT IS IMPRESSIVE.
I AM COMPLETELY SCARED TO OPEN MY EYES BECAUSE I DON'T WANT TO LOSE--
RRROOOOOMMMMM
CONCENTRATION.
HEY, FOXY LADY!
WE'LL BE BACK TO PICK YOU UP LATER!
HEY!
NOT REALLY!
CRUNKLE
CRAASH
DAMN!
CLONK
CLANG
HEY!!!
THAT'S MY JEEP!
WHY ARE YOU PEOPLE ALWAYS STEALING MY--?!
THINGS.
LOGAN--
THAT'S MY MOTORCYCLE, HANK.
LOGAN, IT WAS--
THAT'S MY MOTORCYCLE, HANK.

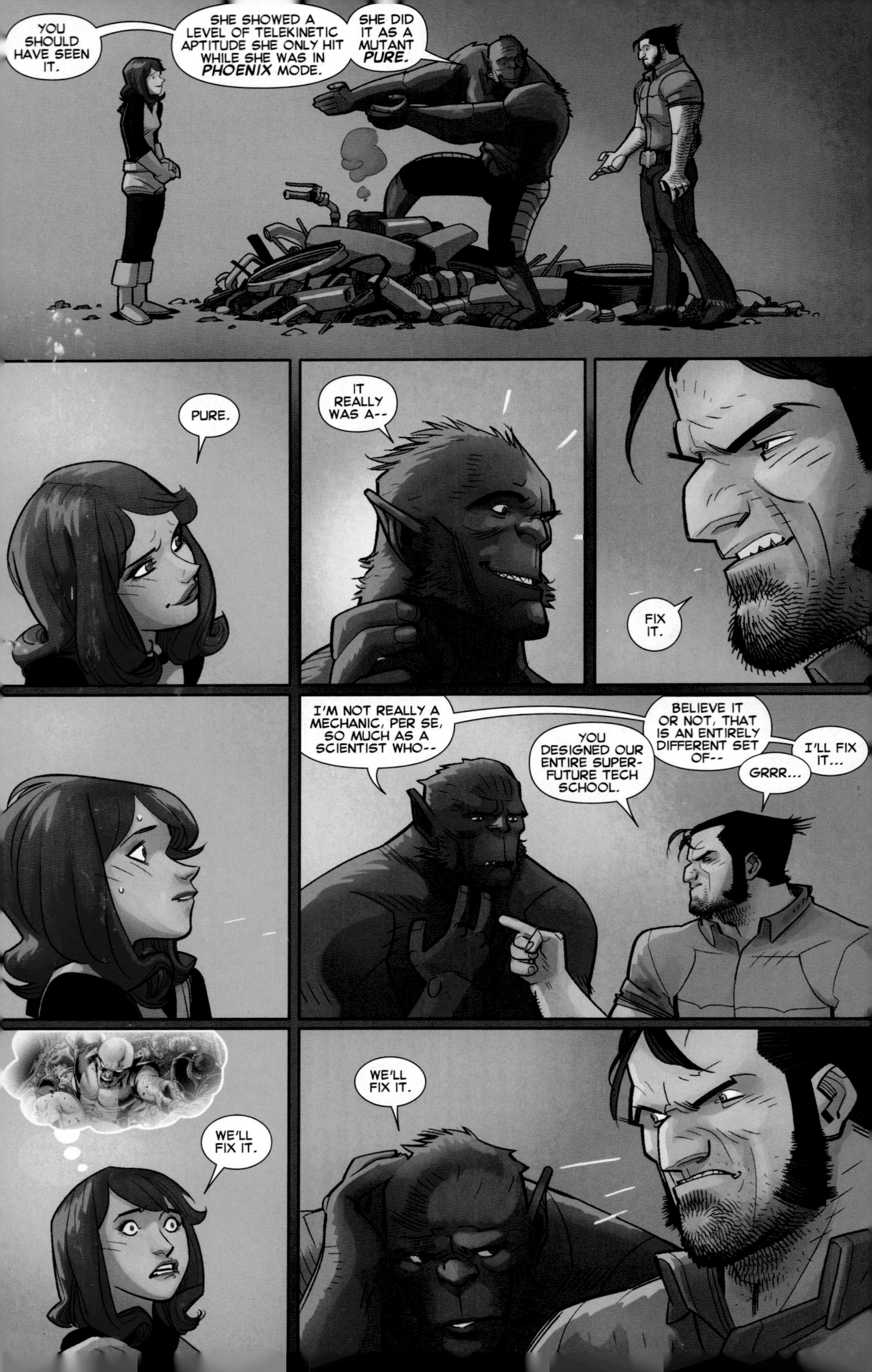
YOU SHOULD HAVE SEEN IT.
SHE SHOWED A LEVEL OF TELEKINETIC APTITUDE SHE ONLY HIT WHILE SHE WAS IN PHOENIX MODE.
SHE DID IT AS A MUTANT PURE.
PURE.
IT REALLY WAS A--
FIX IT.
I'M NOT REALLY A MECHANIC, PER SE, SO MUCH AS A SCIENTIST WHO--
YOU DESIGNED OUR ENTIRE SUPER-FUTURE TECH SCHOOL.
BELIEVE IT OR NOT, THAT IS AN ENTIRELY DIFFERENT SET OF--
I'LL FIX IT...
GRRR...
WE'LL FIX IT.
WE'LL FIX IT.

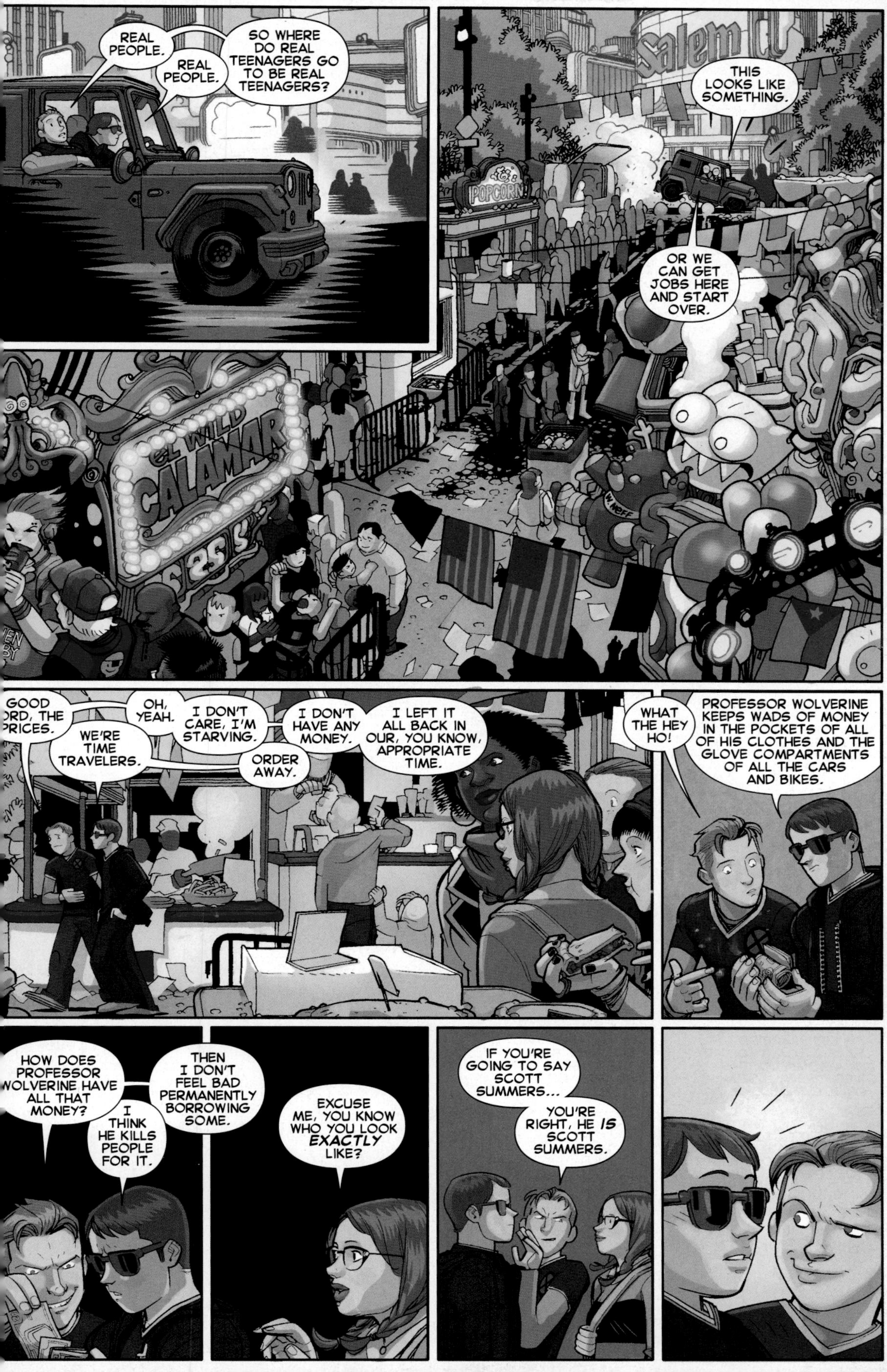

REAL PEOPLE.
REAL PEOPLE.
SO WHERE DO REAL TEENAGERS GO TO BE REAL TEENAGERS?
THIS LOOKS LIKE SOMETHING.
OR WE CAN GET JOBS HERE AND START OVER.
POPCORN
Salem
EL WILD CALAMAR
GOOD LORD, THE PRICES.
OH, YEAH.
WE'RE TIME TRAVELERS.
I DON'T CARE, I'M STARVING.
ORDER AWAY.
I DON'T HAVE ANY MONEY.
I LEFT IT ALL BACK IN OUR, YOU KNOW, APPROPRIATE TIME.
WHAT THE HEY HO!
PROFESSOR WOLVERINE KEEPS WADS OF MONEY IN THE POCKETS OF ALL OF HIS CLOTHES AND THE GLOVE COMPARTMENTS OF ALL THE CARS AND BIKES.
HOW DOES PROFESSOR WOLVERINE HAVE ALL THAT MONEY?
I THINK HE KILLS PEOPLE FOR IT.
THEN I DON'T FEEL BAD PERMANENTLY BORROWING SOME.
EXCUSE ME, YOU KNOW WHO YOU LOOK *EXACTLY* LIKE?
IF YOU'RE GOING TO SAY SCOTT SUMMERS...
YOU'RE RIGHT, HE *IS* SCOTT SUMMERS.

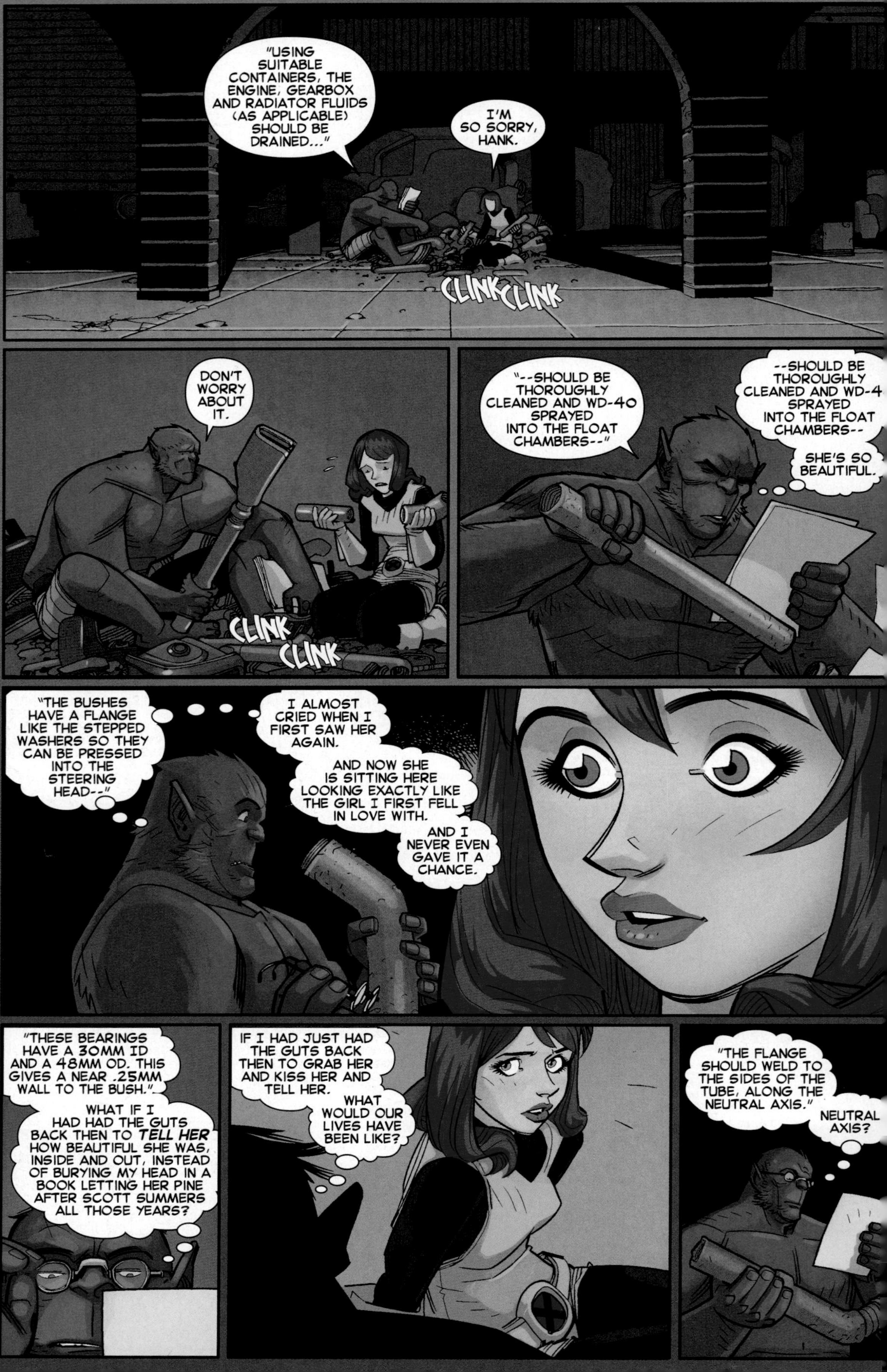
"USING SUITABLE CONTAINERS, THE ENGINE, GEARBOX AND RADIATOR FLUIDS (AS APPLICABLE) SHOULD BE DRAINED..."
I'M SO SORRY, HANK.
CLINK CLINK
DON'T WORRY ABOUT IT.
CLINK
CLINK
"--SHOULD BE THOROUGHLY CLEANED AND WD-40 SPRAYED INTO THE FLOAT CHAMBERS--"
--SHOULD BE THOROUGHLY CLEANED AND WD-4 SPRAYED INTO THE FLOAT CHAMBERS--
SHE'S SO BEAUTIFUL.
"THE BUSHES HAVE A FLANGE LIKE THE STEPPED WASHERS SO THEY CAN BE PRESSED INTO THE STEERING HEAD--"
I ALMOST CRIED WHEN I FIRST SAW HER AGAIN.
AND NOW SHE IS SITTING HERE LOOKING EXACTLY LIKE THE GIRL I FIRST FELL IN LOVE WITH.
AND I NEVER EVEN GAVE IT A CHANCE.
"THESE BEARINGS HAVE A 30MM ID AND A 48MM OD. THIS GIVES A NEAR .25MM WALL TO THE BUSH."
WHAT IF I HAD HAD THE GUTS BACK THEN TO TELL HER HOW BEAUTIFUL SHE WAS, INSIDE AND OUT, INSTEAD OF BURYING MY HEAD IN A BOOK LETTING HER PINE AFTER SCOTT SUMMERS ALL THOSE YEARS?
IF I HAD JUST HAD THE GUTS BACK THEN TO GRAB HER AND KISS HER AND TELL HER.
WHAT WOULD OUR LIVES HAVE BEEN LIKE?
"THE FLANGE SHOULD WELD TO THE SIDES OF THE TUBE, ALONG THE NEUTRAL AXIS."
NEUTRAL AXIS?

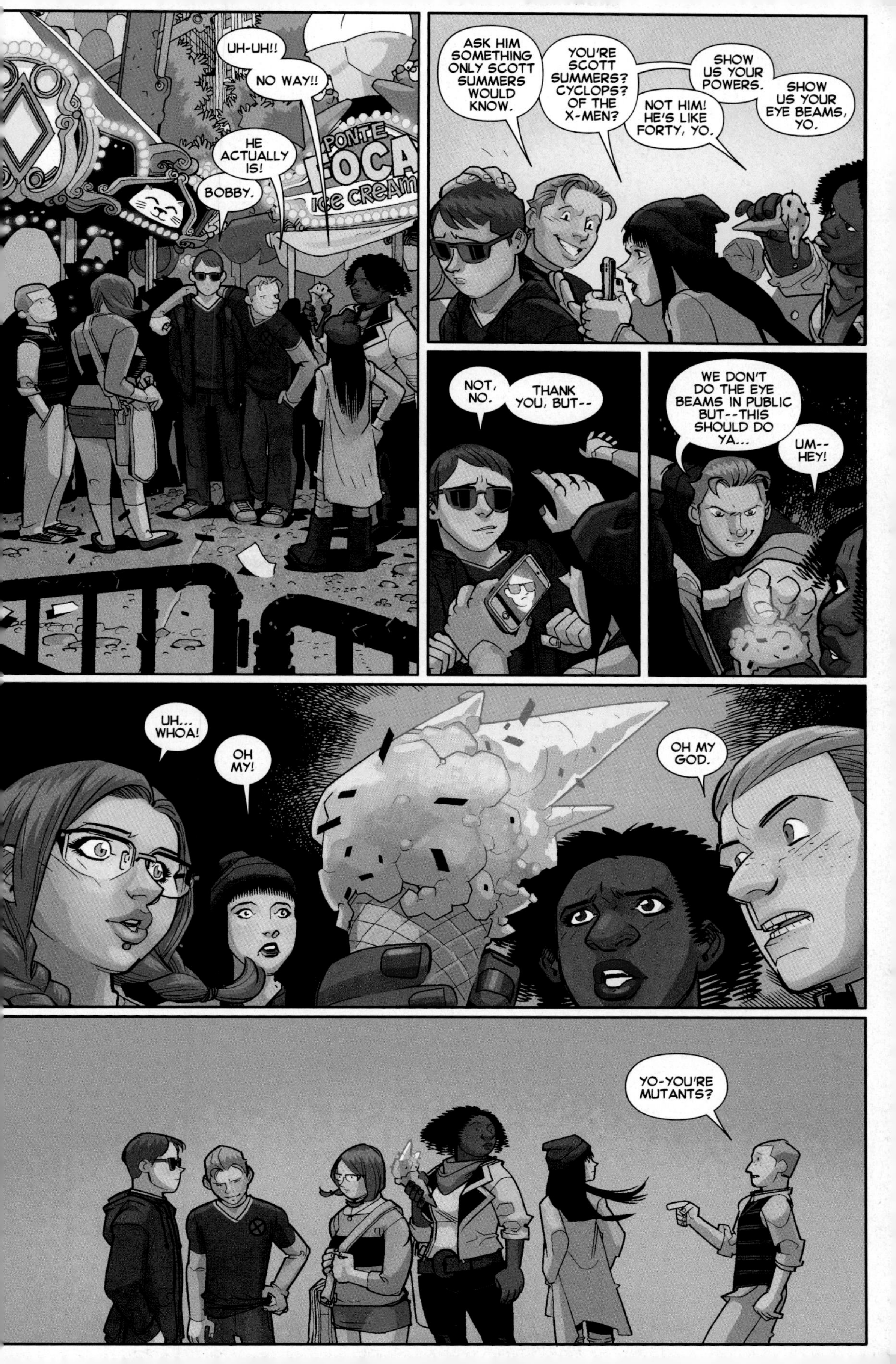
UH-UH!!
NO WAY!!
HE ACTUALLY IS!
BOBBY.
PONTE
FOCA
ICE CREAM
ASK HIM SOMETHING ONLY SCOTT SUMMERS WOULD KNOW.
YOU'RE SCOTT SUMMERS? CYCLOPS? OF THE X-MEN?
SHOW US YOUR POWERS.
NOT HIM! HE'S LIKE FORTY, YO.
SHOW US YOUR EYE BEAMS, YO.
NOT, NO.
THANK YOU, BUT--
WE DON'T DO THE EYE BEAMS IN PUBLIC BUT--THIS SHOULD DO YA...
UM-- HEY!
UH... WHOA!
OH MY!
OH MY GOD.
YO-YOU'RE MUTANTS?

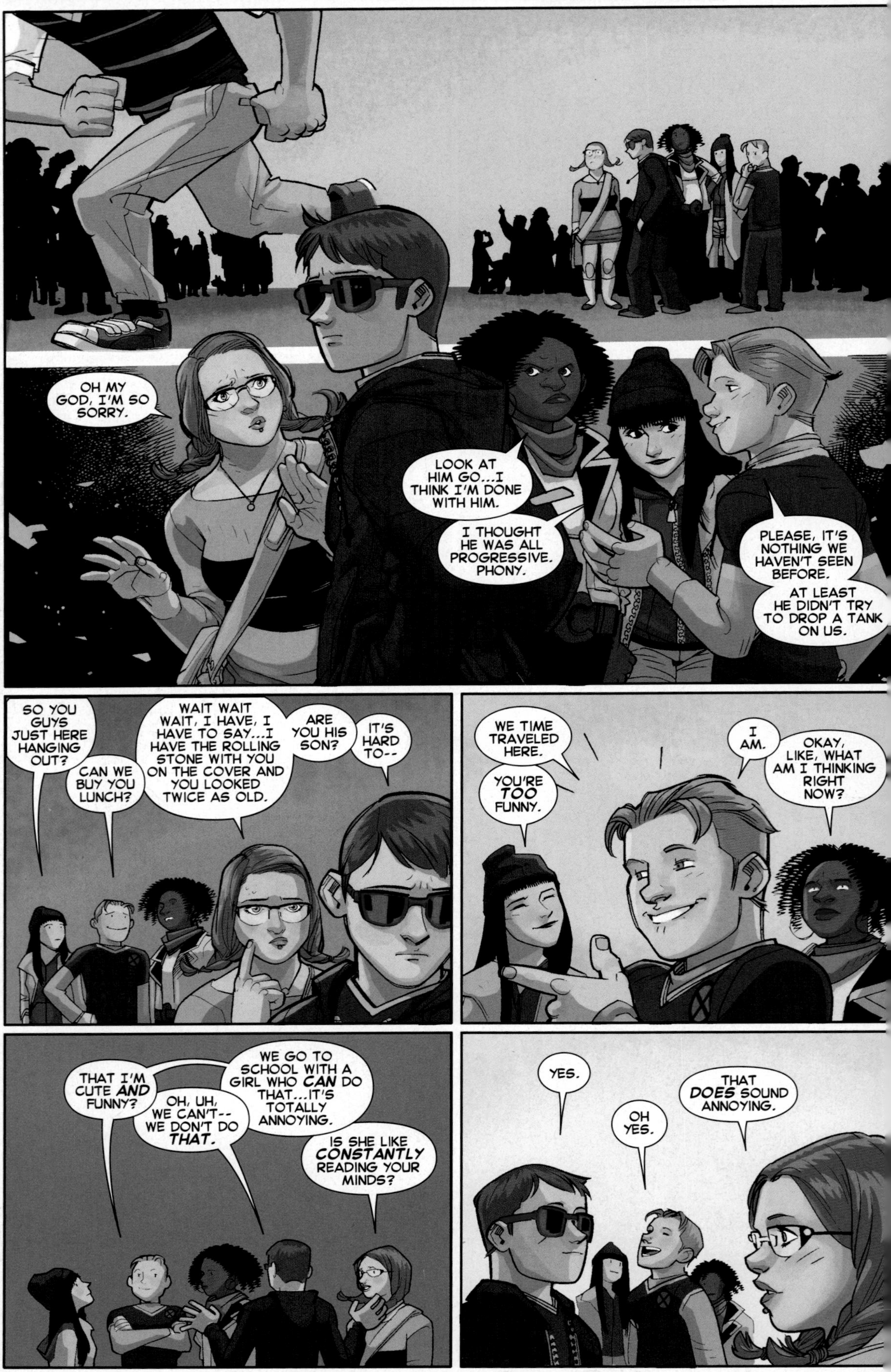
OH MY GOD, I'M SO SORRY.
LOOK AT HIM GO...I THINK I'M DONE WITH HIM.
I THOUGHT HE WAS ALL PROGRESSIVE. PHONY.
PLEASE, IT'S NOTHING WE HAVEN'T SEEN BEFORE.
AT LEAST HE DIDN'T TRY TO DROP A TANK ON US.
SO YOU GUYS JUST HERE HANGING OUT?
CAN WE BUY YOU LUNCH?
WAIT WAIT WAIT, I HAVE, I HAVE TO SAY...I HAVE THE ROLLING STONE WITH YOU ON THE COVER AND YOU LOOKED TWICE AS OLD.
ARE YOU HIS SON?
IT'S HARD TO--
WE TIME TRAVELED HERE.
YOU'RE *TOO* FUNNY.
I AM.
OKAY, LIKE, WHAT AM I THINKING RIGHT NOW?
THAT I'M CUTE *AND* FUNNY?
WE GO TO SCHOOL WITH A GIRL WHO *CAN* DO THAT...IT'S TOTALLY ANNOYING.
OH, UH, WE CAN'T-- WE DON'T DO *THAT.*
IS SHE LIKE *CONSTANTLY* READING YOUR MINDS?
YES.
OH YES.
THAT *DOES* SOUND ANNOYING.

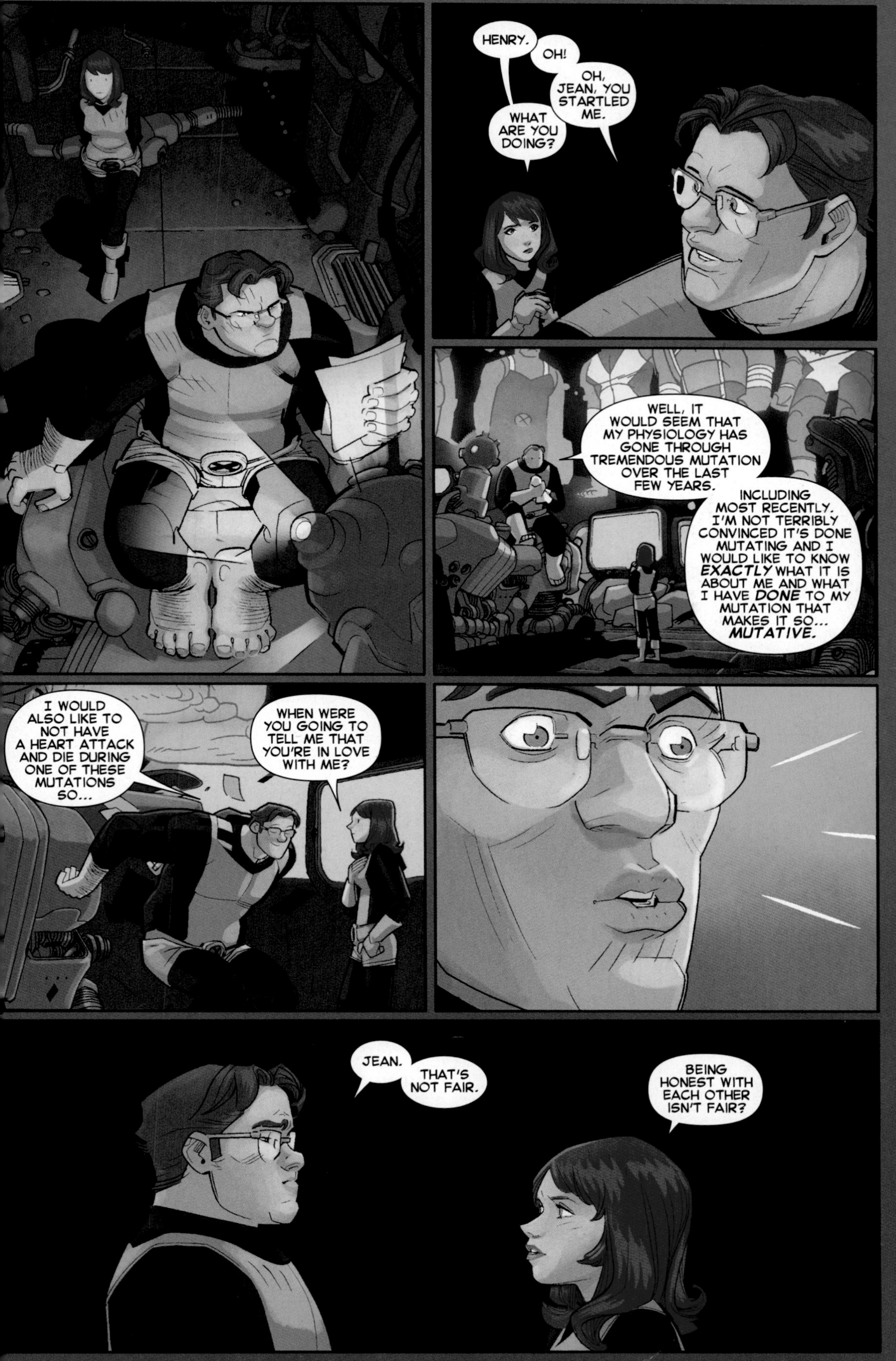
HENRY.
OH!
OH, JEAN, YOU STARTLED ME.
WHAT ARE YOU DOING?
WELL, IT WOULD SEEM THAT MY PHYSIOLOGY HAS GONE THROUGH TREMENDOUS MUTATION OVER THE LAST FEW YEARS.
INCLUDING MOST RECENTLY. I'M NOT TERRIBLY CONVINCED IT'S DONE MUTATING AND I WOULD LIKE TO KNOW *EXACTLY* WHAT IT IS ABOUT ME AND WHAT I HAVE *DONE* TO MY MUTATION THAT MAKES IT SO... *MUTATIVE.*
I WOULD ALSO LIKE TO NOT HAVE A HEART ATTACK AND DIE DURING ONE OF THESE MUTATIONS SO...
WHEN WERE YOU GOING TO TELL ME THAT YOU'RE IN LOVE WITH ME?
JEAN.
THAT'S NOT FAIR.
BEING HONEST WITH EACH OTHER ISN'T FAIR?

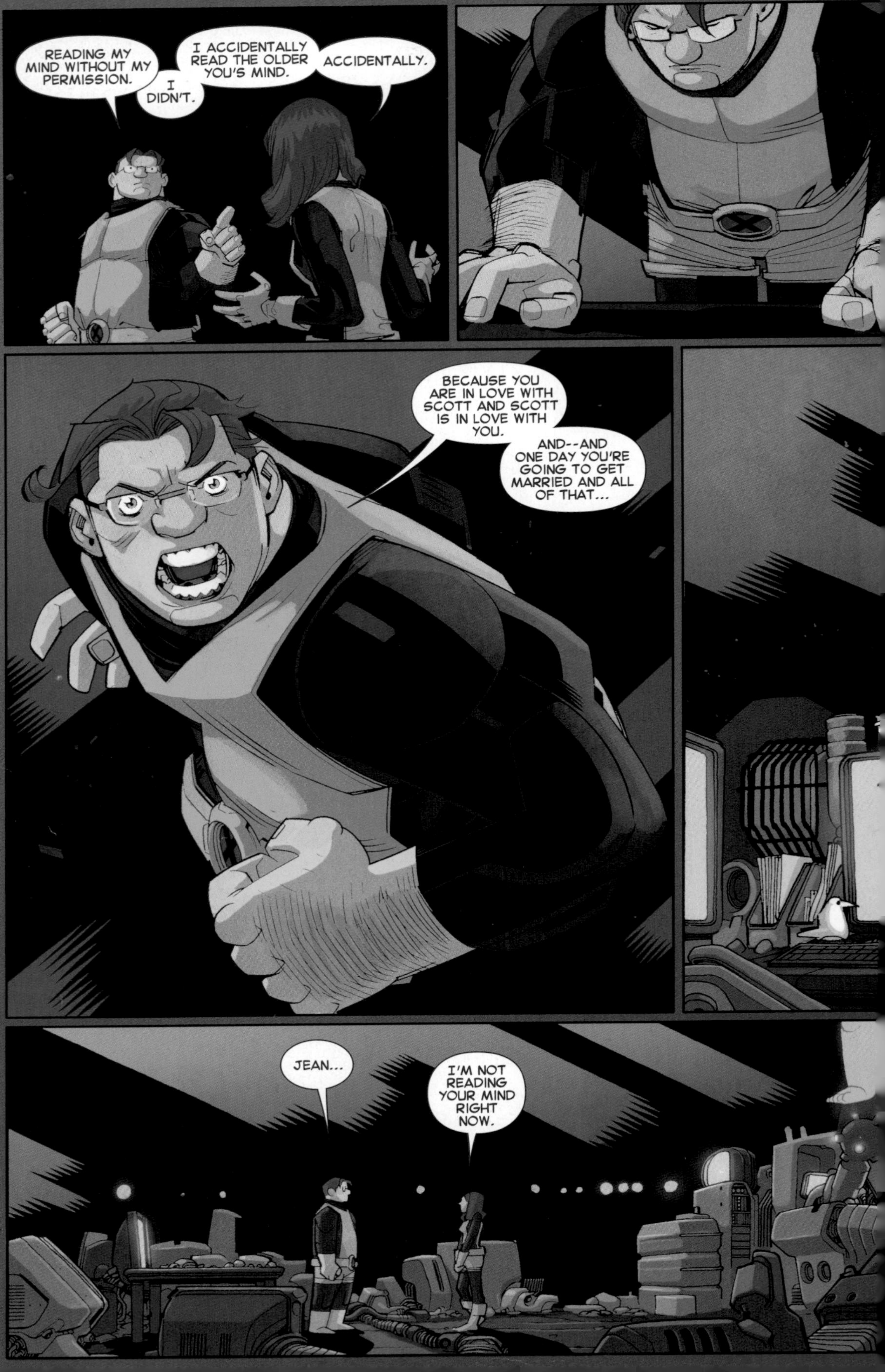
READING MY MIND WITHOUT MY PERMISSION.
I DIDN'T.
I ACCIDENTALLY READ THE OLDER YOU'S MIND.
ACCIDENTALLY.
BECAUSE YOU ARE IN LOVE WITH SCOTT AND SCOTT IS IN LOVE WITH YOU.
AND--AND ONE DAY YOU'RE GOING TO GET MARRIED AND ALL OF THAT...
JEAN...
I'M NOT READING YOUR MIND RIGHT NOW.

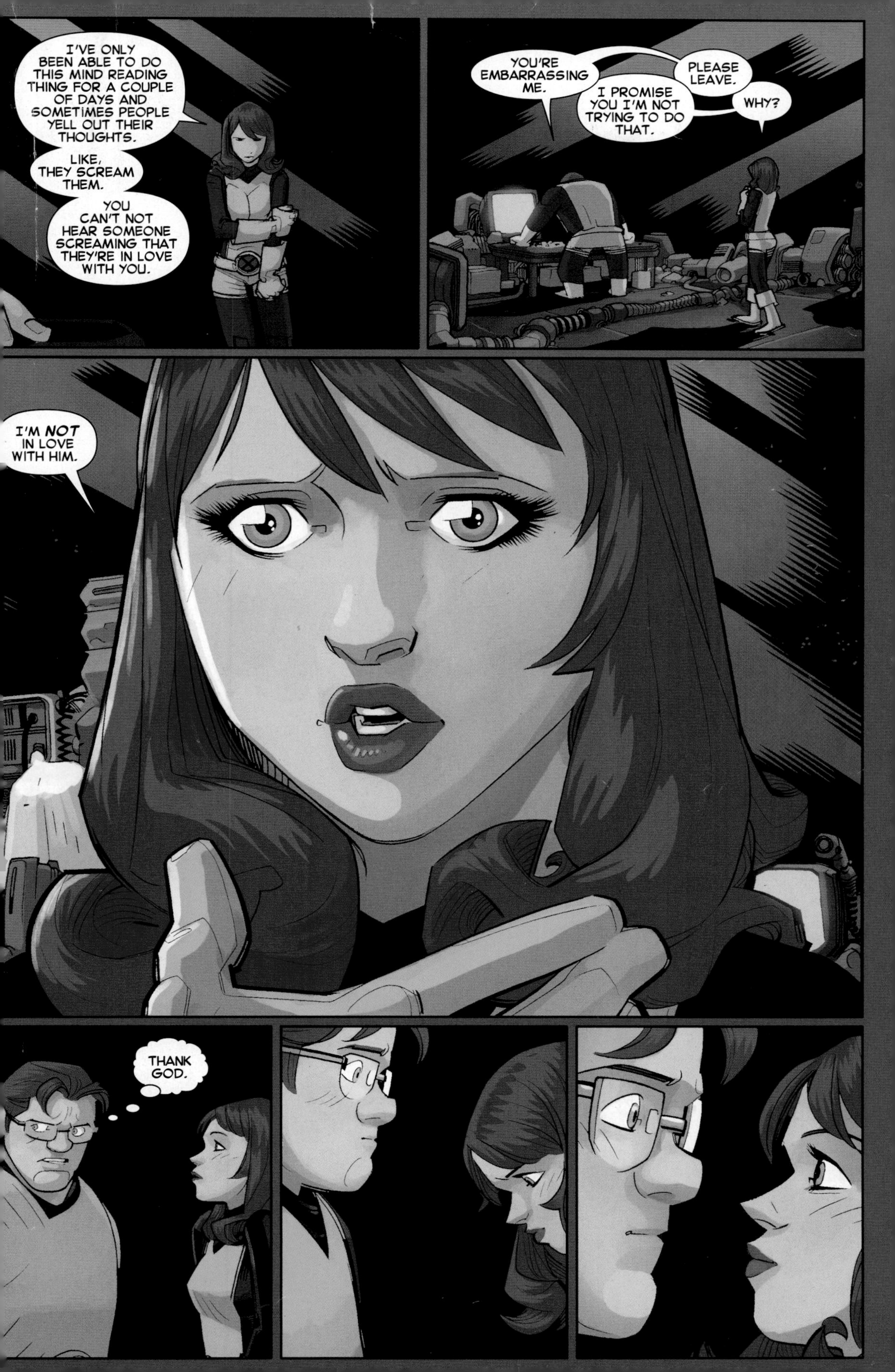
I'VE ONLY BEEN ABLE TO DO THIS MIND READING THING FOR A COUPLE OF DAYS AND SOMETIMES PEOPLE YELL OUT THEIR THOUGHTS.
LIKE, THEY SCREAM THEM.
YOU CAN'T NOT HEAR SOMEONE SCREAMING THAT THEY'RE IN LOVE WITH YOU.
YOU'RE EMBARRASSING ME.
PLEASE LEAVE.
I PROMISE YOU I'M NOT TRYING TO DO THAT.
WHY?
I'M NOT IN LOVE WITH HIM.
THANK GOD.

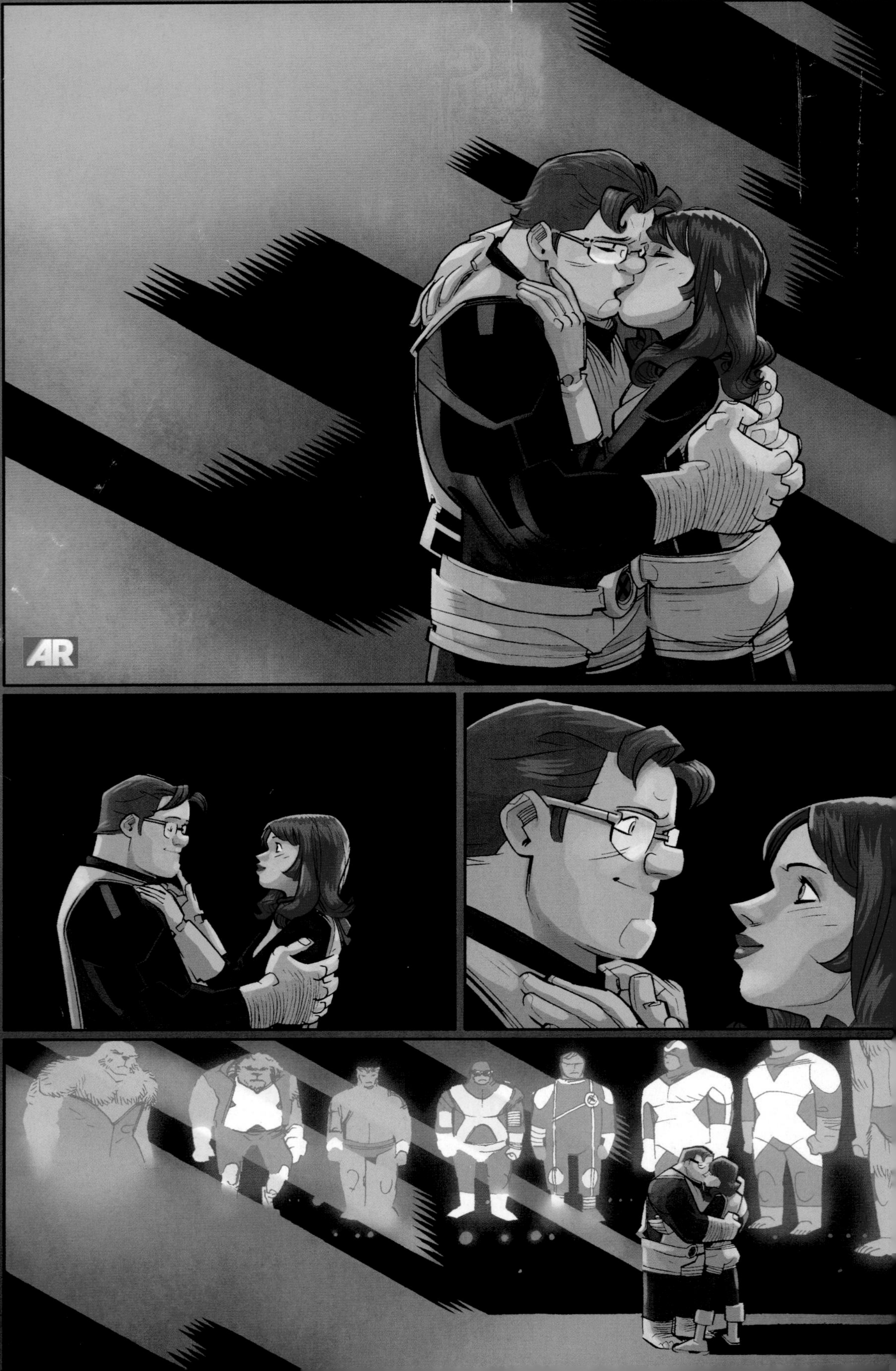

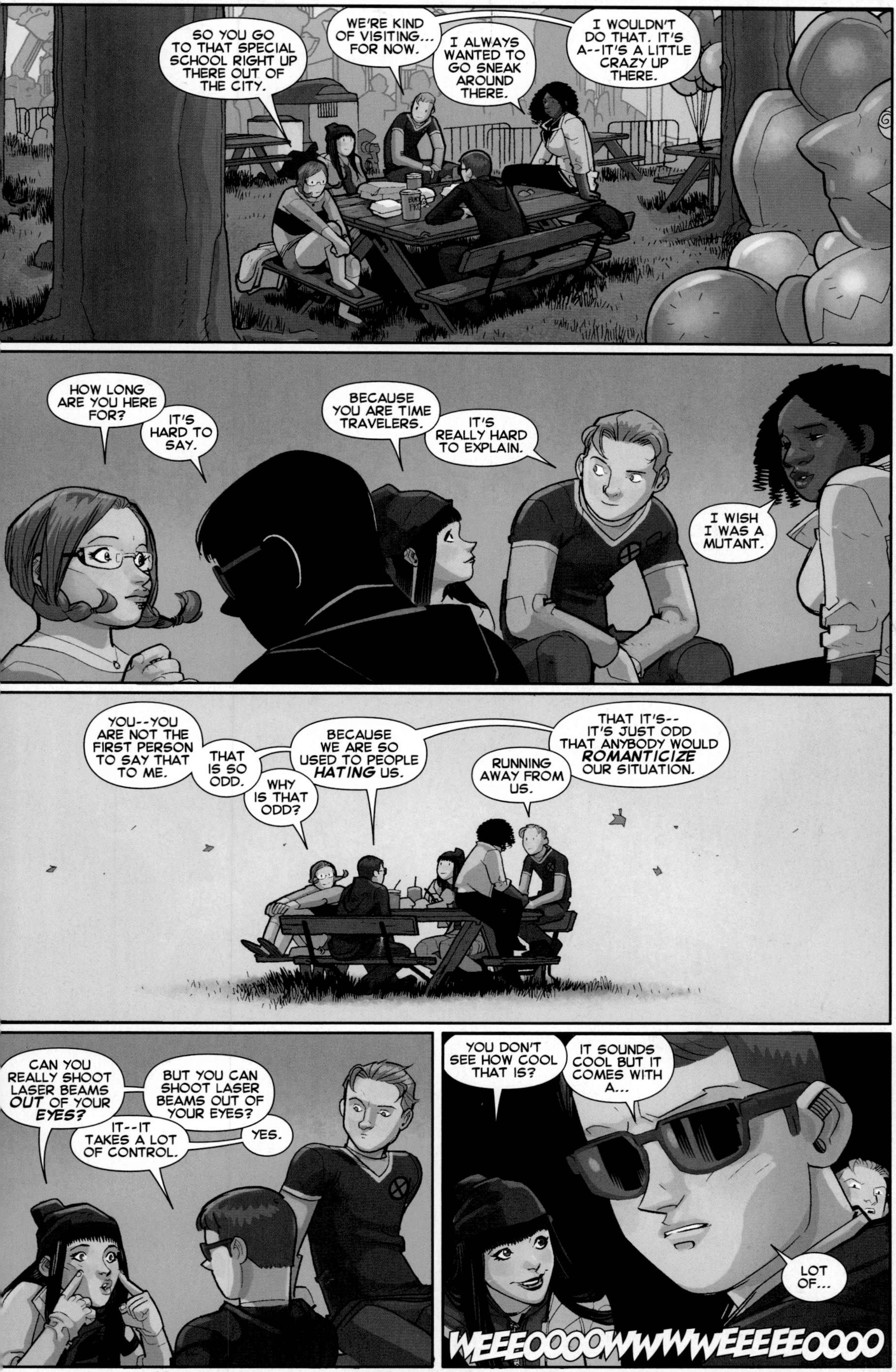
SO YOU GO TO THAT SPECIAL SCHOOL RIGHT UP THERE OUT OF THE CITY.
WE'RE KIND OF VISITING... FOR NOW.
I ALWAYS WANTED TO GO SNEAK AROUND THERE.
I WOULDN'T DO THAT. IT'S A--IT'S A LITTLE CRAZY UP THERE.
HOW LONG ARE YOU HERE FOR?
IT'S HARD TO SAY.
BECAUSE YOU ARE TIME TRAVELERS.
IT'S REALLY HARD TO EXPLAIN.
I WISH I WAS A MUTANT.
YOU--YOU ARE NOT THE FIRST PERSON TO SAY THAT TO ME.
THAT IS SO ODD.
WHY IS THAT ODD?
BECAUSE WE ARE SO USED TO PEOPLE HATING US.
RUNNING AWAY FROM US.
THAT IT'S-- IT'S JUST ODD THAT ANYBODY WOULD ROMANTICIZE OUR SITUATION.
CAN YOU REALLY SHOOT LASER BEAMS OUT OF YOUR EYES?
BUT YOU CAN SHOOT LASER BEAMS OUT OF YOUR EYES?
IT--IT TAKES A LOT OF CONTROL.
YES.
YOU DON'T SEE HOW COOL THAT IS?
IT SOUNDS COOL BUT IT COMES WITH A...
LOT OF...
WEEEOOOOWWWWWEEEEEOOOO

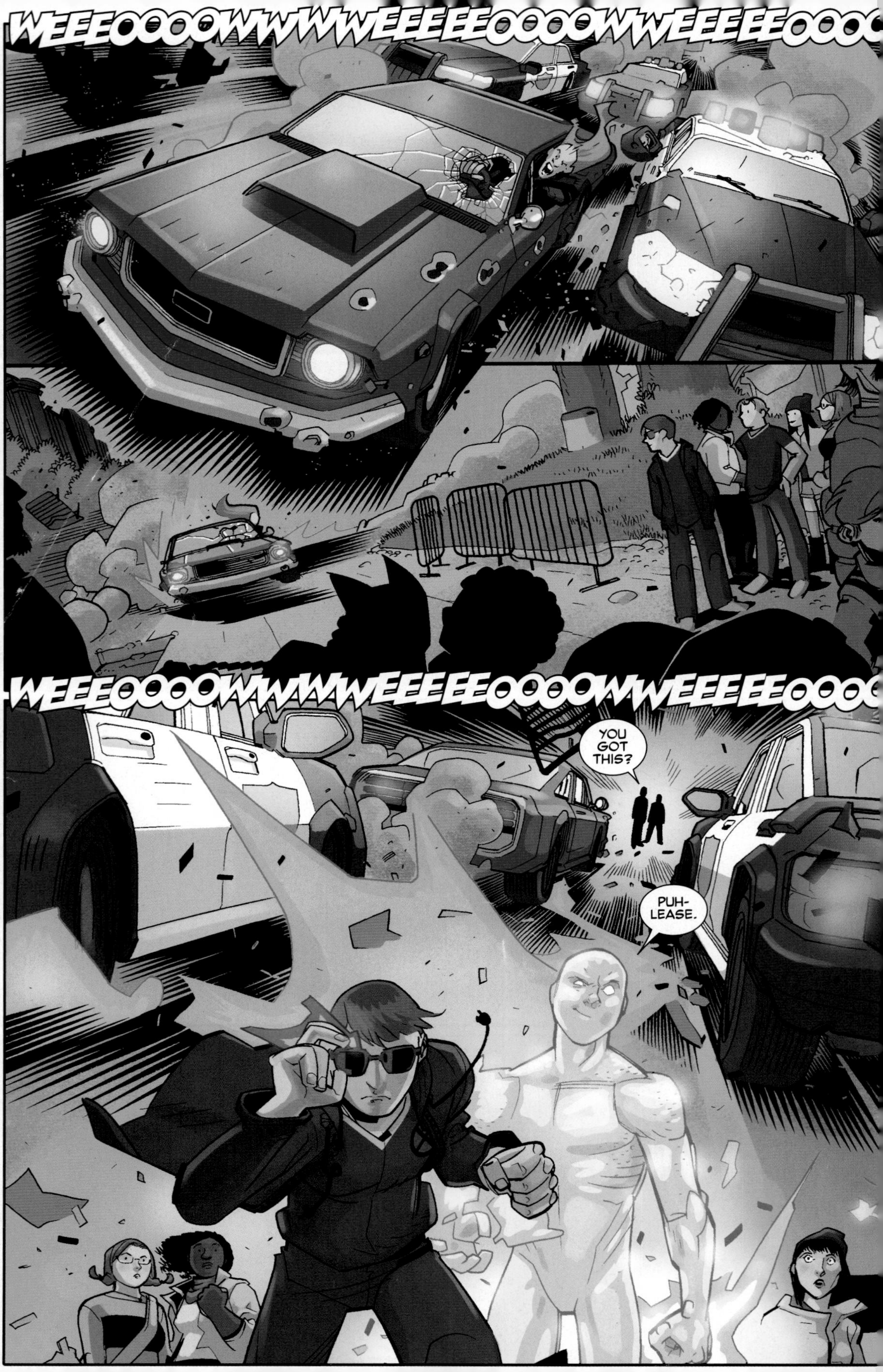
WEEEOOOOWWWWEEEEEOOOOWEEEEEOOOO
WEEEOOOOWWWWEEEEEOOOOWEEEEEOOOO
YOU GOT THIS?
PUH-LEASE.

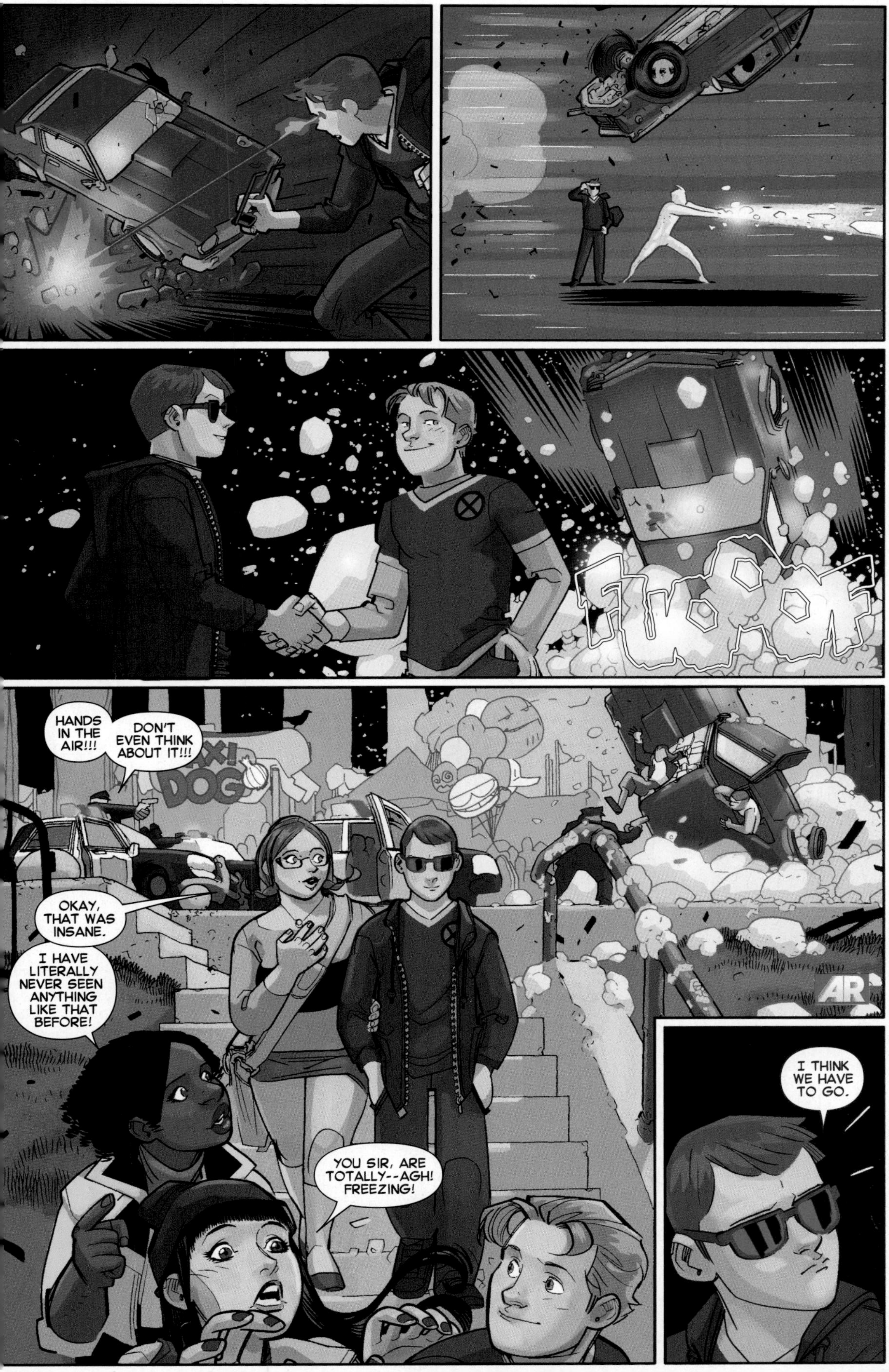
FWOOM
HANDS IN THE AIR!!!
DON'T EVEN THINK ABOUT IT!!!
OKAY, THAT WAS INSANE.
I HAVE LITERALLY NEVER SEEN ANYTHING LIKE THAT BEFORE!
YOU SIR, ARE TOTALLY--AGH! FREEZING!
I THINK WE HAVE TO GO.

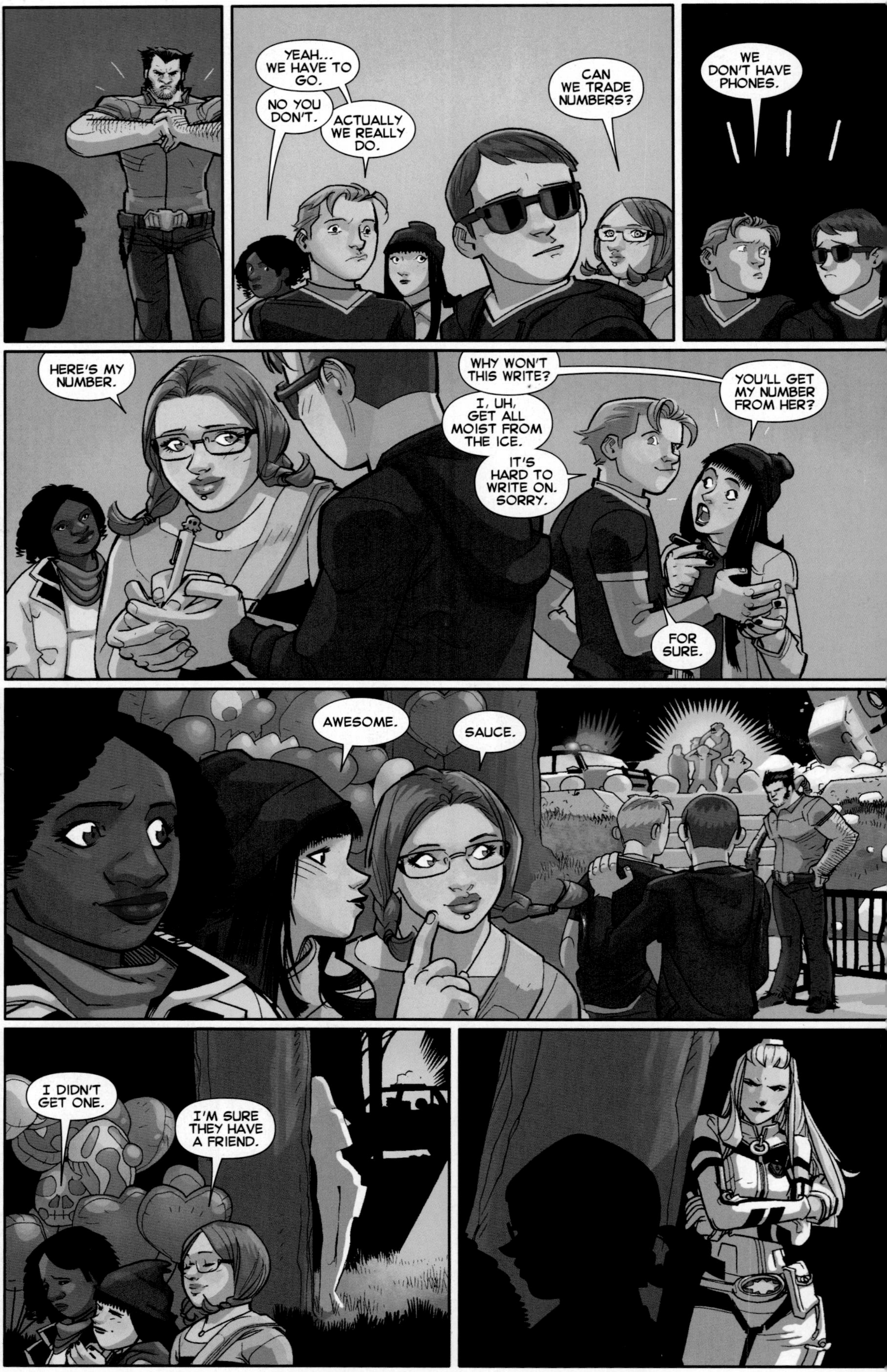
YEAH... WE HAVE TO GO.
NO YOU DON'T.
ACTUALLY WE REALLY DO.
CAN WE TRADE NUMBERS?
WE DON'T HAVE PHONES.
HERE'S MY NUMBER.
WHY WON'T THIS WRITE?
YOU'LL GET MY NUMBER FROM HER?
I, UH, GET ALL MOIST FROM THE ICE.
IT'S HARD TO WRITE ON. SORRY.
FOR SURE.
AWESOME.
SAUCE.
I DIDN'T GET ONE.
I'M SURE THEY HAVE A FRIEND.

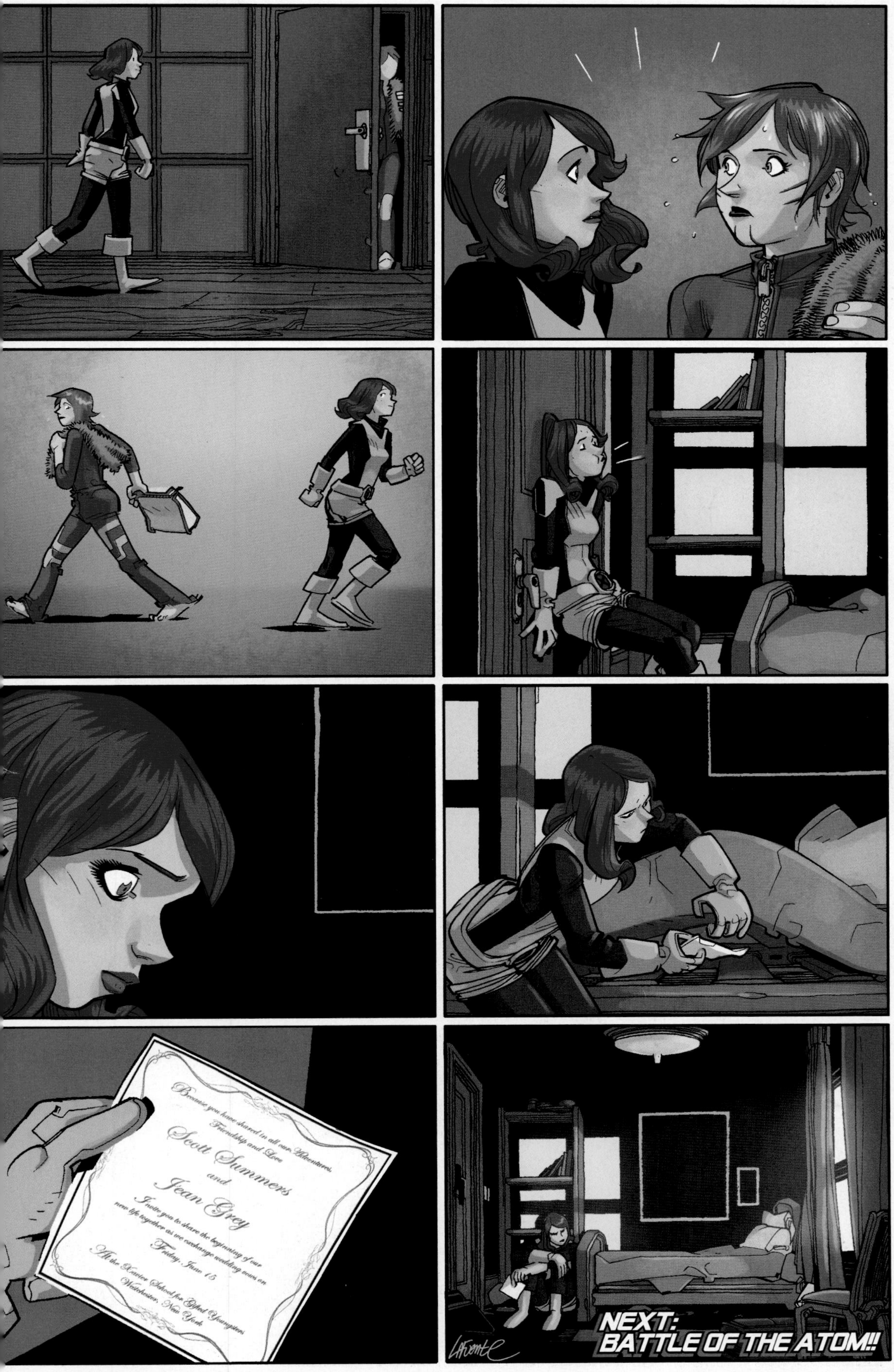
Because you have shared in all our Adventures, Friendship and Love
Scott Summers
and
Jean Grey
Invite you to share the beginning of our new life together as we exchange wedding vows on
Friday, June 15
At the Xavier School for Gifted Youngsters
Westchester, New York
NEXT: BATTLE OF THE ATOM!!

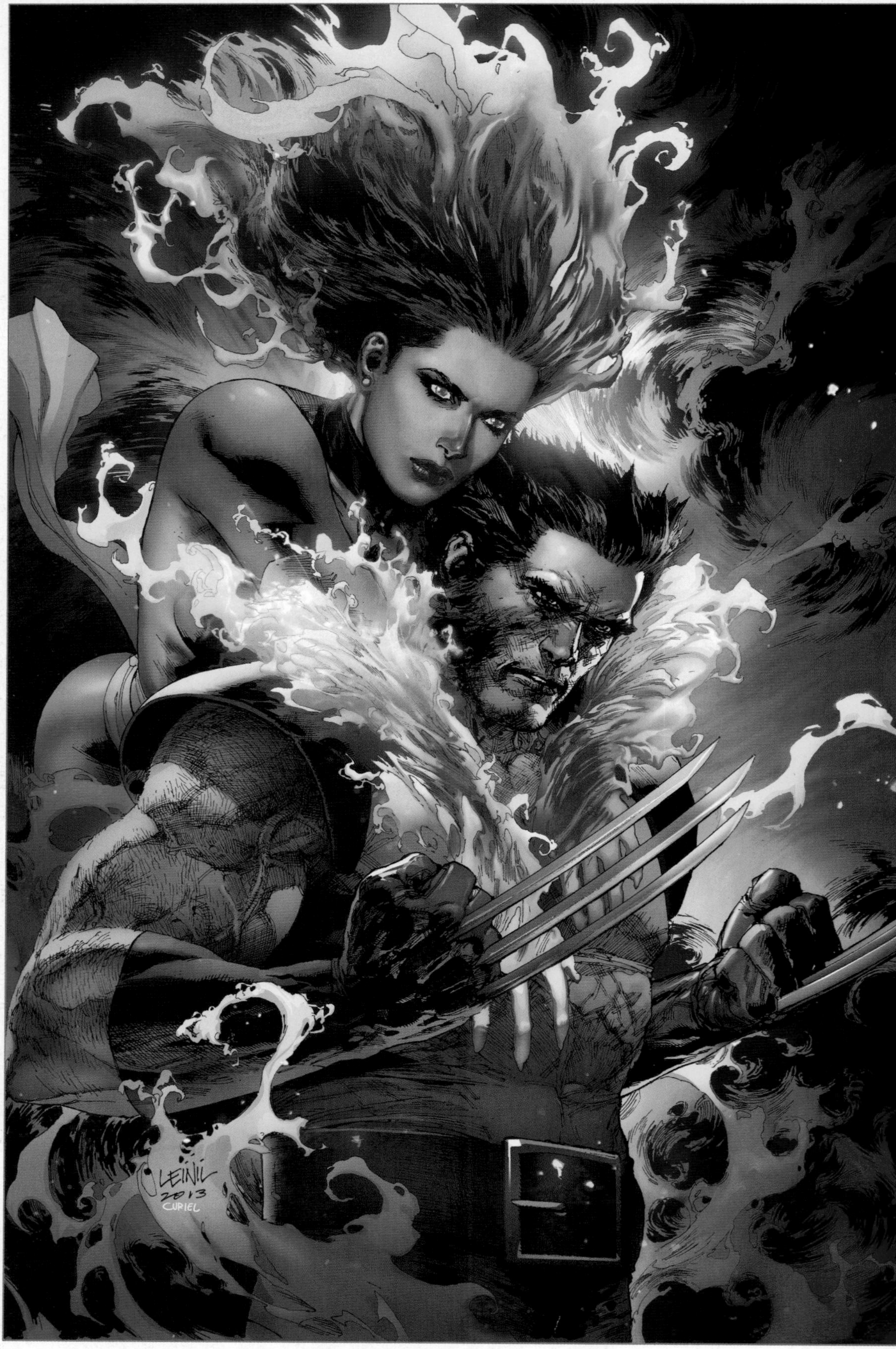
LEINIL
2013
CURIEL

ALL-NEW X-MEN #12 WOLVERINE THROUGH THE AGES VARIANT
BY LEINIL FRANCIS YU & DAVID CURIEL

COVER PROCESS BY STUART IMMONEN

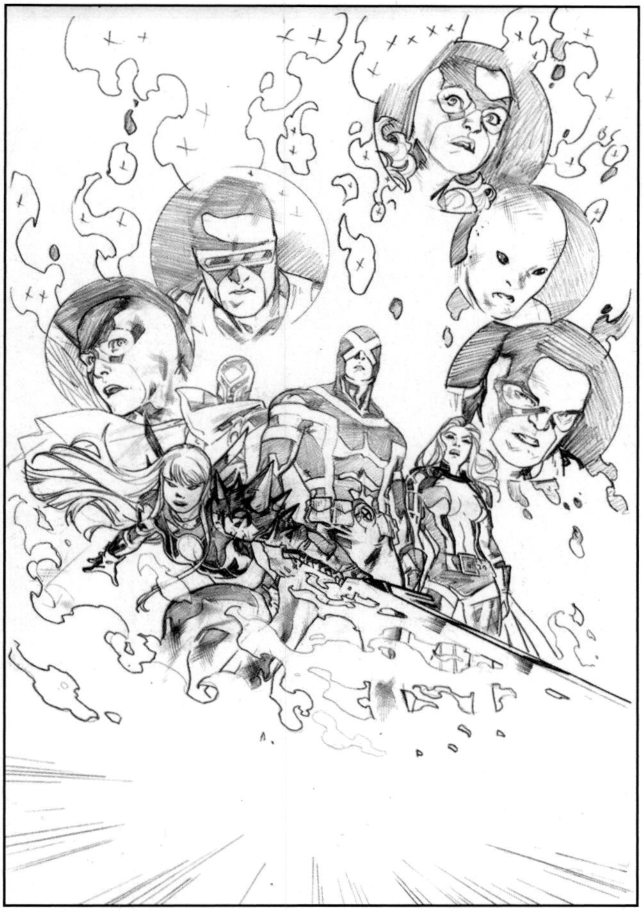

#11 PENCILS

#12 SKETCHES

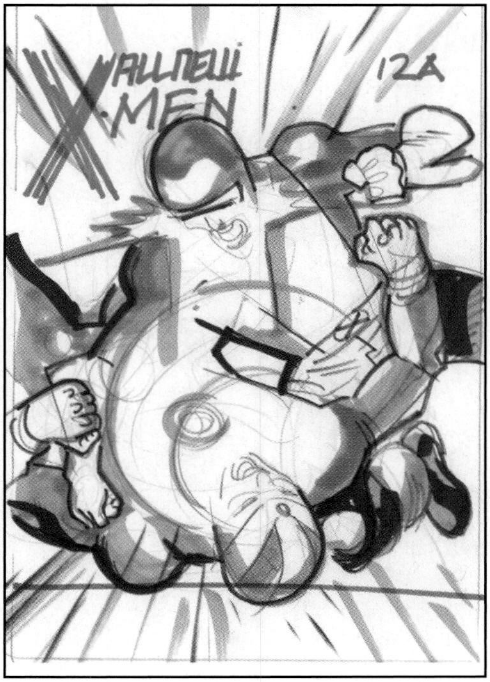
ALL NEW
X-MEN
12A

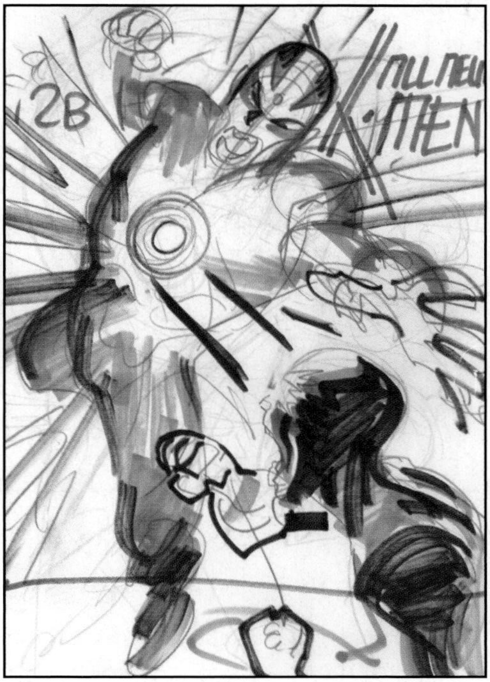
12B
ALL NEW
X-MEN

#13 SKETCHES

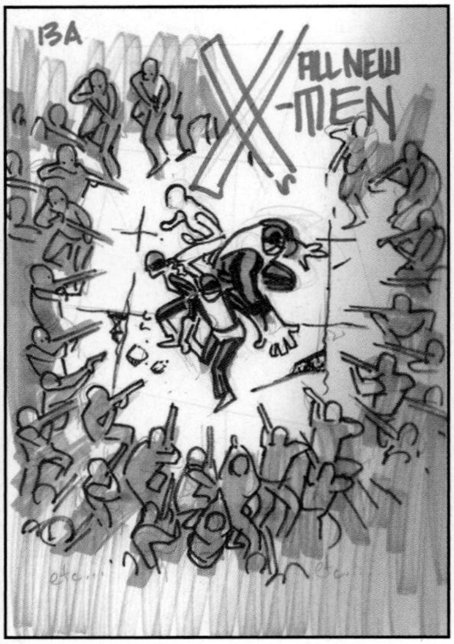
13A
ALL NEW
X-MEN

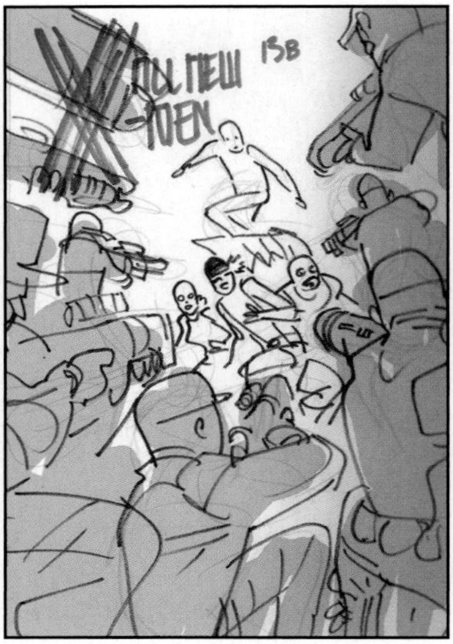
13B
ALL NEW
X-MEN

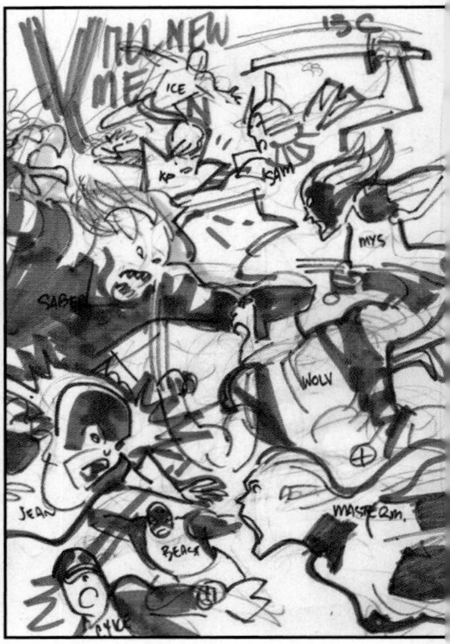
ALL NEW
X-MEN
13C
ICE
KP
SAM
MYS
WOLV
JEAN
BEAST

#14 SKETCHES

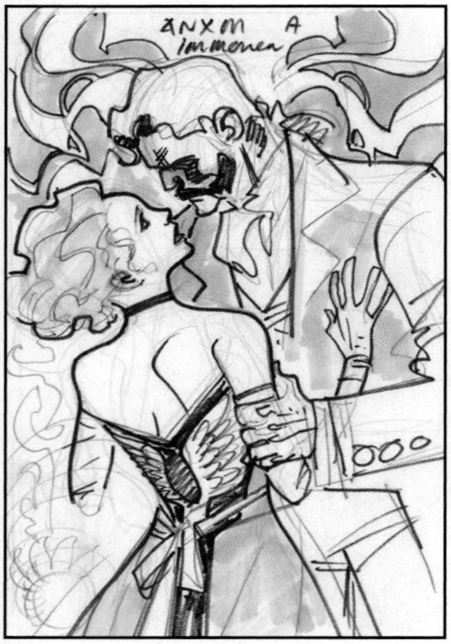
ANXM A
immonen

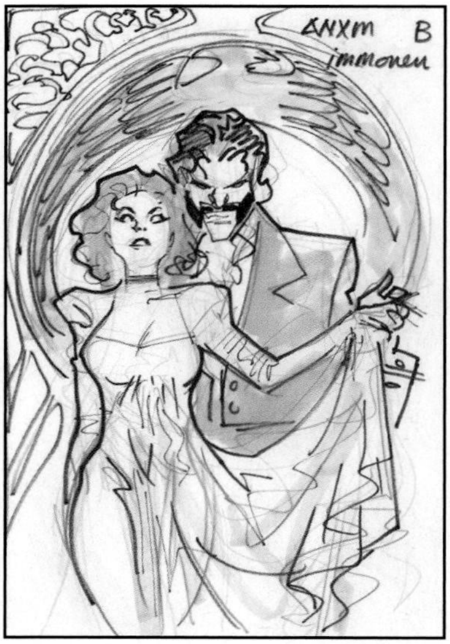
ANXM B
immonen

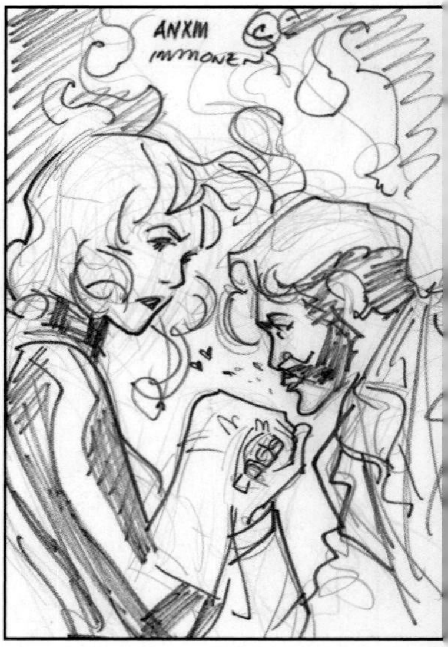
ANXM C
IMMONEN

#14 PENCILS

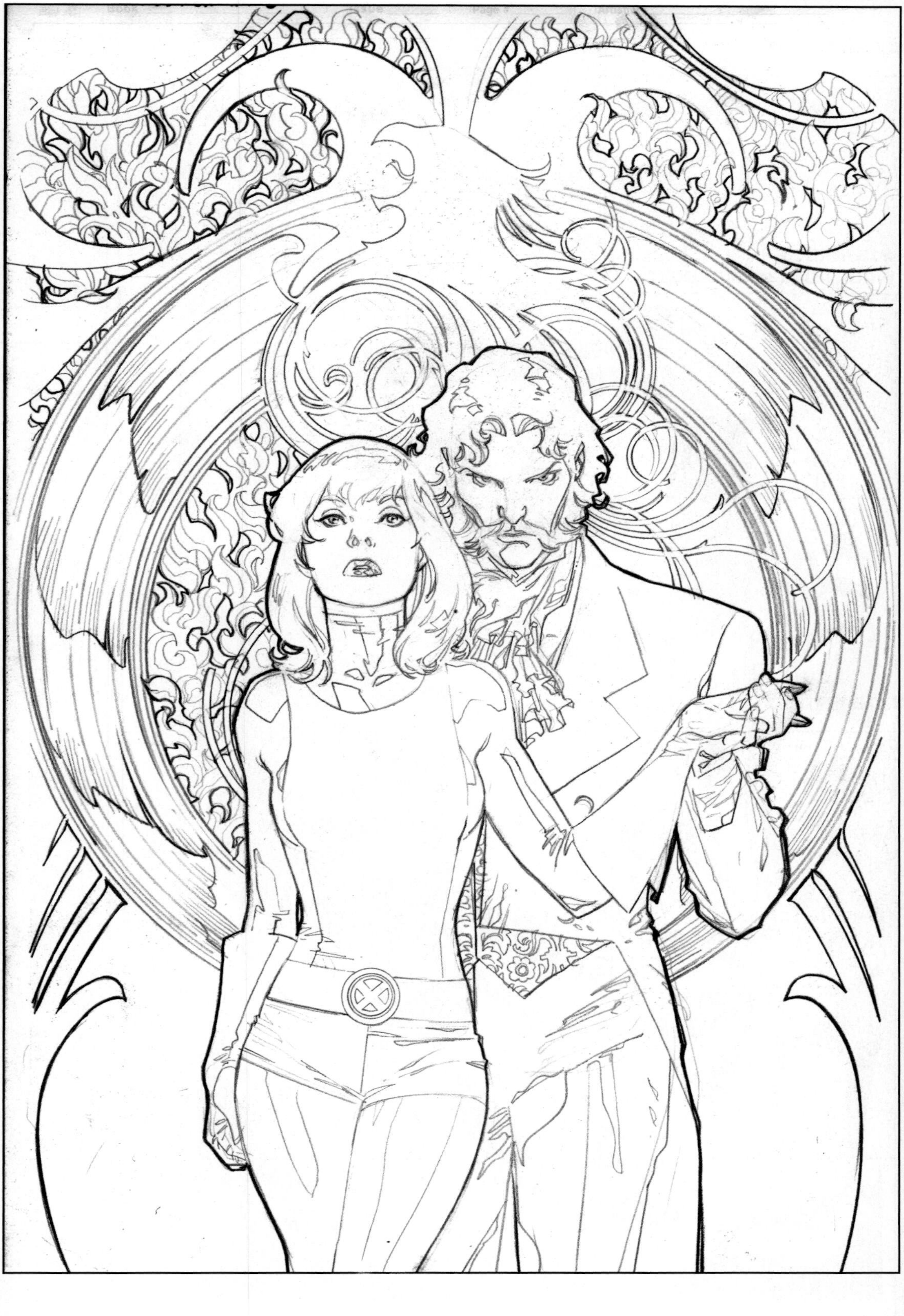

#15 SKETCHES

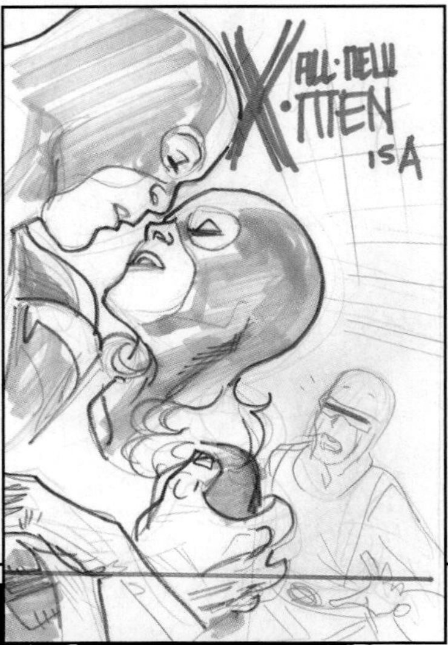
X·ALL·NEW X·MEN
15A

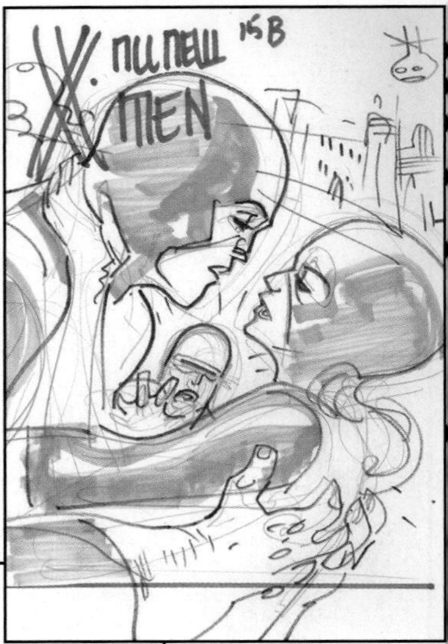
X·ALL NEW X·MEN
15B

#15 INKS BY WADE VON GRAWBADGER

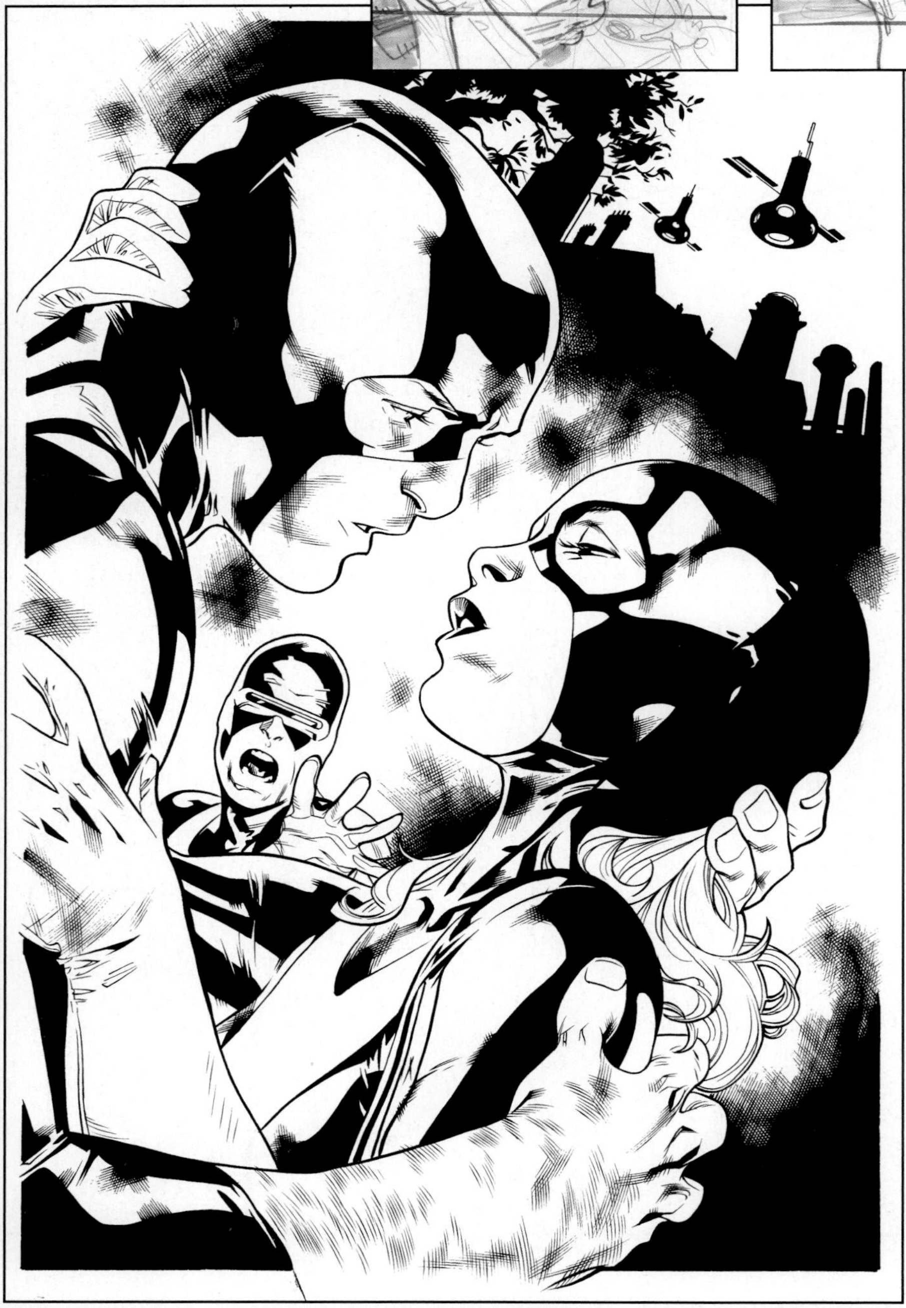

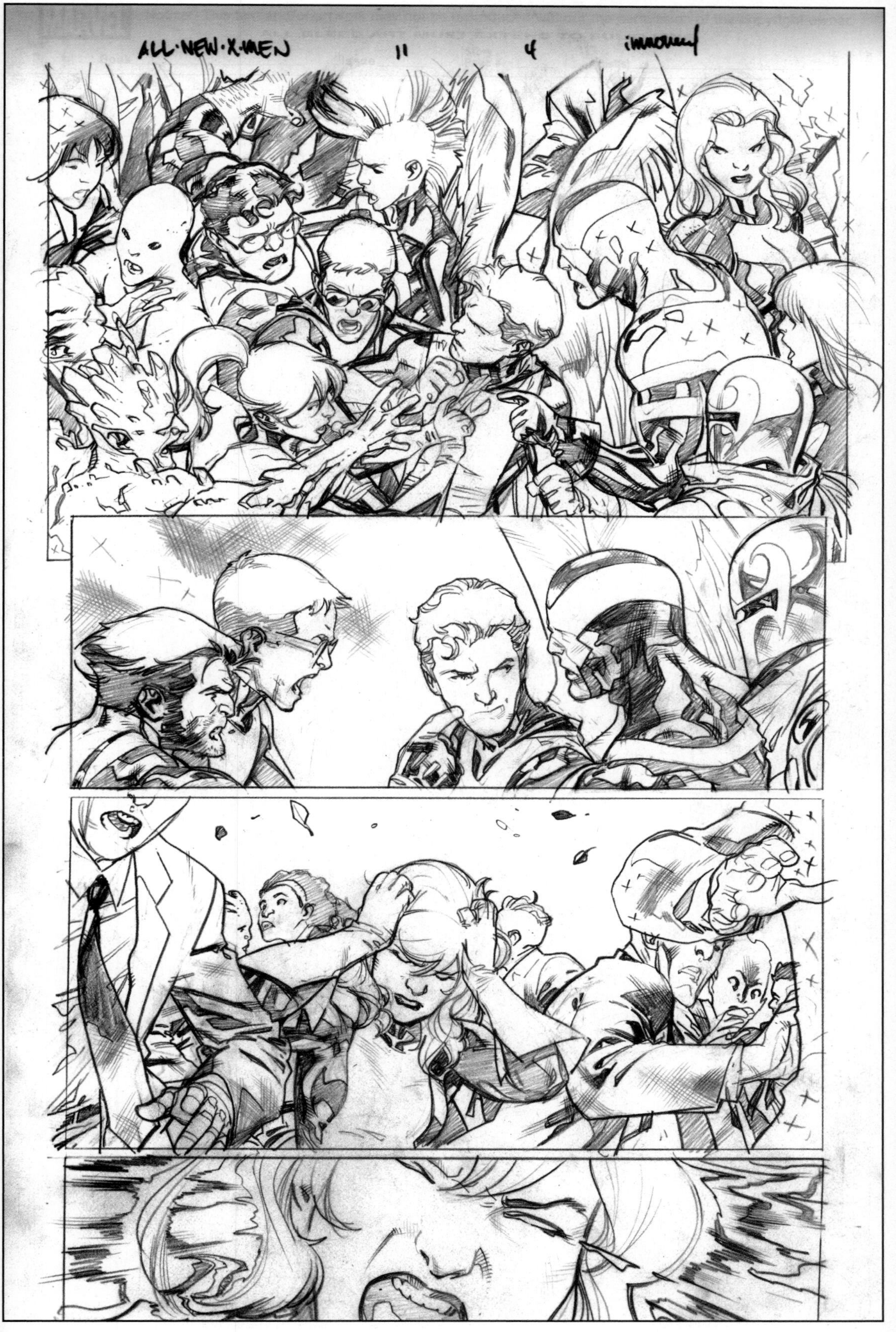
ALL·NEW·X·MEN
11
4

#11, PAGE 16 PENCILS BY STUART IMMONEN

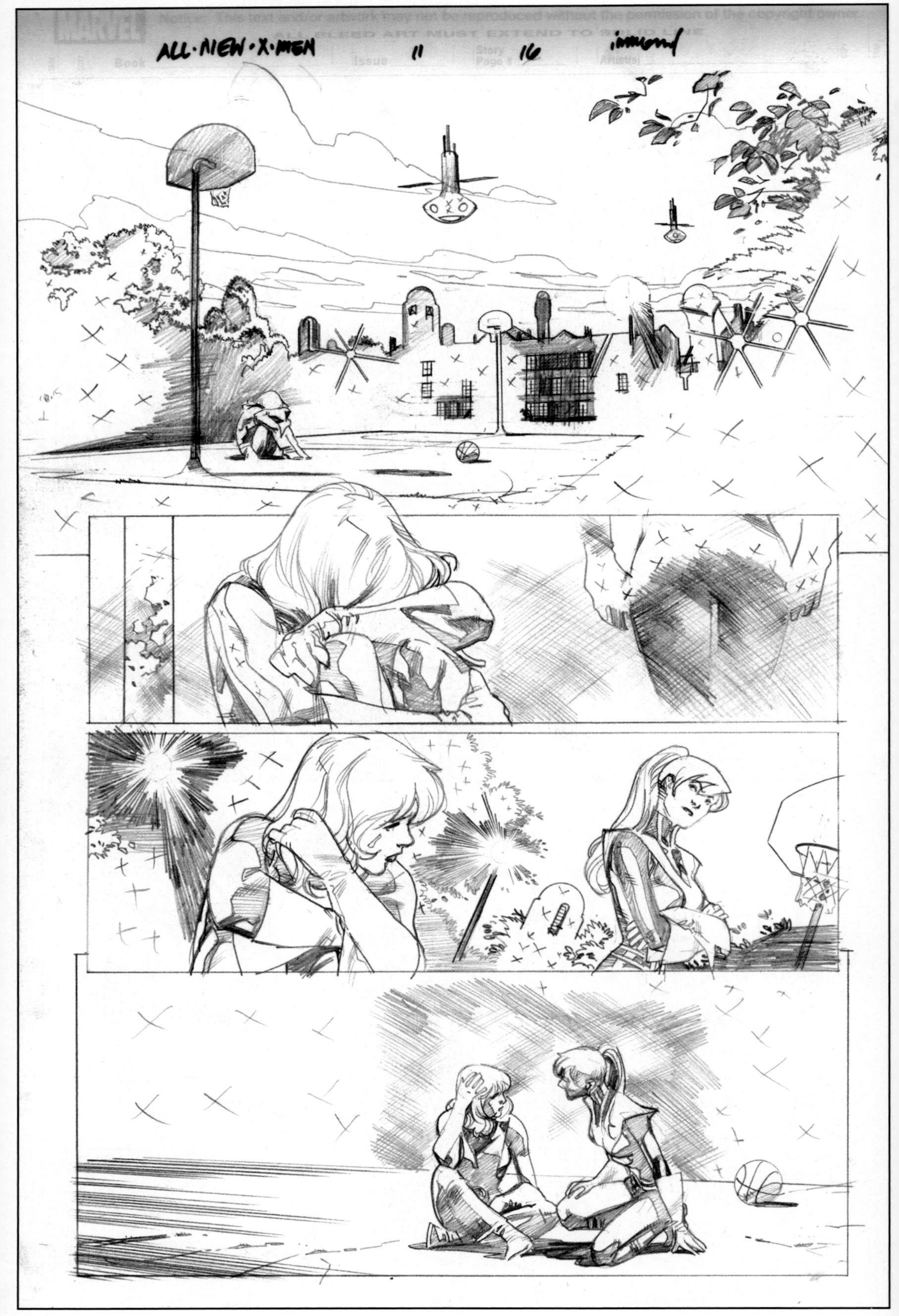
ALL·NEW·X·MEN
11
16

#12, PAGE 6 PENCILS BY STUART IMMONEN

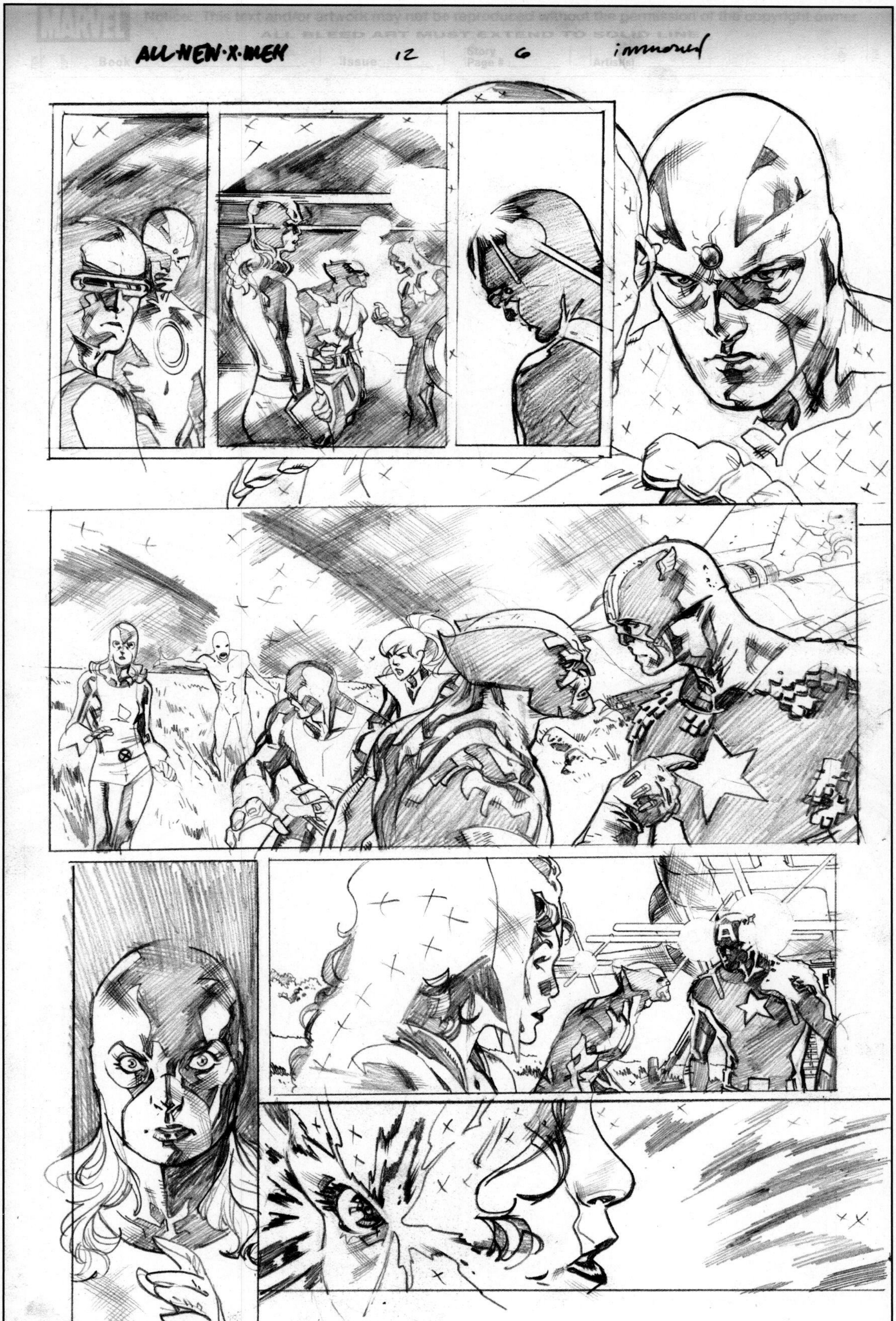

ALL-NEW·X-MEN
12
6
immonen

#12, PAGE 7 PENCILS BY STUART IMMONEN

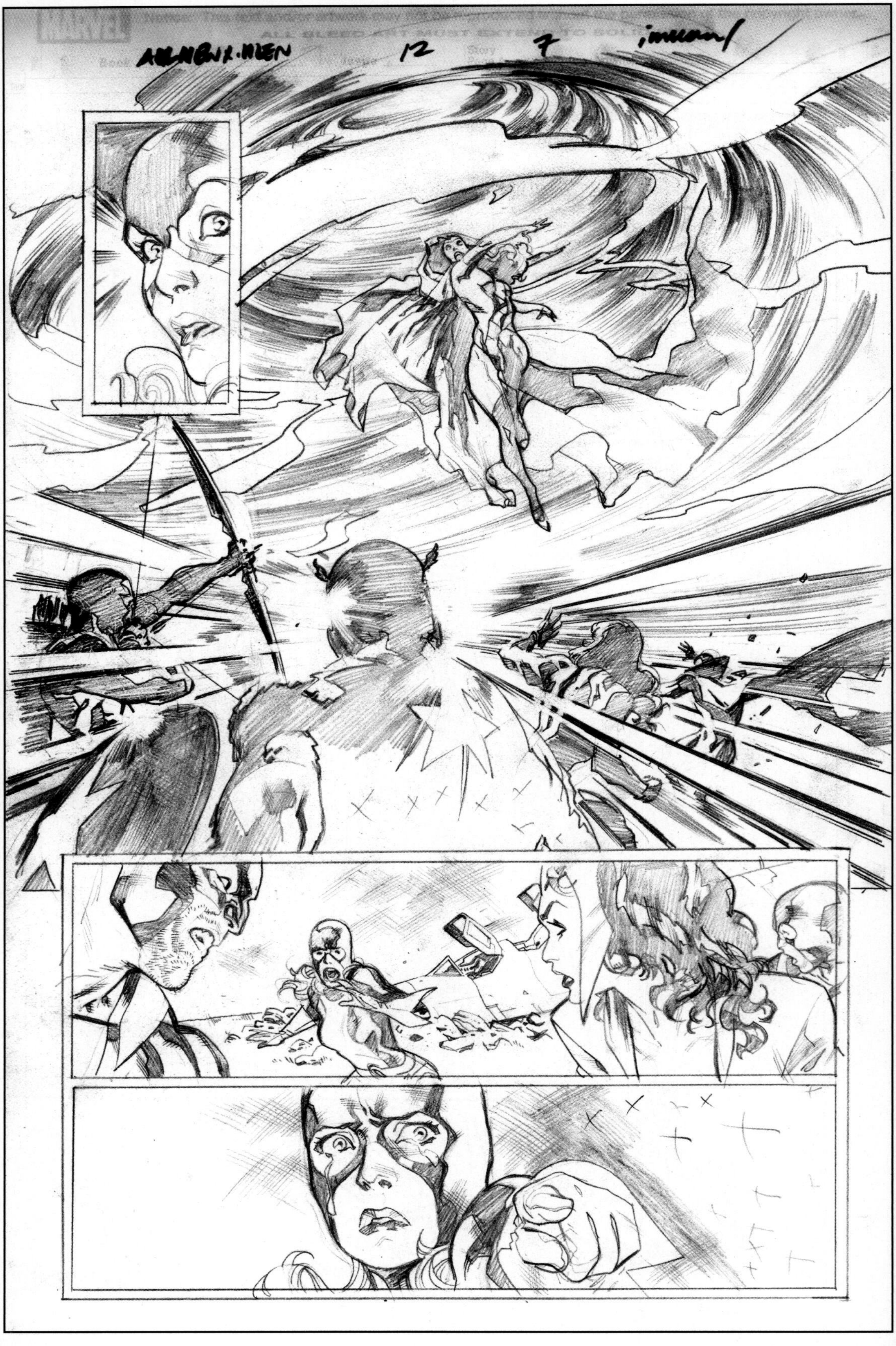
12
7

#12, PAGE 10 PENCILS BY STUART IMMONEN

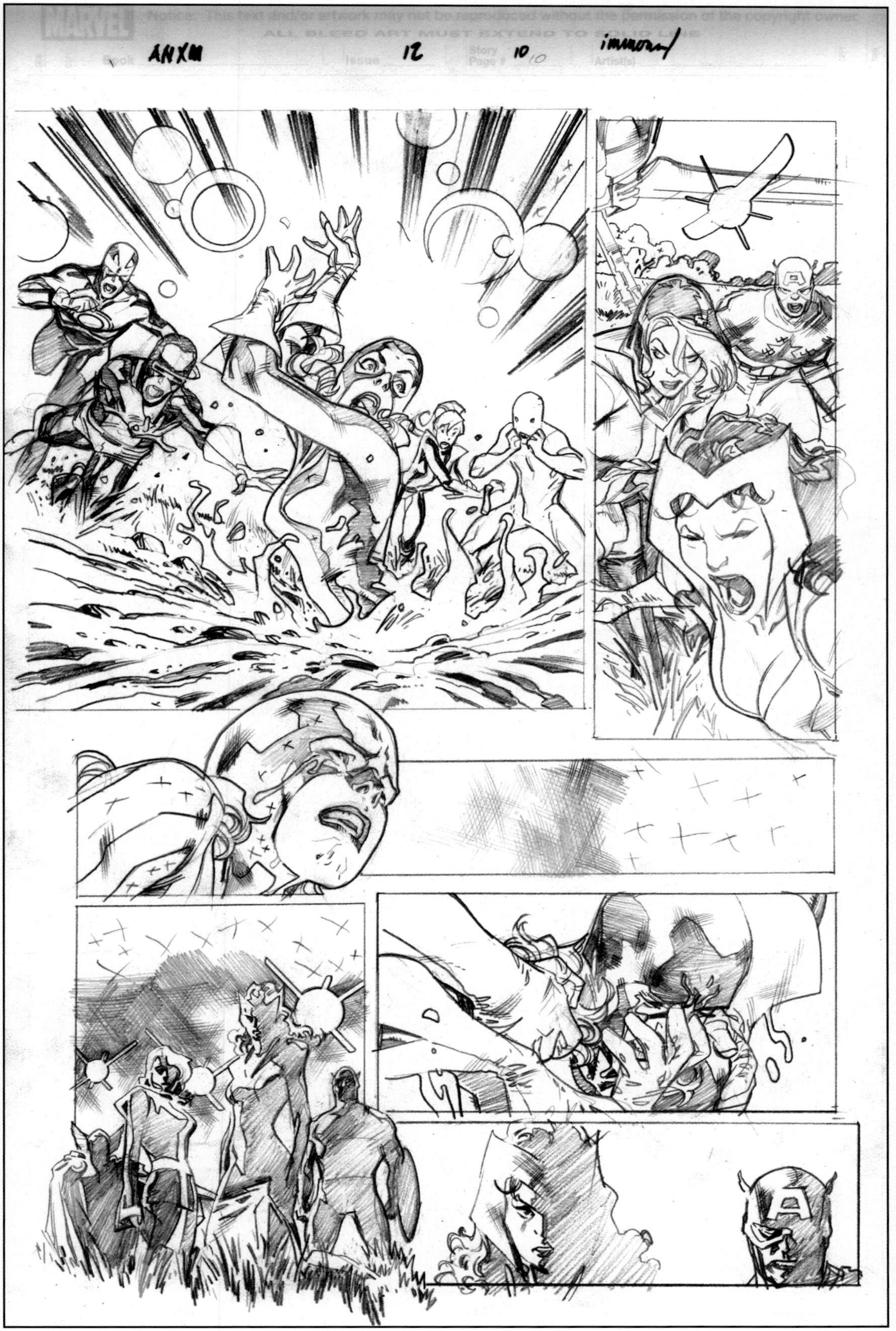

Notice: This text and/or artwork may not be reproduced without the permission of the copyright owner.
ALL BLEED ART MUST EXTEND TO SOLID LINE
Book ANXM
Issue 12
Story Page # 10
Artist(s) immonen

#12, PAGE 15 PENCILS BY STUART IMMONEN

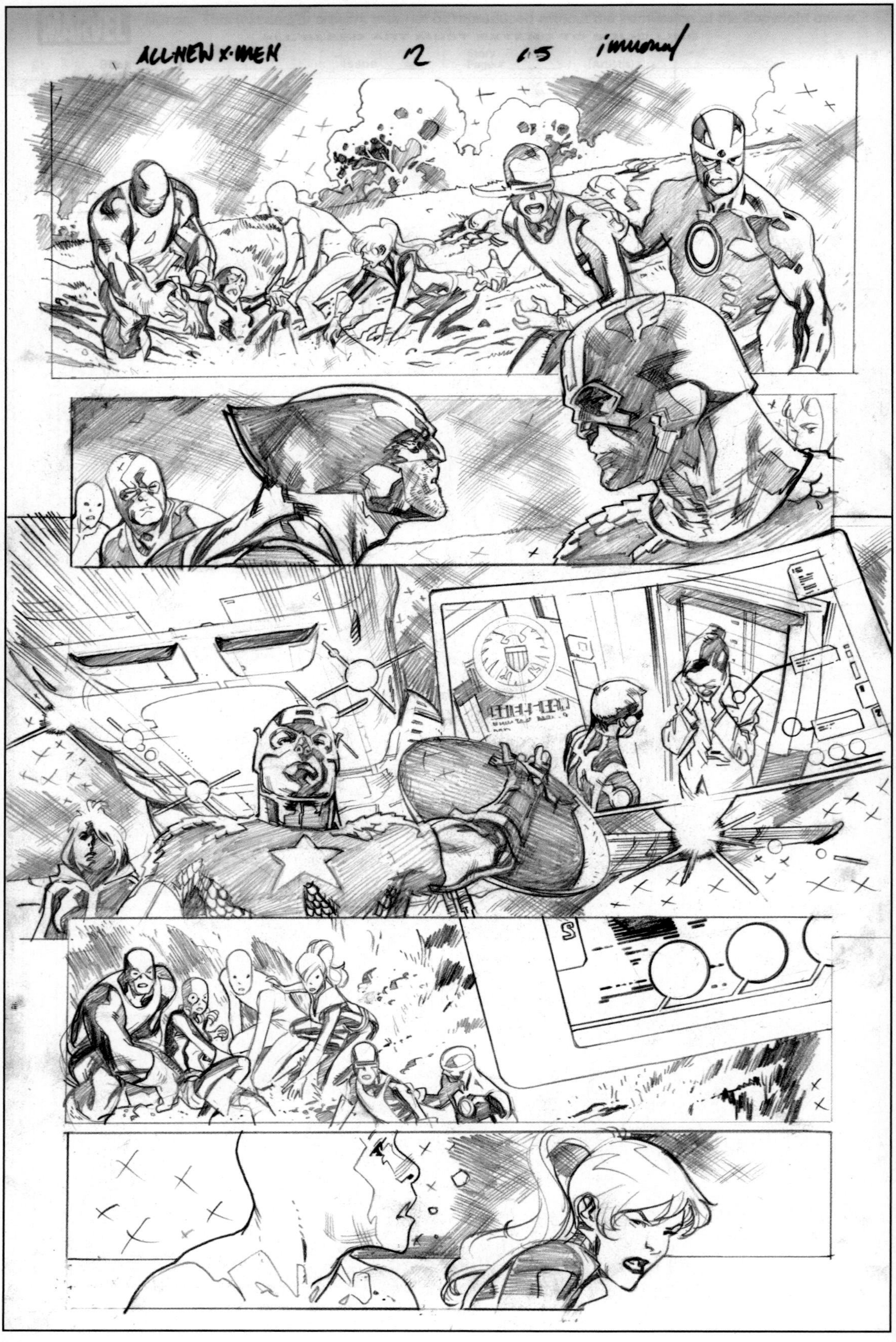
ALL-NEW X-MEN
12
15
immonen

#13, PAGE 13 PENCILS BY STUART IMMONEN

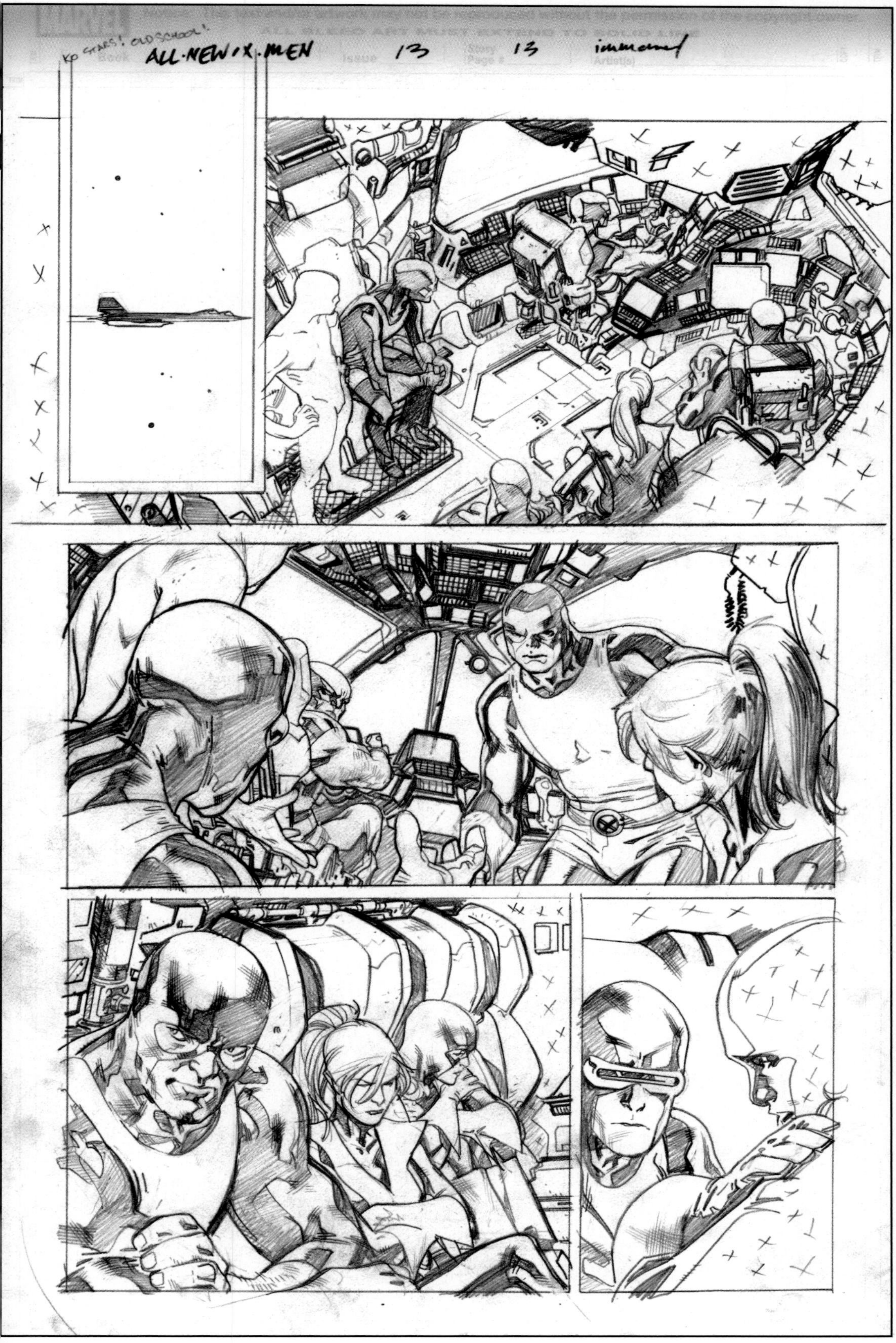
KO STARS! OLD SCHOOL!
Book ALL-NEW X-MEN
Issue 13
Story Page # 13
Artist(s) immonen

#14, PAGE 6 PENCILS BY STUART IMMONEN

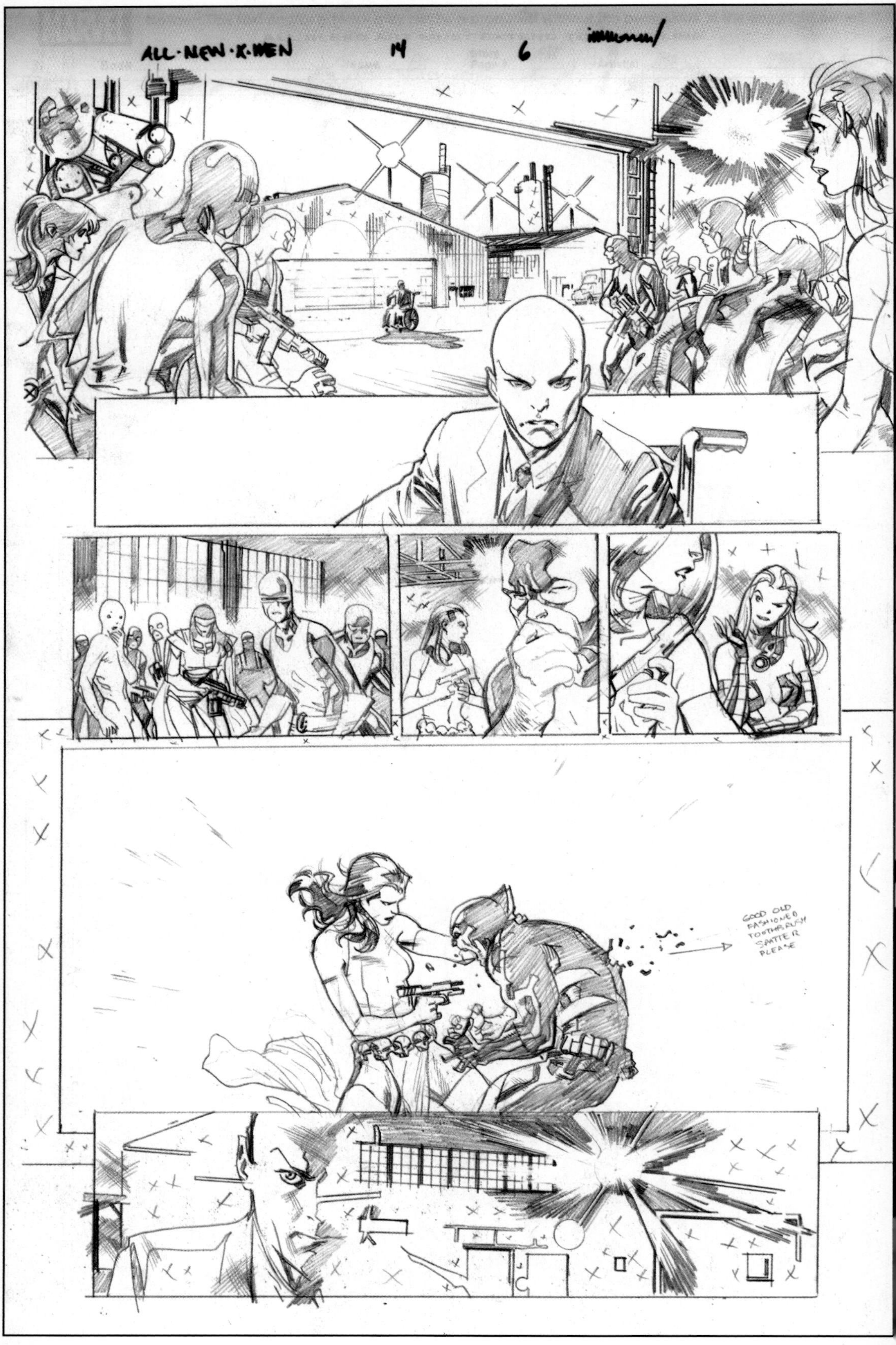
ALL·NEW·X·MEN
14
6
GOOD OLD FASHIONED TOOTHBRUSH SPATTER PLEASE

#14, PAGE 17 PENCILS BY STUART IMMONEN

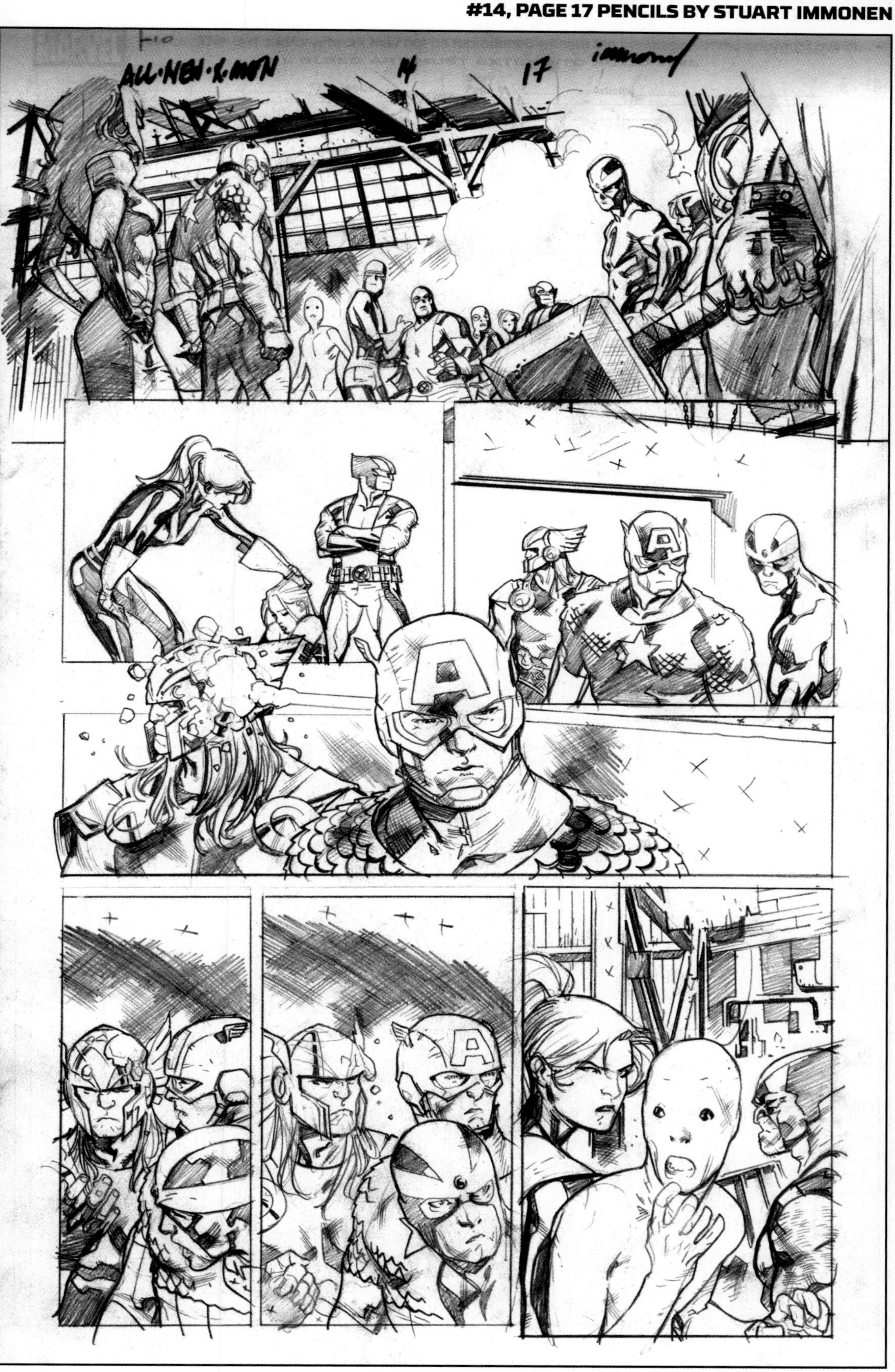
ALL·NEW·X·MEN
14
17

CHARACTER SKETCHES DAVID LAFUENTE

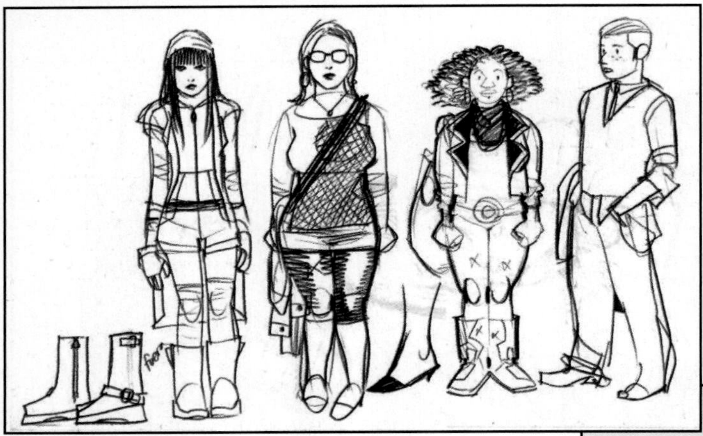

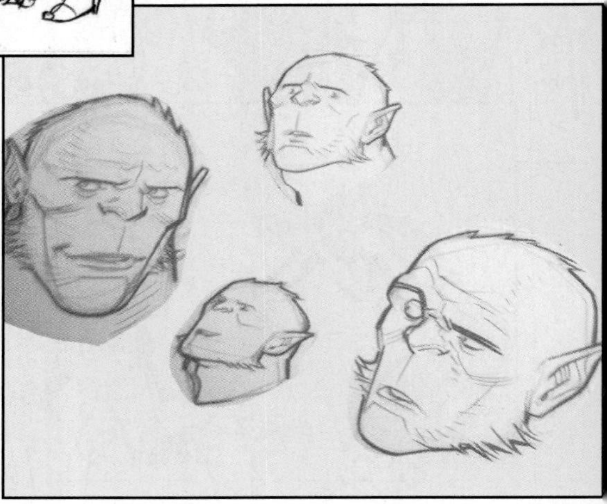

#15 LAYOUTS BY DAVID LAFUENTE

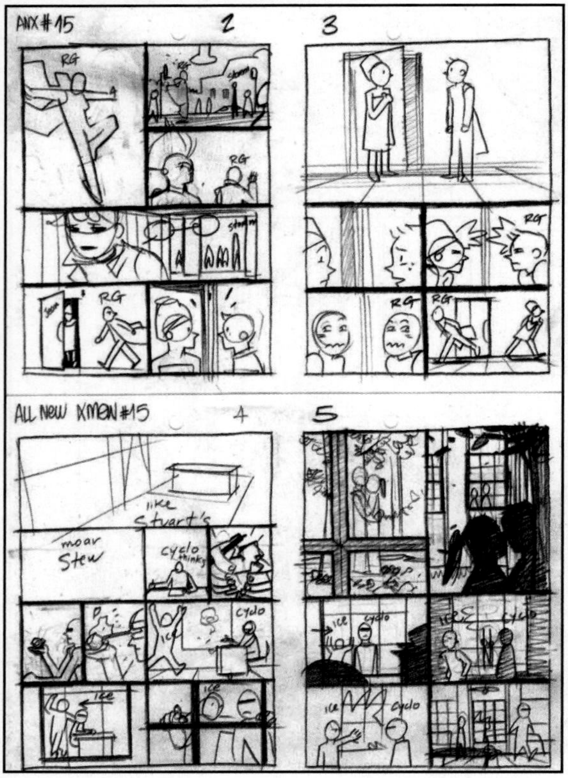
ANX #15
2
3
ALL NEW XMEN #15
4
5
like Stuart's
moar Stew
cyclo thinks
ice
cyclo

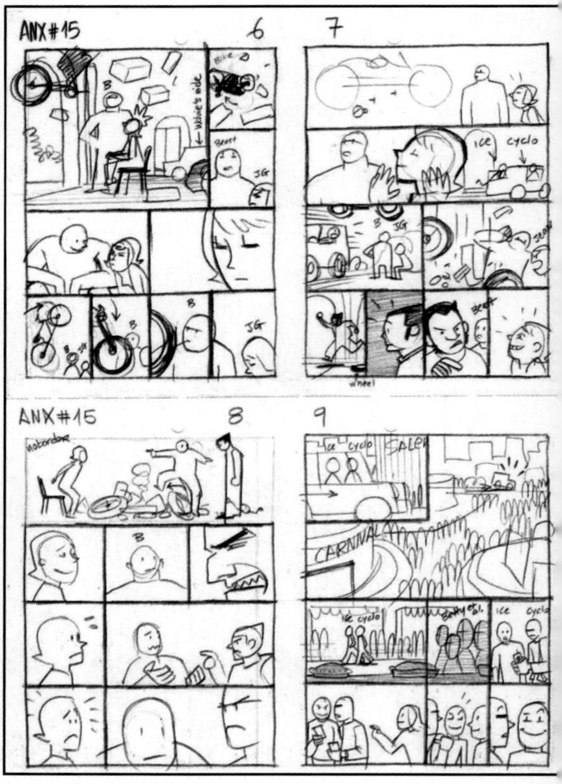
ANX #15
6
7
ANX #15
8
9
Beast
ice
cyclo
CARNIVAL

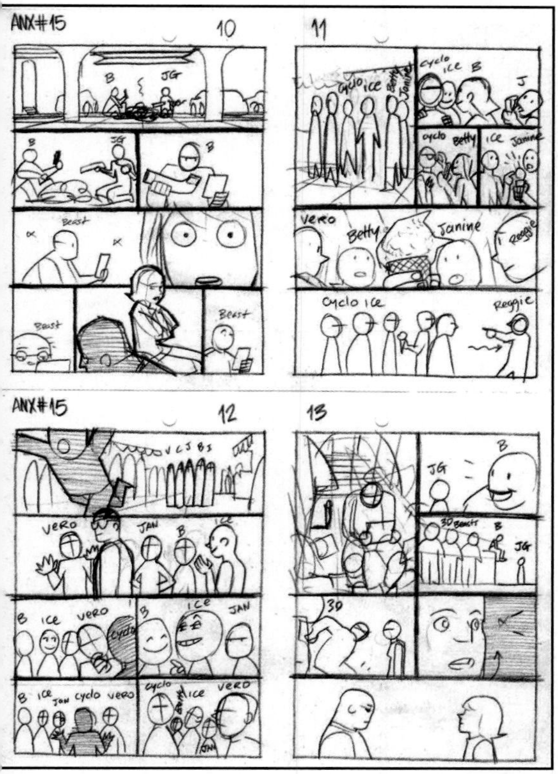
ANX#15
10
11
B
JG
Beast
cyclo
ice
Betty
Janine
J
vero
Reggie
ANX#15
12
13
VERO
JAN
B
ICE
cyclo
JG
3D Beasts
3D

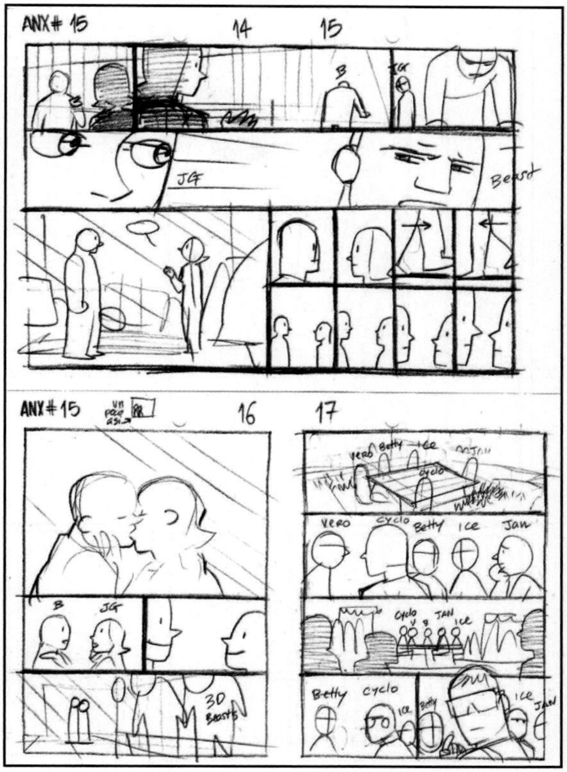
ANX# 15
14
15
B
JG
Beast
ANX# 15
16
17
B
JG
vero
Betty
ice
cyclo
Jan
3D Beasts

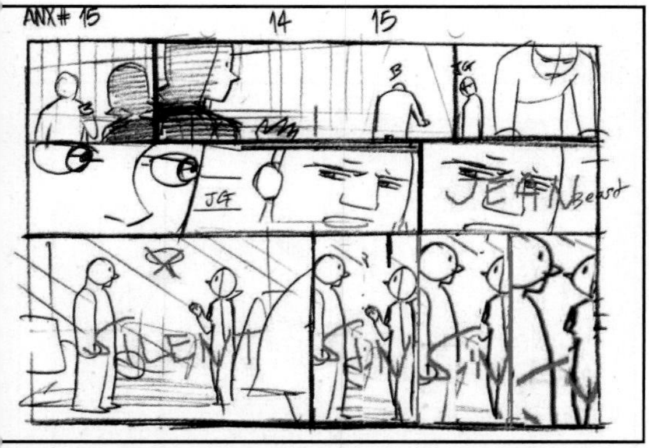
ANX# 15
14
15
B
JG
Beast

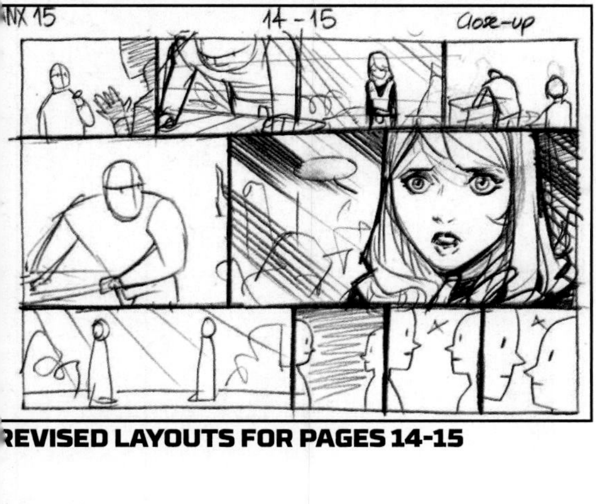
ANX 15
14 - 15
Close-up

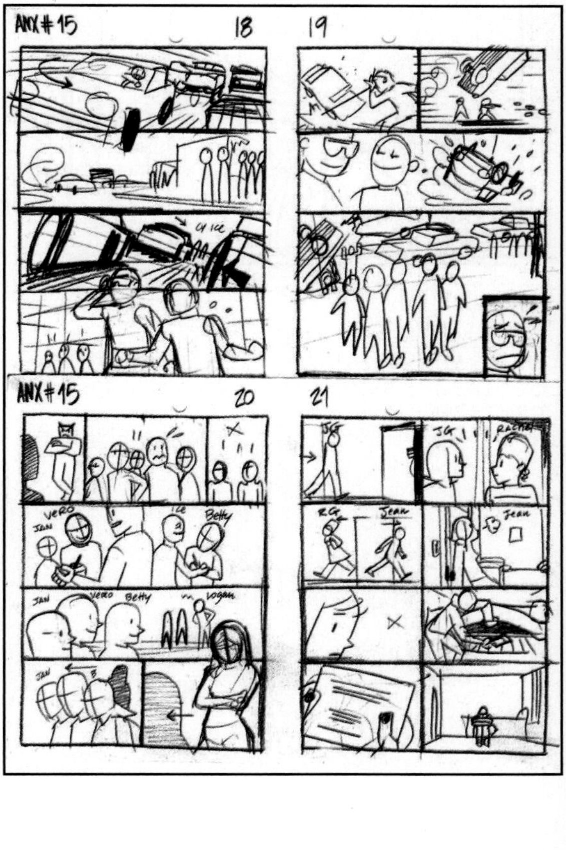
ANX#15
18
19
ANX#15
20
21
vero
JAN
ice
Betty
Logan
JG
Jean
B

REVISED LAYOUTS FOR PAGES 14-15

#15, PAGE 5 PENCILS & INKS BY DAVID LAFUENTE

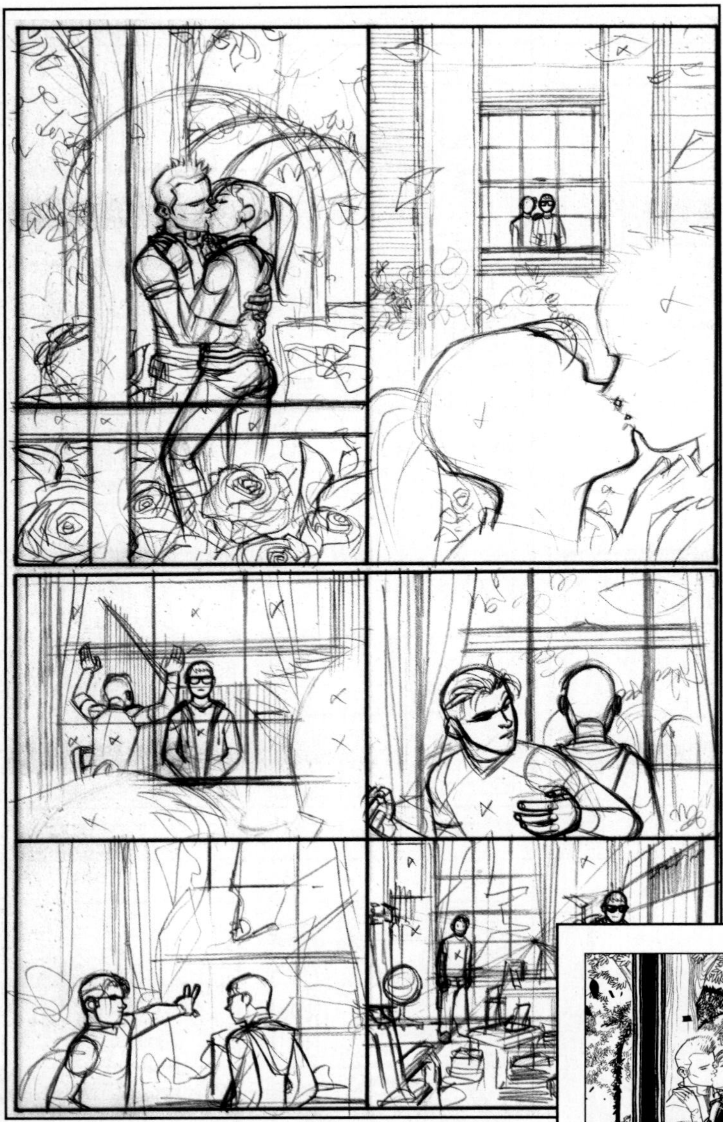

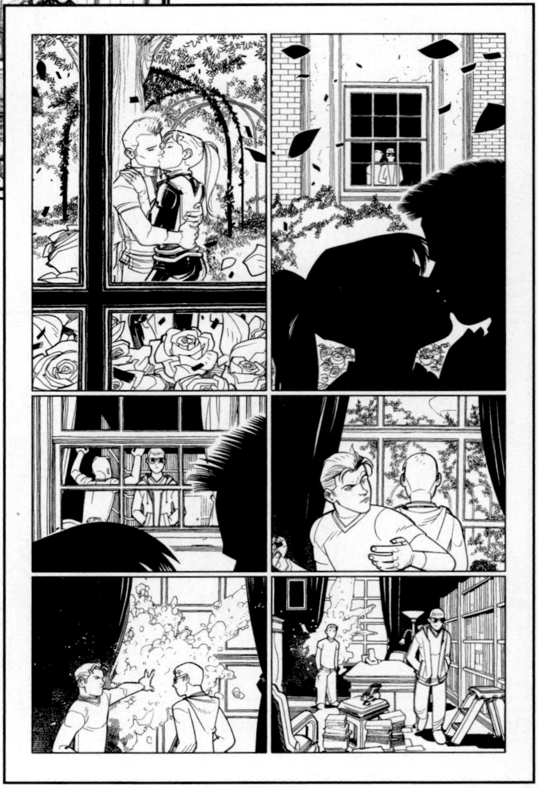

#15, PAGE 7 PENCILS & INKS BY DAVID LAFUENTE

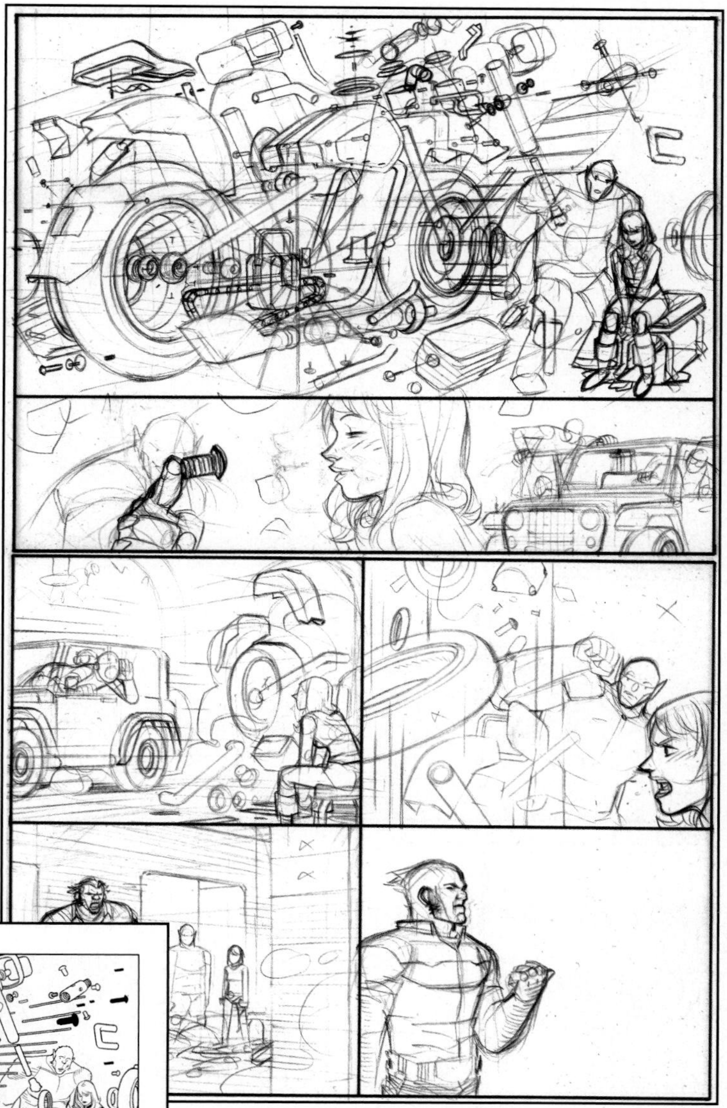

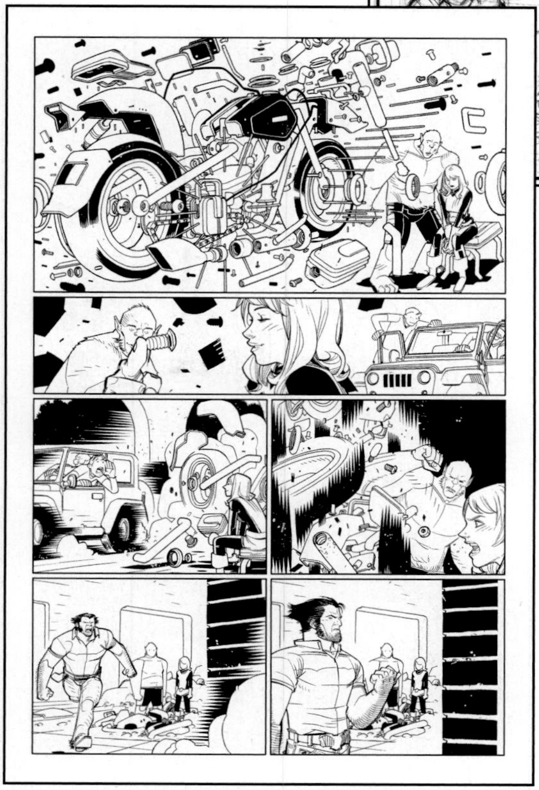

#15, PAGE 13 PENCILS & INKS BY DAVID LAFUENTE

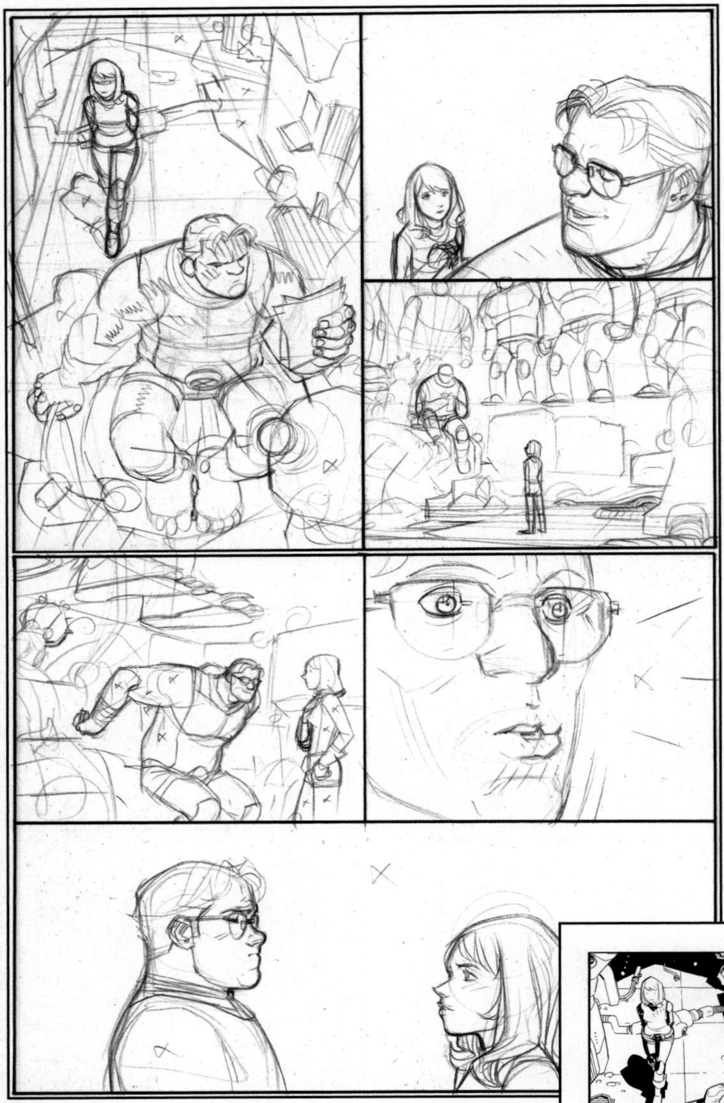

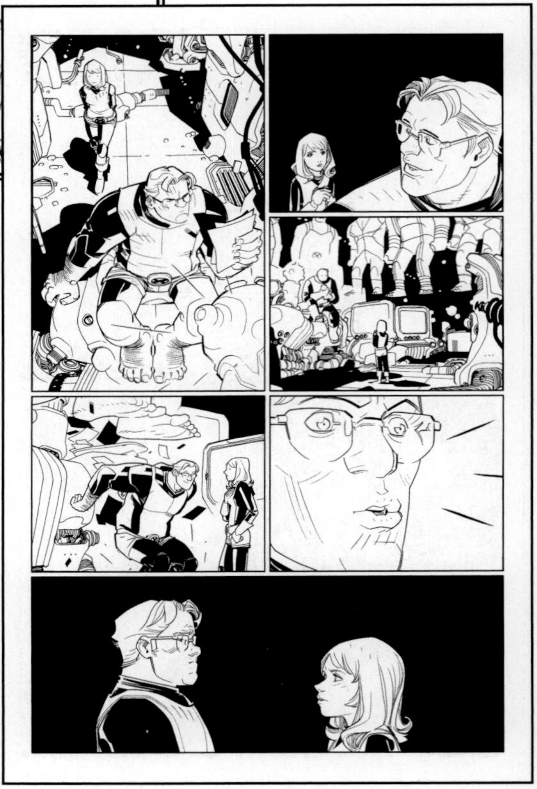

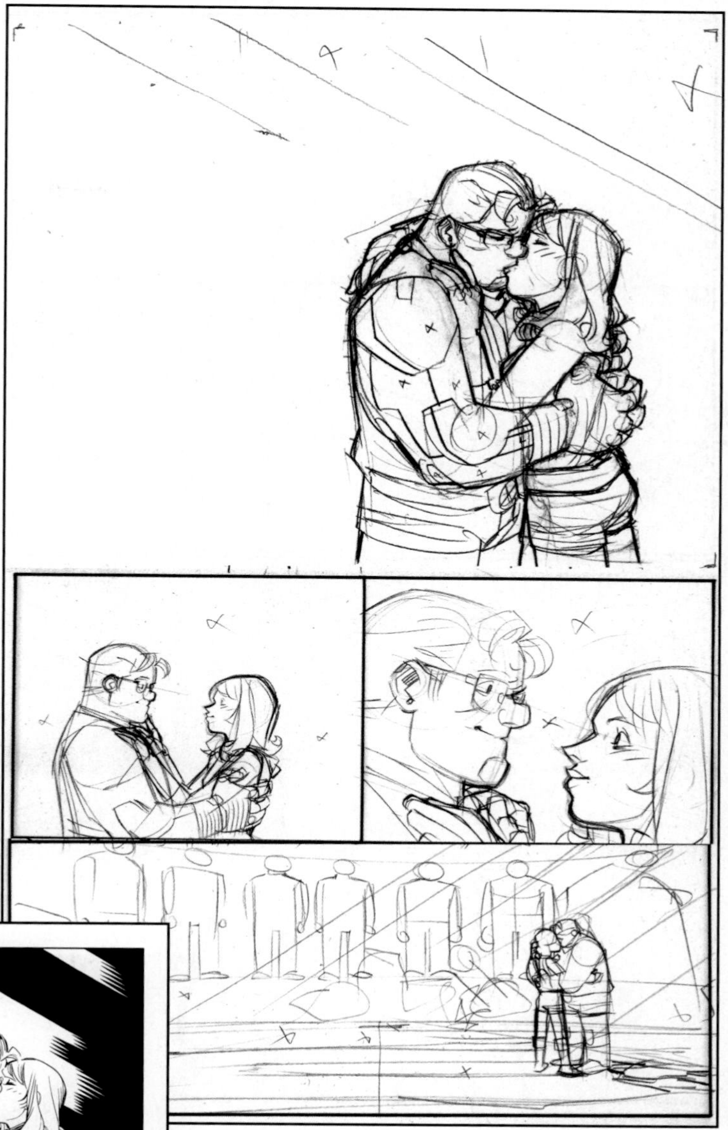

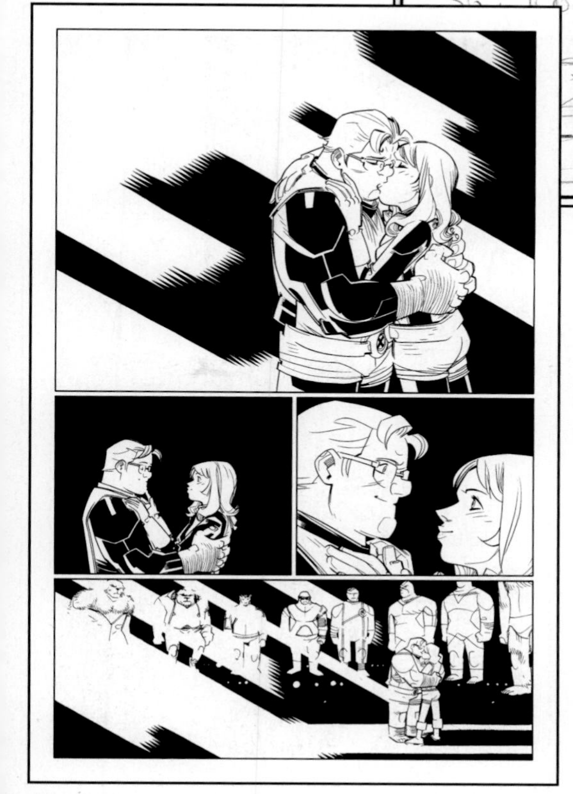

#15, PAGE 18 PENCILS & INKS BY DAVID LAFUENTE

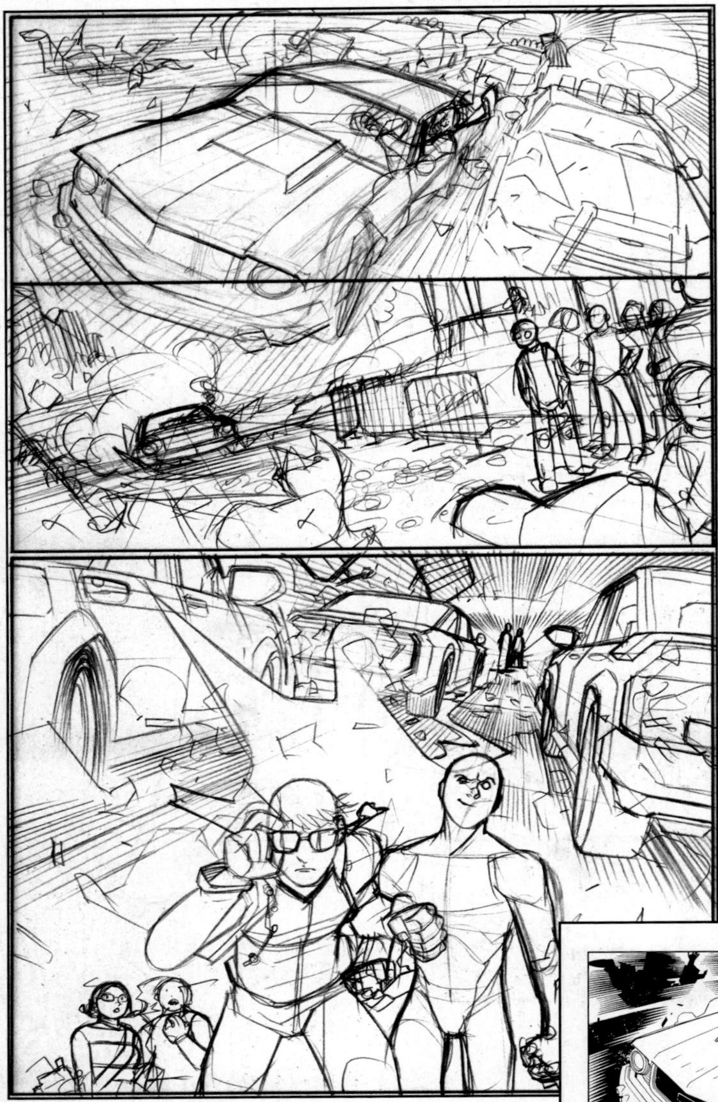

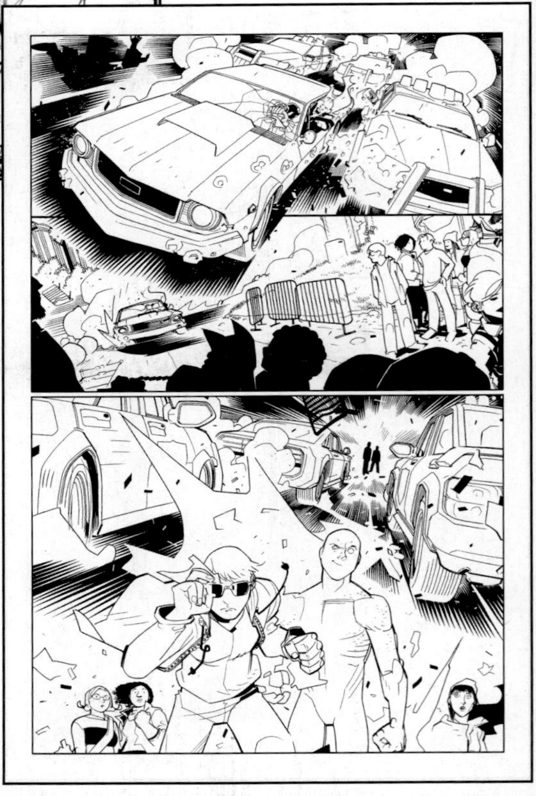

UNCANNY AVENGERS VOL. 1: THE RED SHADOW
WRITTEN BY RICK REMENDER • ART BY JOHN CASSADAY
978-0-7851-6844-7 • DEC130776

© 2013 MARVEL

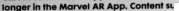